Successful San Diegans

The Stories Behind
San Diego's Most Successful People
Both Past and Present

Successful San Diegans

The Stories Behind
San Diego's Most Successful People
Both Past and Present

by Lee T. Silber

Foreword by Larry Himmel

TALES FROM
THE TROPICS
• Publishing Co. •

Tales From The Tropics Publishing Co.
P.O. Box 4100-186
Del Mar, California 92014

Author: Lee T. Silber
Editor: Johanna Hawkins
Additional Editing: Annette Silber, Beth Hagman
Page Design and Layout: Beth Hagman
Cover Design: Jeff Yeomans
Author Photograph: Martin Mann
Foreword: Larry Himmel

The publisher wishes to express appreciation to the following, who granted permission to use the following photographs: Martin Mann for permission to use photographs of Stephen Bishop, Tim Flannery, Tony Gwynn, Rolf Benirschke, Sue Delany and the Rubio family. The Photo Lab of the Zoological Society of San Diego for photograph of Joan Embery. The San Diego Historical Society for photographs of Max Miller, George Marston and T. Claude Ryan. Hill & Knowlton for photograph of Anthony Robbins.

Library of Congress Catalog Card Number: 92-094220

ISBN: 0-9628771-1-5

Printed in San Diego, California, USA

First Edition

To all those who are proud to be called San Diegans
and still believe this is "America's Finest City."
I salute you.

This book is dedicated with sincere appreciation
to my mom and dad for their continual support,
to my brothers Mark and Scott,
to Andrea for her patience and love
and, as always, to J.B.

Special Thanks

I would like to give credit where credit is due and express my appreciation to all the talented writers, known and unknown, whose books, articles and publicity notes helped in researching this book. I would especially like to thank Evelyn Kooperman, Thomas K. Arnold, Del Hood, R.H. Growald, Karla Peterson, Clark Judge, Bill Center, Virginia Butterfield, John Freeman, Roger Showley and Arthur Salm.

Without the contributions of the following people, this book would not have been possible: Annette Silber for additional writing and her dedication to perfection; Johanna Hawkins, whose creativity and enthusiasm for the project can be felt on every page; Beth Hagman, who took the raw material and honed it into publishable form and Andrea, for putting up with it all.

For a number of months, the California Room in the San Diego Public Library became my second home. I want to thank all the staff, who not only put up with me but always made me feel welcome. Their help is very much appreciated. Thank you, Mary, Paul, Eileen, Edna, Marie, Linda, Joann, Cyndi and Sidney. Thanks also to Lois Horowitz.

I owe a big debt of gratitude to Frank Kern and the San Diego Hall of Champions Sports Museum and Breitbard Hall of Fame in Balboa Park. For membership information, write: The San Diego Hall of Champions Sports Museum, 1649 El Prado, Balboa Park, San Diego, CA 92101 or call (619) 234-2544. P.S.: "Bunny" Hand, thanks for convincing me to become a member and for letting me hang around for hours taking it all in.

Another organization for anyone seriously interested in San Diego's history is the San Diego Historical Society, located in Balboa Park. For membership information, write: San Diego Historical Society, P.O. Box 81825, San Diego, CA 92138 or call (619) 297-3258.

Other organizations that deserve recognition for their support and assistance are: the Advertising Arts College, Del Mar Toastmasters, The Learning Annex, San Diego Writers/Editors Guild, the Surfrider Foundation and the Robert Hays International Fan Club (232 S. 76th St., Franksville, WI 53136).

Others who unselfishly offered their help include: Sally Gary, to whom I am deeply grateful for all her help over the past three years; Elliott Fischoff and Jan Jones, who helped set up the Anthony Robbins interview, and Elizabeth, who gets to work in the castle; Lee "Hacksaw" Hamilton, who answered numerous sports-related questions over the phone and never once complained; Bill Johnston and the San Diego Chargers; Andy Strasberg and Jim Ferguson of the San Diego Padres; Guy, John, Neil and Matt at the Sports Card Club; Denise MacMillin of SAG — a huge thank you; Debbie from Tom Blair's office, who was very helpful; Kirsten at CEO Speakers Bureau, who assisted me in pinning Tim Flannery down for an interview and Marna McClure and Gayle Falkenthal from KSDO.

And thanks to Beth Hagman, Jeff Yeomans, Peter H. Karlen, Ian Rose, Betty Abell Jurus, Peggy Lipscomb, Jane Bernard, Mavis Hancock, Russell Moore, Daris Gringeri, Jeff Marriott, Bruce Walton, Charles Elster, Judy Vance, Barbara Ayers, Kelly Oden, Doris Heckman, Bob Warwick, Barbara Christman, Bobbi Bagel, Marie Anderson, Doug Smith, Tony Angellotti, Adolf Gross, Theresa Hukari, Betsy Mill, Carol Mendel, Laura Gilbert, Margaret McWhorter, Sharon Hancock, Michelle at ARA Services and Don's Photo Services.

Whenever I was suffering from writer's block or worked up an appetite, I usually headed for the Islandia Bar & Grill, Johnny Rockets, Harry's Coffee Shop or the Barefoot Patio Bar. Thanks for the delicious food.

Special thanks to Jimmy Buffett, whose words, music, lifestyle and efforts to preserve the environment have been a constant source of inspiration to me for years. Thanks, Jimmy!

I would like to thank those who believed in what I was doing and offered their moral support: My grandfather, who showed me how to overcome adversity; Rona, a nonstop whirlwind of energy and enthusiasm; Olga, a great listener and one of the wisest people I know; Bruce, who remained a true friend through it all; Darko, my partner in adventure both above and below water; "Boris," who calls to let me know every time there's a swell, testing my ability to stay focused on work; John Aliano who, better than anyone, understands the creative process; Mark Huetter and all my friends on Maui. How could I forget Dina, Diana, Debbie, "Dolfun," Jonnelle, Michelle, Leanne and little Stephen? To anyone I've inadvertently forgotten, I beg your forgiveness. I thank you all!

For a free copy of the newsletter, *Success in San Diego,* or information about The SuccessShop™, write to: Tales From The Tropics Publishing, P.O. Box 4100-186, Del Mar, CA 92014 or call (619) 792-5312.

Foreword

Recently, an old college professor of mine rolled through town. We met for lunch and he told me how proud he was of my accomplishments. His exact words were: "Never has anyone done so much with so little." Yet the pages of this book are filled with inspirational anecdotes of determined people who persevered, overcame and rose to positions of prominence in their chosen professions. Some are internationally famous, others have nationwide or statewide reputations. In my own case, I'm known throughout my entire zip code (92127).

A youngster once asked me, "What's the best way for me to have a successful career on television?" I told him, "Don't ever stop and don't ever let anyone tell you that you can't achieve your goals. Of course, it couldn't hurt if you married into a family that owns a television station."

There are common threads woven through the stories of the people included in this book. All of them were driven, all of them were focused and they all had a sense of purpose, a passion for what they were doing. One of the things I have in common with everyone included here is that I was not paid for appearing in it, either. Nor did I want to be.

It's the biggest thrill of my life to be included in the same book with local heroes like Florence Chadwick and Dr. Seuss, George Marston and Ted Williams. After all, the "Splendid Splinter" has an entire freeway named in his honor. There's an omelette named after me on the menu at The Big Kitchen restaurant. Whoopi Goldberg once worked at The Big Kitchen, and she starred in the movie *Sister Act* – which makes me closer to God, by association. There's the inspirational story of former San Diego Charger Rolf Benirschke, who once hosted *Wheel of Fortune*. I know Rolf personally – which makes me closer to Vanna White, by association.

There's also the story of Ted Giannoulas. His landmark court battle with KGB Radio determined, once and for all, who came first, the Chicken or the man. There's a profile of Tom Blair, who promised to mention me in his column if I mentioned him in this Foreword. There are celebrities and entrepreneurs, athletes and media people and (thank God) no mimes.

I'm not the only weatherman included in this book. Mike Ambrose, whose work I've admired for years, is also profiled. Captain Mike taught me everything you need to know to be a San Diego meteorologist: "Night and morning low clouds, afternoon sunshine."

In many ways, all San Diegans are successful. Those who moved here and those who stayed have successfully realized that this is truly America's Finest City. Just living here makes them one of the privileged few (million). When you first come to San Diego, you're impressed by the ocean, the mountains, the desert and the close proximity to over 200 Roberto's. After you're here awhile, you realize the city's greatest natural resource is its people. Many of those who have helped give this city its charm and character are profiled in this book.

Finally, a few comments about the author. Lee Silber is a remarkable young man. I'm delighted to write the Foreward for his book, because I admire his dedication and how hard he worked to make his dream of writing this book a reality. In *Successful San Diegans,* Lee not only shows off the great people of San Diego, but he also shows you just how these people came to be so successful. He has written a truly uplifting book that is a must-read for every San Diegan.

I loved the book so much I'm giving it to my mother as a birthday gift. She, too, knows that "Never has someone done so much with so little."

Larry Himmel
December 1992

Introduction

I am proud to introduce *Successful San Diegans,* possibly the most complete collection of biographies ever written about San Diego's most accomplished and successful people in the fields of entertainment, sports, media and business. This book represents many hundreds of hours of writing, research and interviews to bring you the over 100 full-length and in-depth profiles, as well as an additional 175 shorter biographical sketches. This incredible book is packed full of facts, trivia, photographs, inspiration and advice. Many of the names are instantly recognizable. Just flip through the pages and I'm sure you'll agree. But if you think you know all there is to know about these successful individuals, think again. They candidly talk about San Diego, their trials and tribulations and, of course, their success and how they achieved it.

These are inspiring and illuminating human stories about personal accomplishment, courage, determination, hard work, struggle and the ability to overcome adversity.

Not only is this work inspirational and informative, it is also especially entertaining and fun. There are even trivia questions included in a section called "Just for Fun." *Successful San Diegans* is designed to accommodate even the busiest reader, as each story can be read in roughly ten minutes. You may find yourself unable to put it down — but if you must, this book can be read over a period of time or whenever you feel you need a lift.

Although the book is intended to be primarily entertaining, I hope you also find it motivating to read about the lives and accomplishments of these very successful people. It's my wish that *Successful San Diegans* will have a lasting impact on you, and that you will be moved by this celebration of effort and achievement.

It may seem that you are sitting in the same room with these people as they share their stories and advice with you on their search for success, fulfillment, wealth, health and, above all, happiness. Chapter by chapter, you see some recurring themes and common traits which are later explored in the section on success. These insights and ideas can be used by everyone, whether you're striving for success or simply want to maintain it. These proven concepts are common factors that have contributed to the success of those included in this book. These are effective "what to do" and "how to do it" ideas that you can use and learn from.

As with any book of this kind, the question arises why certain subjects were included and others omitted. Not a day went by that I didn't ask myself the same question – sometimes several times a day. I want to make it clear that not one person in this book was charged a fee to be in it. I also want to point out that there were a few people I approached to be in this book who turned me down or never responded to my requests for information.

Who qualifies for inclusion in this book? There is no single valid method for judging success. Just look at the varying definitions of success used by the people included here. Yet most would agree that money alone is certainly no criteria for success. It's much easier to set the criteria for defining a San Diegan. For the purposes of this book, a San Diegan is anyone who was born here, grew up here, became successful while living here or substantially impacted the community. There are a couple of exceptions to this rule, but when you read their stories I hope it's clear why they were included anyway. Please keep in mind that this book provides only a sampling of successful San Diegans and is not meant to imply that those selected are the only or even the most successful people in their respective fields. Finally, the book only profiles success stories in the fields of entertainment, sports, media and business. I originally intended to include a section on influential San Diegans, but there are far too many. I opted instead to assiduously file this information away for use at a future date.

I would like to express my regrets about the many successful San Diegans I may have missed or have reluctantly omitted from this work. Space restrictions simply do not permit the inclusion of all the men and women who should have been included. I have in fact profiled several successful San Diegans who had to be pulled at the last minute, when I realized the book had swelled to well over 600 pages. These stories, as well as information on countless others, will be used for subsequent editions. Incidentally, many more profiles will appear in our companion newsletter, *Success in San Diego.* For a free copy of *Success in San Diego,* or to submit information on someone worthy of inclusion, please write to *Success in San Diego,* P.O. Box 4100-186, Del Mar, CA 92014.

This book is intended for both young and old, long-time San Diegans and newcomers alike. All are sure to be filled with a sense of pride in San Diego and its people while reading and reminiscing about the legends of years past and learning about the success stories of today.

No matter what your background, no matter what your purpose, this book is for you!

"The people we admire in our lives

are ordinary people who have been able

to accomplish some extraordinary things.

The things that make them extraordinary

are things that we all possess."

Rolf Benirschke

Table of Contents

Entertainment

Chapter 1: Actors

Chapter 2: Musicians

Chapter 3: Celebrities

Chapter 4: Writers

Sports

Chapter 7: Other Sports

Media

Chapter 8: Television

Chapter 9: Radio

Chapter 10: Print

Business

Chapter 11: Big Business

Entertainment

Chapter 1: Actors

Robert Duvall

Whoopi Goldberg

Robert Hays

Tawny Kitaen

David Leisure

Cleavon Little

Gregory Peck

Briefs

Desi Arnaz · Annette Bening · Victor Buono

Michael Damian · Jimmy "Schnozzola" Durante

Faye Emerson · Dennis Hopper

Julie Kavner · Kathy Najimy

Cliff Robertson · Marion Ross

Charlene Tilton

Raquel Welch

Robert Duvall
Academy Award-Winning Actor

It's almost impossible to pin down exactly who Robert Duvall is. He's always so integrated into the character he plays that Robert Duvall the man simply disappears. You'll never catch him acting. His work is consistently excellent in whatever medium he chooses – television, stage or film.

A native San Diegan, Duvall was born January 5, 1931. His father was a rear admiral who hoped his son would follow in his footsteps and attend Annapolis. Instead, Duvall chose Principia College in Illinois, earning a degree in dramatic arts. He served a hitch in the army and is a Korean War veteran. After his military tour, he headed to New York to study at The Neighborhood Playhouse, palling around with struggling young actors Gene Hackman and Dustin Hoffman. During those lean years, Duvall worked the midnight shift at the Post Office, sorting mail to pay the rent.

In 1957, Duvall snagged the lead role in Arthur Miller's *A View from the Bridge,* which led to several television roles. These included regular appearances on *Naked City* and *The Defenders,* but he created his favorite character, Gus, for the 1989 TV miniseries *Lonesome Dove.*

His big screen debut came in 1963 as Boo Radley in *To Kill A Mockingbird.* He made his mark as an "actor's actor" in the *Godfather* films (I and II) and as an American colonel in the hit *Apocalypse Now.* His extraordinary, Oscar-winning performance in *Tender Mercies* earned him the acceptance and true star status he deserves.

With four Oscar nominations under his belt, Duvall finally won the coveted Best Actor Award for his 1983 portrayal of a down-and-out country western singer/songwriter in *Tender Mercies.* Many contend that he warrants top awards for all his roles. From his screen debut in *To Kill A Mockingbird* to *The Godfather (Parts I and II), Apocalypse Now, The Great Santini, The Natural* and, more recently, *Days of Thunder, Ramblin' Rose* and HBO's *Stalin,* he never delivers less than a mesmerizing performance. Duvall throws himself body and soul into his parts. In *Tender Mercies,* he sang every song on a demanding soundtrack himself and danced a mean two-step for the role.

Spreading his wings a little, Duvall also worked on Broadway in *American Buffalo* and directed the much-praised film, *Angelo, My Love.*

Today, Robert Duvall lives on a ranch in Virginia and spends his spare time playing tennis and riding horses in competition. For Christmas one year, Tom Cruise (Duval's co-star in *Days of Thunder),* sent him a jumper as a gift. Duvall also lists country music as one of his interests — one he really got to explore when making *Tender Mercies.*

Whoopi Goldberg
Actress/Talk Show Host/Comedienne

Whoopi Goldberg never cared about being famous. She just wanted to do what she loved — acting. In pursuing that goal, she has seen some very lean times, indeed. To support her love of theater, she held a string of odd jobs, working as a bricklayer, bank teller and cosmetician in a funeral parlor. She spent many of these struggling years in San Diego, where she helped found the San Diego Repertory Theater while washing dishes at The Big Kitchen Restaurant in Golden Hill. A single mother, there were times when she was forced to collect welfare to help pay the bills for herself and her daughter.

San Diego is where Goldberg began her ascent into stardom. The climb to the top was incredibly tough, but she beat the odds and is now one of the biggest stars in Hollywood (a fact confirmed by her recent hit movie, *Sister Act,* which grossed over $125 million in 1992). But, as Whoopi quickly found out, once you're on top, the trick is to stay there. After a string of mediocre movies including *Jumpin' Jack Flash* (1986), *Burglar* (1987), *Fatal Beauty* (1987) and *Clara's Heart* (1988), some critics were ready to write her off. But then she was nominated for Best Supporting Actress in the 1990 blockbuster hit, *Ghost.*

"Back from the dead," Goldberg's career is reaching new heights. She enters a new phase as late-night talk show host with her own syndicated half-hour talk show, *The Whoopi Goldberg Show.* She was able to make a joyous statement with the 1992 film *Sarafina!* shot on

Whoopi Goldberg

location in South Africa. And 1993 opens with another film where she plays opposite Ted Danson in *Made in America.*

Goldberg is well-known for her tireless humanitarian efforts on behalf of children, the homeless, human rights, substance abuse (as an ex-substance abuser herself) and many other worthwhile causes and charities. Always outspoken on a number of issues, Goldberg has received many death threats, but she refuses to let them stop her.

In 1992, Goldberg made her literary debut with *Alice,* a children's book she wrote with illustrations by John Rocco. She also occasionally plays the consummate listener as a regular cast member of *Star Trek: The Next Generation.* She continues to do *Tales from the Whoop* specials for Nickelodeon, more HBO Specials, Comic Relief and is the voice of Gaia in the environmental series *Captain Planet and the Planeteers.*

Whoopi Goldberg (her real name is Caryn Johnson) began performing at the age of eight in New York children's theater. In 1974, she moved to San Diego, where she honed her comedic skills as part of an improvisational group called Spontaneous Combustion. In 1983 she caught the attention of Mike Nichols, who offered to present her in a new Broadway show, which later became an HBO special, *Whoopi Goldberg: Direct from Broadway.* The record album from the show won a Grammy Award as Best Comedy Recording of the Year in 1985. Her act also caught the attention of Steven Spielberg, who subsequently cast her in his film version of Alice Walker's *The Color Purple.* Her portrayal of Celie earned her an Oscar nomination as well as a Golden Globe award in 1985. In 1986, she acquired an Emmy Award nomination as Best Guest Performer in a Dramatic Series for her appearance on an episode of *Moonlighting.*

Since then, Goldberg has made many television appearances, many of them award-winners. In 1987, Whoopi, Billy Crystal and Robin Williams co-hosted HBO's now historic *Comic Relief benefit,* raising millions of dollars for the homeless. Her role as Oda Mae Brown in the 1990 hit movie *Ghost* garnered her the Academy Award for Best Supporting Actress and ended any talk that she would never reach the career heights many predicted for her just a few years earlier.

In 1991, Goldberg hosted the *34th Annual Grammy Awards* telecast. Her immense success is a source of constant inspiration for many aspiring actors who now call San Diego home — as Whoopi once did.

Robert Hays
Actor

More than handsome, Robert Hays is a nice guy. Ask anyone who knows him, on-screen or off. He's starred in twelve motion pictures, three television series and numerous movies for television since leaving San Diego for Hollywood in the late 1970's. His acting career took off when he played the neurotic young pilot in the comedy hit *Airplane!*, which led to many more roles in both film and television. You've seen him in *Take This Job And Shove It, Utilities, Scandalous, Airplane II* and Stephen King's *Cat's Eye.*

Hays made his television debut in the San Diego-based detective series *Harry O* before landing a starring role as Doctor Brad in the comedy series *Angie.* His other series credits include *Starman* — a cult favorite — and more recently the character Ted Costas on the half-hour comedy series *FM.* He's also starred in several made-for-TV movies and mini-series.

Known for both comedic and dramatic performances, his latest role was in the action-adventure film *Fifty-Fifty,* where he's cast as a sarcastic mercenary opposite Peter Weller. The movie was filmed entirely in Malaysia.

With the success he enjoys in Hollywood, you'd think Hays would forget the less-than-prosperous days of his early career. The fact is, he looks back fondly on his years in San Diego, when he learned his trade at Grossmont Community College and the Old Globe Theatre, earning $45 a week, living in his Volkswagen bus and eating large quantities of brown rice. "I had an incredible time — the time of my life in San Diego," he says.

Born in Bethesda, Maryland, Robert Hays is the son of a retired Marine Corps colonel who was a much-decorated fighter pilot in three wars. Hays and his family moved to a different city every two or three years throughout his childhood — even living in Izmar, Turkey for three years. He comes from a solid family background despite all the moving around, and is very close to his parents, who still reside in the San Diego area.

As a teenager, Hays had no idea what he wanted to do with his life, so he enrolled at the Grossomont Community College, taking whatever classes he could get. Discovering a passion for acting, Hays devoured every class that had anything to do with theater, studying and rehearsing up to ninety hours a week.

Recently, Hays was in San Diego for the dedication of a plaque in his honor at Grossmont College. When in town, he also visits with his

Robert Hays

first drama teacher, Clark Mires, who encouraged him to pursue a career in acting. The Old Globe Theatre also gave him a chance to learn his art in a variety of plays, including *The Glass Menagerie, The Man in the Glass Booth, Richard III* and *Say Who You Are,* for which he won an Atlas Award for Best Actor. He was so hooked on acting that on his occasional days off he'd drive to Indian reservations and give dramatic readings from the back of the 1966 Volkswagen bus which doubled as his residence. He owns that VW bus to this day.

Acting wasn't making him wealthy, but he wasn't complaining. He took odd jobs to pay the bills, working as a janitor at San Diego State University, where he attended for one semester and serving as a messenger at Channel 10, where he made some money on the side by taking pictures of the actors for their portfolios. "I was collecting $47 a week unemployment, and then I lost the unemployment because I got a job making $45 a week," he says ruefully. "It was so incredibly wonderful. I look back on that stuff and I wouldn't give it up for anything. It was so great. I mean, I was living in my van. Then I got an apartment with a friend of mine, Don Sparks, who's a great actor. He and I roomed together, and I think it was $110 a month, $55 each, and I was making $45 a week. They say your rent should be about one week's salary, so I was pushing it a little bit."

Despite the fact that he was just scraping by, he put his father's advice to good use. "From when I was little, my dad taught me how to save money. Before you pay your bills, you first pay yourself. So you take 10% and put it in the bank. Ten percent of my $45 a week was $4.50, so I rounded it up to $5 and I would always stop by the savings and loan on Laurel and Fifth and stick my $5 in there, and I'd use the rest of my salary to pay bills. At the end of the season, I remember some of the equity actors at the Globe getting paid five times as much as I was every week were tapped out. They'd spent all their money, and I had $300 saved up!"

After Hays landed his first television role playing a psychiatrist in an episode of the David Janssen series *Harry O,* he moved to Los Angeles. Within two years he'd acted in more than twenty-five shows. While appearing as a series regular on *Angie,* he also managed to squeeze in his big screen debut in *Airplane!* Since then, he's found success on television and in films.

"You never feel like you've gotten whatever it is you're trying to get to. One time I was at a party at a friend's house and this young guy came up to me and said, 'Wow! What's it like?' I asked, 'What's what like?' He said, 'Man, you made it! You're on top of the mountain! What's it like?' And I thought, 'Wow, that's pretty interesting. Here I am just struggling along and this guy thinks I'm on top.' So I said, 'Well, basically it's really nice, but every time you get up to what you think is the top of the mountain, you realize it's just a plateau, so you're never going to see the top of that mountain. You're just going to reach plateaus over and over. It's really great, and a lot of fun to sit here and relax, but you can't do that very long because as soon as you do, everything starts to pass you by. Unless you keep moving up, that's all you're ever going to have. It's a constant struggle.'"

Hays is married to actress-singer Cherie Currie. Their son, Jake, was born in February 1991, exactly nine months from their wedding night. Hays, who waited until his forties to get married and start a family, has always kept himself busy. A pilot, he claims he's been too busy with projects lately to get in the air. "The last flying I did was toward my helicopter rating. I haven't got the rating yet, but I've got about thirty-two hours towards it. I haven't done any fixed-wing flying for awhile."

His other hobbies include mountain climbing (he hiked the Matterhorn in 1989), auto racing (he's won several pro-am races), horseback riding (his family has always kept horses) and tennis. The second annual Robert Hays Celebrity Tennis Classic was held at the Le Meridien in San Diego this year to benefit needy kids. One sport he enjoyed while living in San Diego was surfing. "I remember surfing Black's when it was a nude beach. I had these baggy painter's pants that I lived in because they were only $2.50 each. You know, white, with hooks on 'em to hold brushes, and pockets all over. I'd wear those things until they'd start wearing out in the knees, and I'd cut them off and make shorts out of them. That's what I used to surf in. I remember one time at Black's, I was on a six or eight foot wave. I was screaming down this wave, cranked a bottom turn and crouched in the tube when I felt a rip in my shorts... and then another... and pretty soon my trunks were just shredded and I was holding them overhead, swinging them in a circle. Great ride – and hey, it was a nude beach, anyway."

Tawny Kitaen
Actress

Tawny Kitaen has made her dreams come true by achieving fame and fortune both as a model and as a highly sought-after actress. "There have been times when I haven't gotten anything that I've wanted or anything that resembles what I wanted, but I have always been able to pick myself up by the bootstraps and go forward," she says. After growing up in San Diego, Kitaen appeared in rock videos, handed out MTV music video awards, starred in movies like *Bachelor Party* and *Witchboard* and had numerous television parts before landing a regular role on the new *WKRP in Cincinnati.* On top of all that, she recently became the new co-host of *America's Funniest People.* Kitaen has come a long way from the girl who once cruised the Pacific Beach boardwalk on her bike.

Julie Kitaen (she changed her name to Tawny when she was six) was born in Grossmont Hospital in 1961 and comes from a long line of San Diegans. Both her grandparents and parents attended Hoover High, and most of her family still resides in San Diego. Kitaen grew up in El Cajon, Pacific Beach and La Jolla before graduating from Mission Bay High in 1978. Although she now lives in Newport Beach, she still calls San Diego home. "I love San Diego. It's my favorite place on earth," she says earnestly.

Kitaen's fondest memories are of her teen years. "We used to get on our bicycles and ride down Diamond Street to the beach and just cruise the boardwalk, back and forth, and watch all the good-looking guys carry their surfboards into the water." She also recalls going to Straight Ahead Sound and hanging out with bands like Ratt before they became international rock stars.

"I worked at Burger King on Mission Boulevard and, believe it or not, it was one of my favorite jobs," Kitaen remembers. "My boss was really cool. Usually you had to pay your dues by making burgers in the back for awhile so you could get up to the front. I did not dig cooking in the back because it was always too hot and you couldn't see the beach." She quickly worked her way up to cashier. At sixteen, she worked at Mission Bay Hospital, making announcements over the intercom from 11:00 p.m. to 7:00 a.m. That was her last regular job before becoming a model at seventeen.

Kitaen certainly had the looks for a successful modeling career, but because she was short for a fashion model, she never thought it would last. About this time, she won a national talent contest called *Faces of Tomorrow* along with Arsenio Hall. At nineteen, she accepted a role in *The Perils of Gwendolyn*, filmed in France and Spain. Returning to the States, she starred opposite Tom Hanks in *Bachelor Party*

Tawny Kitaen

and went on to star in four more feature films. She broke into television as the rich, snobby New York heiress in the HBO comedy series, *Glory Years.* Kitaen was also visible in music videos featuring hard rock bands Ratt and Whitesnake. She eventually married David Coverdale, lead singer for Whitesnake, putting her career on hold. When they broke up, she returned to television as Mona Loveland, a sexy late-night DJ with a big heart on the new *WKRP.* She's currently working on an animated cartoon for Fox as the voice of an 800-pound cat named Annabelle in *Eek, the Cat.*

Things have worked out well for the girl who turned down the opportunity to compete for San Diego's Over The Line Tournament's Miss Emerson. "I was talking to Kathy [Estocin, childhood friend and celebrity hairdresser] the other day during makeup before we started shooting," says Kitaen, "and I said, 'When we were fourteen or fifteen, what was more important to me – to be famous or to be rich?' And she said, 'I think at that point it was more important to be famous.'" And now? "Rich!" is Kitaen's reply.

Tawny Kitaen has achieved both fame and fortune in her career and takes solace in the security her earnings give her. "It means a certain freedom and a certain security to me," Kitaen says seriously. "I think all of us have a fear of ending up a bag lady, and I have a good chance of not – unless I'm stupid and I'm foolish with money. If I play my cards right, I'll be able to retire one day and travel. As a single female, it's really important to have that kind of security."

She has the drive and determination to make it in almost every endeavor she undertakes. As Kitaen puts it, "I always knew that there ain't nothin' I can't do."

Kitaen is an excited mother-to-be. She and California Angels pitcher Chuck Finley are expecting their first child early in 1993.

David Leisure
Actor

David Leisure, better known as the sleazy car salesman Joe Isuzu or as Charley, the conniving neighbor on NBC's prime-time sitcom, *Empty Nest,* found that the road to success was long and hard, and sometimes had him sleeping curbside. Through incredible perseverance and a burning desire to make his dream of becoming a working actor a reality, he was able to overcome the many years of frustration and financial hardship. Things were so bad during those tough times that he twice ended up living out of his 1964 Volkswagen bus, and it cost him his first marriage. Those days are behind him now and Leisure, who is entering his forties, turned his big break as TV pitchman Joe Isuzu into a solid career doing what he wanted to do all along – act for a living.

As an overweight student at Grossmont High School (220 pounds), Leisure developed a sense of humor about himself. It was a defense mechanism that proved useful later in his career. After losing over sixty pounds the summer before his junior year, he decided to join the drama club. He quite simply fell in love with acting. He thrived on the audience's response and applause, finding his self-worth on the stage. He went to Grossmont College and then on to San Diego State University, earning a degree in fine arts. At State, he roomed with Robert Hays, another San Diegan who would make good in Hollywood (best known as the star of the movie *Airplane!*).

After graduation, Leisure headed to Los Angeles to begin his acting career. Unfortunately, he didn't land his first part until six years later, and he had to shave his head to do it. After four auditions, he finally landed the role of a Hare Krishna for the 1980 film *Airplane!* that his old roommate Robert Hays was starring in. Soon after, Leisure's career hit another dry spell, and he waited tables and slept in his van, hoping that his next acting bit was just around the corner. His marriage fell apart under the pressure, and it was years before he found work as an actor again. After attending a workshop on making commercials, he landed his first role as a TV pitchman. He did a series of ads for the Bell Atlantic Yellow Pages and then hit it big when he was hired over eighty others to play Joe Isuzu, the soon-to-be-famous center of a hilariously different auto ad campaign. In these ads, the fibbing car salesman found it impossible to tell the truth. In many of the ads, he's seen making bold and deceitful claims about Isuzu cars and trucks while the words "He's lying" are superimposed on the bottom of the screen. In one of the most memorable of these ads, Joe Isuzu is making a pitch for the Isuzu I-Mark: "It gets ninety-four miles per gallon, city, 112 highway. Its top speed is 300 miles per hour and, if you come in tomorrow, you'll get a free house. You have my word on it." Leisure parlayed his huge success into the role of Charley, the obnoxious neighbor on *Empty Nest.* Typecasting – even as a slithering sleazeball – is working in Leisure's favor.

Many people would have given up their dream if they had to face even a few of the low points David Leisure has had to overcome. He never quit and, through sheer determination and a will to succeed, became living proof that dreams don't have to die young. He achieved success in his mid-thirties after years of rejection, a broken marriage and real financial hardship, but he's now doing what he most enjoys. He remarried, plays golf regularly and earns over fifty-five million dollars a year. (I'm lying about that last part. But he does earn enough so he won't have to take up residence in his Volkswagen ever again.)

Cleavon Little
Tony Award-Winning Actor

Cleavon Little was a major success on and off Broadway, as well as in motion pictures and television. He won a Tony in 1970 for his outstanding performance in the musical *Purlie*. His movie credits include the hilarious, classic cowboy spoof *Blazing Saddles, Once Bitten, Toy Soldiers, Arthur II, On the Rocks* and *Fletch Lives.* He was awarded an Emmy for his appearance on television's *Dear John,* and has also been seen in *All in the Family, Temperatures Rising, Police Story, Bagdad Cafe, Midnight Caller* and *Simon and Simon,* which was shot in San Diego.

Little's rise to the top wasn't without its share of hard times. He was born in Oklahoma in 1939, but his family moved to San Diego when he was three. His childhood was underprivileged, but he was proud of who he was, if uncertain what the future held. He once told *TV Guide* (April 28, 1973), "My mother and my father gave me a sense of pride in myself, as a man and as a black man. They never told me I was anything less than that. And I never had any complexes about it. I never wished I was anything else... They made me feel good about myself. A lot of people feel so terrible about themselves that they never pursue the talents they have. And every human being has a talent. The trick is finding it and knowing it once you've found it."

Little discovered and began to explore his special talent for acting when he was at Kearny High School. He pursued acting at San Diego City College and the Old Globe Theatre before becoming discouraged at San Diego State University. A constant worrier, Little developed an ulcer while he was still a teenager. He dropped out of acting and took a job working with gifted children at the Jewish Community Center. When his father fell ill, Little became the sole provider for his family of

Cleavon Little

seven, working nights at his dad's janitorial job.

Eventually, Little was able to return to school and graduated from San Diego State University in 1965. He won an ABC competition for a two-year scholarship to the American Academy of Dramatic Arts in New York, where he did some important and impressive stage work. He had parts in *MacBird!* and *Scuba Duba* and became close friends with Dustin Hoffman when they worked together in *Jimmy Shine*. In 1970 he followed *Jimmy Shine* with his Tony Award-winning performance in *Purlie*. His first television appearance – on *Archie Bunker* –

led to a starring role in the series *Temperatures Rising*. After that, his career was both prolific and steady.

Cleavon Little was held in high regard by his peers and loved by his many fans. And why not? He took his own advice and discovered his special talent – then went ahead and made the most of it. The only thing that could stop him was cancer. Cleavon Little died in October, 1992.

Gregory Peck
Legendary Actor

This Academy Award-winning actor has appeared in over fifty movies since leaving San Diego and becoming an international star. The handsome Peck acted in some of Hollywood's finest films during a long and illustrious career. He is often cast as the "good guy," such as the Southern lawyer in *To Kill A Mockingbird,* a priest, farmer, general, president and, more recently, the proud and stubborn businessman in *Other People's Money*. But despite his amiable good looks, he's been quite convincingly sinister, most notably as Josef Mengele, the evil and despicable Nazi in *The Boys from Brazil*. Peck has been nominated for an Academy Award five times, winning one for *To Kill A Mockingbird.*

Peck was born in La Jolla on April 5, 1916. His father owned the only pharmacy in town, right on Prospect Street. La Jolla was just a sleepy little seacoast village when Peck was growing up. Everybody knew everybody else. For the most part, his childhood was a happy one, and he spent a lot of time at La Jolla Cove. Then his father lost his business, and his parents divorced while Peck was still very young. He sold papers and shined shoes to earn extra money, until he was sent off to St. John's Military Academy in Los Angeles at the age of ten.

During his late teens, the tall and lanky Peck lived with his father, attending San Diego High School. At eighteen, he quit school to become a truck driver, but quickly realized there was no future in that. He enrolled at San Diego State University, then transferred to UC Berkeley as a pre-med student, working his way through school waiting tables and parking cars. When Peck, who was somewhat of a loner, was offered a chance to act, he accepted, despite his awkwardness and lack of self-confidence. He relished the idea of making new friends, and he liked acting – so much so that he ended up graduating with a B.A. in Drama.

Soon after graduation, Peck set off for New York to see if he could make a career of acting. It didn't take long to get his answer. He worked briefly on Broadway before becoming a star in RKO's *Days of Glory* and *Keys to the Kingdom.* Peck's most memorable hits include *Spellbound, The Yearling, Gentleman's Agreement, Twelve O'Clock High, The Snows of Kilimanjaro, Moby Dick, The Guns of Navarone* and *To Kill a Mockingbird.* Like many successful actors these days, Peck turned to producing films. He is partly responsible for bringing *Cape Fear* and *Pork Chop Hill* to the screen.

Not one to ignore his roots, Peck co-founded the La Jolla Playhouse along with Dorothy McGuire and Mel Ferrer in 1947. He held the distinguished position of President of the Academy of Motion Picture Arts and Sciences from 1967 through 1970. He has also been active in the American Cancer Society, the National Council on the Arts and The American Film Institute.

Peck has been happily married for over thirty years to his second wife, Veronique. They met when she interviewed him. They have two children; Peck had three children from his first marriage. His eldest son, Jonathan, tragically committed suicide in 1975 at the age of thirty. His son Stephen is a documentary filmmaker, Carey is a banker and Tony and Cecilia are aspiring actors. Tony was married to ex-supermodel Cheryl Tiegs and Cecilia starred in the feature film *Torn Apart* in 1990.

Today, the legendary Gregory Peck lives with his wife on their estate in the Holmby Hills section of Los Angeles.

Briefs

Desi Arnaz (1917-1986).

He will always be remembered for his portrayal of Ricky Ricardo on the perennially-popular television series *I Love Lucy*. In addition to his on-screen accomplishments, however, Arnaz was an innovator behind the scenes. His grandfather founded the Bacardi Rum Company, but the Cuban Revolution stripped his family of its wealth. Arnaz fled to the U.S., where he first worked cleaning birdcages in Florida. The musician-turned-actor married Lucille Ball and achieved both fame and fortune with the syndication of their semi-autobiographical television show, but he also appeared in several films. He spent the last two decades of his life in Del Mar.

Annette Bening

This talented actress has received considerable attention recently from gossip columns regarding her marriage to Warren Beatty and the child born to the unmarried couple in early 1992. Yet even before they met during the filming of *Bugsy,* Bening attracted attention as an accomplished actress with some very impressive credentials. She was nominated for the coveted Tony Award in 1987 for her role in the Broadway play *Coastal Disturbances* and earned an Oscar nomination in 1991 for her portrayal of the sexy con artist Myra Langtry in *The Grifters* (partially filmed in San Diego). Bening's family moved to San Diego when she was seven. After deciding to become an actress, she took drama classes at Patrick Henry High School. Graduating in 1975, she pursued another of her interests, scuba diving, working as a cook aboard a charter boat in San Diego. Meanwhile, she continued her drama studies at Mesa College, making her Old Globe debut as a belly dancer in the 1977 production of *Timon of Athens.* After years of stage work, Bening made it to Hollywood with several prime time television appearances, including *Miami Vice.* Her feature film debut was opposite John Candy and Dan Aykroyd in *Great Outdoors.* Other film credits include *Postcards from the Edge, Guilty by Suspicion* and *Regarding Henry.*

Victor Buono (1938-1981)

Born in San Diego in 1938, Victor Buono first began acting at St. Augustine High School and in San Diego Junior Theater. He went on to become one of San Diego's most renowned actors. He first left San Diego for Hollywood in 1957 at the age of nineteen, but returned after eight months, ready to throw in the towel. Fortunately, he was "discovered" while performing at the Old Globe. During his career as a character actor, Buono appeared in more than twenty-five films, portrayed evil King Tut in *Batman, the Series* for several television seasons and played more than twenty roles at the Globe. In 1962, Buono was nominated for best supporting actor for his role in *Whatever Happened to Baby Jane?* also starring Bette Davis and Joan Crawford. He won his first Atlas Award at the ripe old age of eighteen, eventually winning two more for his commanding stagework. At six feet tall and over three hundred pounds, Buono cut an imposing figure equally at home with comedy and drama. He died at the age of forty-three.

Michael Damian

To thousands of soap opera fans, Damian is better known as Danny Romalotti, a character he created and has played on *The Young and the Restless* for over a decade. Many San Diegans also remember him as one of the vocalists in the 1970's progressive rock band, the Weirz, which included other members of his family. The second youngest of nine siblings, Damian grew up in Escondido but moved to Los Angeles in 1978. Soon after relocating, he struck out on his own and released "She Did It" in 1980, a song that led Dick Clark to invite him to perform on *American Bandstand.* That break led to an audition for a role on *The Young and the Restless.* The producers of the soap designed a character around his unique talents, and Danny Romalotti, a struggling singer by night and a waiter by day, was born. "It was funny, because that's exactly what was happening to me in real life," Damian laughs, "so I basically went into the role playing myself." Off the screen, his music career really took off. His version of "Rock On" sold over five hundred thousand copies, earning Damian a gold single. His two other hits include "Cover of Love" and a ballad he wrote as well as performed, "Was It Nothing At All."

Ted Danson

Although Danson's family moved away from San Diego when he was a child, he was born here in December, 1947. He needs no introduction — his portrayal of Sam Malone, ex-baseball player and owner of everyone's favorite bar has made him a star. The award-winning NBC comedy series *Cheers* has made his name a household word. After several seasons of being nominated for an Emmy Award as best actor in a comedy series, Danson finally received the honor in 1990. But Danson didn't start out on top. He paid his dues performing in several commercials, playing a box of lemon-chiffon pie mix in one. His first important role came in the steamy thriller *Body Heat* in 1981. The box-office success of *Three Men and a Baby,* starring Danson, Tom Selleck and Steve Guttenberg gave him stature as a film star. Currently, Danson devotes much of his free time to cleaning up ocean pollution through an organization he and his wife helped found.

Jimmy "Schnozzola" Durante (1893-1980)

The big-nosed, gravel-voiced entertainer appeared in numerous movies, his last being *It's a Mad, Mad, Mad, Mad World* in 1963. That year he was also made honorary mayor of Del Mar, a place he called home every summer since 1937 and his second residence for thirteen years. With a few friends from Hollywood, Durante helped build the track and establish Del Mar's thoroughbred racing scene, making it a popular summer destination for the "movie crowd" for many years. Long after he retired, his distinctive profile could often be seen at the horse races or along the beach, surf fishing. The road and the bridge leading to the fairgrounds were renamed in his honor.

Faye Emerson

The late actress was successful in film, on stage, radio and television. She came to San Diego while still in her teens and studied drama first at Point Loma High School and later at San Diego State University. A lovely blonde, she was discovered in 1941 while acting at the Old Globe. After success as an actress, she hosted her own talk shows, *The*

Faye Emerson Show and *Fay Emerson's Wonderful Town.* She was an early advocate of women broadcasters and producers.

Dennis Hopper

In a career that has spanned over three decades, this talented actor/director from Lemon Grove has had his share of ups and downs. But each time the resilient Hopper has been down, he fought his way back, and today he has both life and career in order. After his family moved to the San Diego area, Hopper attended Lemon Grove Junior High. He was voted "most likely to succeed" by his Helix High School classmates in 1954. At Helix, he was very active in both the drama and speech clubs while apprenticing at the La Jolla Playhouse. He left San Diego in his late teens with $200 he earned working at the Old Globe. Quickly signed by Warner Brothers, he starred in his first film, *Johnny Guitar,* in 1954. The following year he was cast opposite James Dean in the classic *Rebel Without A Cause.* He was blackballed and labeled difficult to work with shortly after appearing in *Giant,* and resorted to television work while moonlighting as a photographer to earn a living. In 1969, he made a Hollywood comeback in dramatic fashion, writing, directing and co-starring in the award-winning film, *Easy Rider.* Hopper's years of drug and alcohol abuse caught up with him, though, and he bottomed out in the early 1980's. Again, he made a dramatic come-back, returning completely drug and alcohol free to portray a recovering alcoholic in the 1986 film *Hoosiers,* which earned him an Oscar nomination. In 1987 he returned to directing, scoring a box-office hit with the controversial *Colors,* starring fellow San Diegan Robert Duvall. Making up for lost time, he has been busy acting and directing ever since, only taking time out to indulge his other passion, collecting art.

Julie Kavner

This San Diego State University drama graduate (1973) has done her alma mater proud. She has worked steadily in show business since 1974, but has only recently received the recognition due her. Before starring in the 1992 film *This Is My Life,* about a single mother's struggle to make it as a stand-up comic, Kavner was probably best known as the voice of Marge on *The Simpsons.* While growing up, she always wanted to become an actress although, slightly overweight and introverted, she certainly didn't look the part. Even her parents had their doubts. She worked as a typist to make ends meet until breaking into television as the awkward kid sister in *Rhoda.*

Since then she has made her mark, winning an Emmy Award in 1978 for Best Supporting Actress in a comedy series for her work in *Rhoda* and garnering two other Emmy nominations as well. She showed her versatility as one of the ensemble players on *The Tracy Ullman Show,* appeared in five Woody Allen films and had roles in the movies *Awakenings* and *This Is My Life.*

Kathy Najimy

Playing an eternally upbeat nun opposite Whoopi Goldberg in the 1992 smash hit *Sister Act* made Kathy Najimy a star. A graduate of Crawford High School, she told *People Magazine* (6/22/92) what it was like growing up on the heavy side: "When you're not thin and blonde, you come up with a personality real quick. Funny people don't have to be Barbie dolls." Her acting career began when she and her three siblings staged their own garage productions. She went on to major in theater at San Diego State University, supporting herself working various odd jobs. She came face-to-face with her idol, Bette Midler, dressed as a rabbit and delivering a singing telegram to an amused Midler after a local concert. Najimy was such a fan she had pictures taken of herself standing in front of Midler's door in New York. Now she's set to star in a Disney movie opposite her idol. Najimy can also be seen in bit parts in *Soapdish, The Fisher King* and *This Is My Life.*

Cliff Robertson

The Oscar-winning actor has appeared in over one hundred television roles, dozens of films and is the corporate spokesperson for AT&T. Born in La Jolla in 1925, Robertson's parents split when he was two. His mother died just months later, and he was raised by his grandmother in La Jolla. Robertson's father was a well-to-do playboy who lived off a large trust fund, but Cliff established a strong work ethic early in life. He lied about his age to get a job selling magazines when he was only nine years old. He later had a paper route and woke at four in the morning to trap lobsters. He rode his bike thirteen miles from La Jolla to wash planes in exchange for an occasional flying lesson, and flying vintage planes remains one of his greatest joys in life. Robertson served in the Merchant Marines during World War II. Afterwards, he financed his education at the Actor's Studio in New York himself, unwilling to accept money from his family. He lived in a tiny apartment and parked cars, bused tables, drove a cab, worked construction and drove a truck to make ends meet when he wasn't acting in off-Broadway productions. One of his first (paying) acting jobs offered free room and board along with a few dollars a week. The years of struggle paid off in 1968, when he won an Academy Award for best actor in the title role of *Charlie,* a film he helped bring to the screen. A few years later, he took a stand against a corrupt Hollywood mogul, turning him in for allegedly embezzling thousands of dollars – a story told in the bestselling book, *Indecent Exposure.* After this incident, Hollywood closed ranks against him and he found it next to impossible to find work until 1981, when he was cast in *Brainstorm.* His comeback included the television series role of a neurosurgeon on *Falcon Crest.* In 1991, Robertson was seen in *Wild Hearts Can't Be Broken* and in 1992 he co-starred in Francis Ford Coppola's *Wind.* He still lives part-time in La Jolla.

Marion Ross

Known to many San Diegans for her years onstage at the Old Globe and the La Jolla Playhouse, Marion Ross is best known to the rest of the world as Mrs. Cunningham, for her role in the successful ABC series *Happy Days* (1974-1984). The Emmy-nominated actress also starred as Sophie Berger on the CBS series *Brooklyn Bridge.* After she decided to become an actress at age thirteen, Marion worked hard to make her dream come true. A real hustler, her drive to succeed and love of her work sees her continuing at a frantic pace to this day. A graduate of Point Loma High School and San Diego City College, she spent many years in San Diego. She currently maintains a second home in Cardiff-by-the-Sea.

Charlene Tilton

Charlene Tilton is best known as Lucy Ewing on *Dallas,* where she played J.R.'s sexy niece. Born in San Diego in 1958, she grew up in the "shack city part of Hollywood, the kind of neighborhood you drive through with your windows rolled up." [*People Magazine,* 5/9/88] She never knew her father, who left when she was born. Her mother was an emigré from Yugoslavia, who did her best to support them both on her secretary's salary. Left for long hours on her own, Charlene decided at a very young age that she would make it as an actress, and she devoted her life to making it happen. She appeared in every school play she could wangle a part in and by age ten was traveling by bus to see agents she'd looked up in the Yellow Pages. She landed her first bit part in Disney's *Freaky Friday* while still in high school. Though her friends tried to discourage her, trying to point her toward a more "sensible" career, she kept looking for her big break. She was "discovered" while working in a t-shirt shop and landed some small roles before making it big on *Dallas* early in 1978. The diminutive actress (a bare 5 feet tall) is known for her continued devotion to fitness, and looks better than ever in her thirties.

Raquel Welch

Raquel Tejada started her career as a cheerleader and a member of the drama club at La Jolla High School. She was crowned "Fairest of the Fair" in 1958, changed her name and turned her ambitions toward Hollywood. During the late 1960's, the voluptuous Raquel Welch worked very hard to bring attention to herself, with fierce determination to become a star. Her relentless pursuit of that goal took her from modeling for a Sunset Strip sports shop to wearing a fur bikini in her debut film, *One Million Years B.C.* Once established as a sex symbol, she spent years trying to be taken seriously as an actress. She finally gained some respect when she earned the Golden Globe Award for Best Actress in *The Three Musketeers.* When producers were unwilling to take a chance on her in a musical comedy, she launched her own one-woman show. It wasn't particularly successful, but she didn't give up. She took more singing and dancing lessons and tried again. This time she packed them in, becoming a regular headliner in Las Vegas. Her books and videos on fitness and beauty also enjoy a great deal of success.

Chapter 2: Musicians

Stephen Bishop

Nathan East

Michael Franks

Joey Harris

Steve Laury

Nick Reynolds

Peter Sprague

Briefs

Peter Allen · A.J. Croce · Bob Crosby
Fattburger · Rosie Flores · Hollis Gentry
Sam Hinton · Iron Butterfly · Frankie Laine
Kevyn Lettau · Bob Magnusson
Barbara Mandrell · Mojo Nixon
Gary Puckett and the Union Gap · Ratt
Roger Reynolds · Gustavo Romero
Jack Tempchin · Earl Thomas
Eddie Vedder · Tom Waits
Frank Zappa

Stephen Bishop
Singer, Songwriter

San Diego native Stephen Bishop has done it all in his up-and-down career in show business. As a musician, he was awarded best male vocalist of the year, garnering gold records with the hit singles "On and On" and "Save It for a Rainy Day." Top artists Phil Collins, Eric Clapton and Sting have been happy to work with him. He has written hundreds of songs, including the Grammy-nominated "Separate Lives" from the film *White Nights.*

As an actor, Bishop has made cameo appearances in a number of movies, including *National Lampoon's Animal House* and has even hosted a TV variety show.

Stephen Bishop, once a *San Diego Union* paperboy, lived in Chula Vista, Mission Valley, North Park and La Mesa with his mother and stepfather. His parents were divorced when he was eight. Young Bishop was heavily influenced by the Beatles. A self-taught musician, he performed locally with a band called the Weeds, which finished runner-up in a local Battle of the Bands contest.

Immediately after graduating from Crawford High School in 1969, Bishop headed to Los Angeles to make it as a rock star. Success didn't come easy. It took him over seven years of frustration and hardship before he finally got a break. During those lean years, Bishop eked out a meager existence, riding his bicycle to auditions. During all that time, he never gave up the dream of making it as a rock star. Then, in 1975, Tom Sullivan sang Bishop's song "One More Night" on the Johnny Carson Show, and his career began to take off.

Bishop's 1977 debut album *Careless* yielded his two biggest hits to date, "On and On" and "Save It For A Rainy Day," establishing him as a pop superstar. His days of poverty over, he moved into new digs in the Hollywood Hills. His 1978 follow-up album, simply titled *Bish,* was also a success, including the hit song "Everybody Needs Love."

After the success of *Bish,* it was an uphill battle to repeat his early string of hits. Bishop recorded a third album, *Red Cab To Manhattan,*

Stephen Bishop   *Photo by Martin Mann*

but it failed to yield any hit songs. He turned to songwriting for films, including *Summer Lovers* and *Arthur,* writing and singing the theme song from *Tootsie,* "It Must Be You."

Bishop's life and career took a turn for the worse after the death of his mother, with whom he was very close. His next album, *Sleeping With Girls,* was never released, and the project left him financially strapped. After a long dry spell, he returned in the late 1980's with the fantastic *Bowling In Paris.* The encouragement and support of his friend Phil Collins helped make that album possible.

In the liners notes on the Rhino release *Best of Bish*, Bishop writes, "I've always felt some people in this business could never figure me out. Songwriter, recording person or a strange guy with weird clothes. Well, I'm all of those..."

Nathan East
Musician, Songwriter

Since graduating from the University of California at San Diego with a degree in music, Nathan East has established himself as one of the top bass players in music today. His credits are so numerous and diverse, it's impossible to list them all. Here's just a sample of the people he has recorded and performed with since leaving San Diego for Los Angeles in 1979: Eric Clapton, Michael Jackson, Dolly Parton, Barbra Streisand, Al Jarreau, Phil Collins, Ray Charles, Kenny Loggins, the Eurythmics, Kenny Rogers, Lionel Ritchie and George Benson. And this doesn't even mention the other work this busy bassist has been doing. He's provided the groove for many movie soundtracks and hundreds of commercials.

As songwriter, Nathan East was one-third of the team that wrote the hit "Easy Lover" for Philip Bailey's *Chinese Wall* album. Phil Collins also produced, sang, played drums and helped pen that one. As part of the jazz super-group Fourplay, East teamed up with old friends Lee Ritenour (guitar), Harvey Mason (drums) and Bob James (keyboards) to again achieve success. The band's debut album, released in 1991, had an extended stay of over 25 weeks at the top of *Billboard's* Contemporary Jazz Album Chart.

East and his brother Marcel co-own a Los Angeles recording studio, and the two are working on their first album. East also toured with Eric Clapton since playing bass for the *Behind The Sun* album in 1986. To say his musical career is a success story is a gross understatement.

East grew up in San Diego, where he attended Crawford High School. Before he picked up the bass guitar at fourteen, he studied the cello for about three years. After learning a few licks on the bass, he played with the band at a school dance and for the first time heard the intoxicating roar of the crowd.

At Crawford, East played bass in the jazz band, orchestra and pep band, giving him valuable sight-reading experience. He also gained stage experience playing proms and dances with a local group called Power, which included Hollis Gentry and Carl Evans, Jr. East developed his ear playing along with the radio, listening to Chicago, Earth, Wind and Fire and Tower of Power. He practiced prodigiously, eventually developing into one of San Diego's top jazz players.

At UCSD, East played in a band six nights a week. With two quarters to go before graduation, he left to go on the road with Power, backing up singer Barry White. He returned to earn his bachelor's degree before moving to Los Angeles to pursue a career as a studio session player. Despite a rough start, once keyboardist Patrice Rushin recommended him for a gig with flautist Hubert Laws, he's been working non-stop. He began what can only be described as an over-loaded studio schedule, becoming "everybody's bassist."

East worked with a variety of musicians, playing everything from jazz to rock to country. Talented and versatile, he's the consummate professional, getting along well with other musicians. He played bass on countless hit songs by many of the top artists in the business. Over the years, his relationship with Eric Clapton grew, and he was involved with Clapton's latest hit, "Tears In Heaven."

A workaholic, East is so busy he rarely gets a day off, but when you love what you do and receive adulation from your peers and top money for your efforts, it's hard to say "no." Especially when Quincy Jones, Peter Gabriel, Michael Bolton, Julio Iglesias and Earl Klugh are all calling for your special touch.

There was a time, in his first six months in L.A., when his phone didn't ring at all. Today, Nathan East's phone is ringing off the hook — and he's happy to hear it, happy to be busy.

Michael Franks
Jazz/Pop Singer, Songwriter

On the title track of Michael Franks' tenth album, *Blue Pacific,* the San Diego native sings about being a hometown boy who makes good. This is something Franks definitely knows about. He's achieved great success and popularity. He's someone San Diegans can be proud to claim as one of their own.

Franks' music is as diverse as his many talents. It's a fusion of pop, contemporary jazz and funk — it is and has always been innovative and original. The singer, songwriter and multi-instrumentalist is known for his smooth, whispery voice and clever lyrics. His songs take a unique look at love and relationships, tropical locales and art.

Franks was born in La Jolla and grew up in the then-sleepy beach town of Mission Beach. His family lived in many San Diego communities, usually near the beach. He played in a number of pop and folk bands at University High School before graduating in 1962. Admiration of The Kingston Trio prompted him to purchase his first guitar from Thearles Music Store in downtown San Diego. Later he left to study at UCLA and the University of Montreal, where he majored in contemporary literature. He eventually earned his degree from UCLA.

Early in his career, Franks opened for Gordon Lightfoot and worked with blues giants Sonny Terry and Brownie McGee. He later recorded his first single, "Can't Seem To Shake This Rock 'n Roll," embarking on a national tour with comedian Robert Klein. His long relationship with Warner Brothers began when he took on a musical research project which led to a contract in 1975. His first album, *The Art of Tea,* came out the following year and yielded Franks' first pop/jazz hit, "Popsicle Toes." The follow-up album, *Sleeping Gypsy,* was another gem, setting the stage for a long and consistent career. His most recent album reached the top of the adult contemporary charts and another is scheduled for the spring of 1993.

On *Sleeping Gypsy,* Franks employed members of the talented jazz group, The Crusaders, establishing his trademark: surrounding himself with the best musicians and producers in the music business. The list of musicians who have appeared on Michael Franks albums reads like a *Who's Who* of contemporary jazz. Larry Carlton, Joe Sample, Jeff Lorber, Steve Gadd, Earl Klugh and David Sanborn are only a few.

Franks and his wife currently live in Florida. Usually, when he comes to San Diego for a show he only stays a day or two, but in October 1989 he spent a whole month in town, writing part of *Blue Pacific.* It was a nostalgic time for him, recalling his youth and the area that was once his home. Interestingly, despite his success as a popular music star, he was seldom recognized during his stay in San Diego.

Franks is a contemporary jazz superstar with many other interests as well. He loves art, is dedicated to fitness and supports a variety of worthy causes. He's been working for many years on a musical based on the life of the artist, Paul Gauguin. Three songs from this long-awaited musical are on his current hit album. An avid runner, Franks jogged around Mission Bay during his visit in 1989 and wrote "Long, Slow Distance" about his love of the sport. He's committed to the environment and the fair and ethical treatment of animals.

Joey Harris
Guitarist-Singer for The Beat Farmers

Joey Harris was born to play guitar. It's in his blood. His uncle is Nick Reynolds, a founding member and deft guitarist of The Kingston Trio, one of the most popular musical groups in recent history. In fact, it was his famous uncle who taught young Joey his first few chords on the ukulele. Reynolds now proudly boasts that Harris is "one of the great guitar players in the country." It's a talent he puts to good use as guitarist-singer with hometown heroes, the Beat Farmers – a band that's legendary around the country for its brand of rowdy, rock-a-billy music. Yet, despite being named group of the year in 1991 at the San Diego Music Awards, the critically-acclaimed band has yet to find commercial success. As they prepare to record a new album for a late-1992 release, they're hoping for increased record sales. But they won't compromise their musical integrity. That's something that's been important to The Beat Farmers since Harris joined them six years ago. "Working with these guys has been just a real great experience, and Country Dick [founding member of the band] is just a constant source of inspiration," he says.

Harris, now thirty-five, was born into a very musical family. "There were always guitars around the house. My grandfather was a great guitar player. In fact, I still have his old Martin. He inspired his three kids, Nick, my mom [Jane] and my Aunt Barbara to sing and play, and that rubbed off on us, too."

Growing up in Coronado, Harris was more influenced by the

Beatles than the Kingston Trio. Ironically, it was the Beatles and the whole British Invasion that knocked his uncle's group right off the top of the charts. His musical tastes evolved from the Beatles to Jimi Hendrix when he "just sort of went crazy." Harris then discovered blues and BB King and Eric Clapton's style of playing. Always in touch with the local music scene, he remembers seeing current Beat Farmers lead guitarist Jerry Raney playing at a place called JJ's while he was still in high school.

After graduating from Coronado High in 1975, Harris began learning his trade by doing it. He auditioned for and won a spot in John Stewart's band. Stewart, who also grew up in Coronado, was a songwriter for and a member of the Kingston Trio and was embarking on a solo tour. Harris toured with Stewart until 1979, all the while learning about songwriting and developing his own unique and witty style. "I went from trying to be a guitar monster to trying to be another Randy Newman. Yikes!" says Harris.

In 1980, Country Dick called, wanting to put together a country band. That's when Country Dick and the Snuggle Bunnies was formed. The band consisted of anywhere from four to ten members, depending on who decided to show up at gigs. In 1982, Harris and his high school pal Bruce Donnelly went to Australia at the urging of a publisher to record a solo album under the name Joey Harris and the Speedsters. The album was not a success. Dejected and disappointed, Harris moved back home to live with his parents and take a job in a Coronado pizza shop. During that time, Country Dick put together the Beat Farmers, and the band really took off. Their first album, *Tales of the New West,* released in 1985, came right at the height of a trend that saw the band touring Europe to rave reviews. When guitarist Buddy Blue left the group, Harris stepped in to play on the Beat Farmers' fourth album, *The Pursuit of Happiness.*

Harris' favorite Beat Farmers' album title is *Poor and Famous,* because it best describes the band's situation. "We have a really huge cult following, and they hunt down the records," says Harris. "They order them, and they do everything they can to get them — but other than that, you're never able to find them in stores, even in San Diego. The records haven't done very well for a lot of reasons. The band's not really commercial in a lot of senses." They've never sold out on their ideals, and they didn't have to go to Los Angeles to make it. That wins points with local die-hard fans.

Harris feels fortunate to be able to perform (the band is on the road six months out of the year) and have an outlet for his songs, even though it has yet to pay off financially. "To me, success is not a big house with a big pool," Harris says. "It's not about driving a fancy car." Still, Joey Harris won't ever be working in a Coronado pizza shop again. He's happy to be where he is today because, as he points out, "There are so many musicians I know in this town who are so capable and really talented who just haven't gotten the breaks I have." His famous uncle readily notes that Harris has earned his breaks. "He bothered to sit for three to four years and learn how to play guitar."

Satisfied with his career, Harris is also happy in his marriage. He and his wife, Miss Vicki, took their wedding vows on stage at the 1990 Street Scene, with Country Dick Montana serving as the minister, two days before holding a more private, family ceremony.

Steve Laury
Jazz Guitarist

Steve Laury first gained national attention as guitarist and songwriter for Fattburger, spending five years with the successful San Diego-based pop-jazz group before going solo in 1990. His debut album, appropriately titled *Stepping Out,* reached number three on the Radio & Records contemporary jazz charts and did extremely well in Japan. His second release, *Passion,* spent three weeks at the Number One spot and is a strong seller in the United States and abroad. But just as his solo career was taking off, Laury was diagnosed with lymphoma, a potentially fatal form of cancer. After undergoing weeks of chemotherapy and facing a fifty to sixty percent chance of recovery, his disease is now in remission. He has resumed his musical career, but with a completely new perspective on life.

Born in Vineland, New Jersey on March 22, 1953, Laury's childhood was filled with tribulation. His parents split up when he was very young, and it had a traumatic effect on him. He didn't do well in school and was somewhat of a rebel growing up. Music was the one uncomplicated thing in his life. "The reason I got so interested in music was because it came really easy for me. I picked up a guitar and started playing it without any lessons at all," he says. He also liked the attention it brought him. "But my stepfather was a cop and a body builder and into things like hunting. He couldn't understand it, so he didn't promote my playing at all. That made me want to play even more."

Laury received his first guitar after winning a bet with his older brother. He wagered that he could learn the introduction to a song on his brother's guitar, despite the fact that he was only eleven years old and had never played before. He easily won the bet, forcing his brother to buy him a ten-dollar, handmade, nylon-string guitar. He kept it for five years. By the time he was seventeen, Laury was getting paid to play, gigging three to four nights a week. Finding it tough to wake up for school, he decided to make music his career and took the G.E.D. test to get his diploma early.

When Laury was twenty-one, he found quality work hard to come by in New Jersey and decided to check out the West Coast music scene. After a brief stint in Los Angeles, he settled in San Diego and began playing with such notable musicians as bassist Nathan East and keyboardist Carl Evans, Jr. After playing in a number of bands around town, he became an integral part of Fattburger, where he was responsible for shaping the groove-oriented sound that helped the band become a national contemporary-jazz sensation. With the band's success came the necessity of touring. Laury had just married and signed a solo deal with Denon Records. He felt it would be too much to go on the road while trying to work on his solo career. He offered to remain in the band and continue to play for their albums, but they gave him an ultimatum. "A lot of people thought I left them high and dry when I got my solo deal," he says ruefully. "It didn't work out that way at all."

As a solo musician, Laury has found a niche for his signature sound. He's fast becoming legendary for his keen sense of melody and his flawless fretboard work. His style is often compared to guitar great Wes Montgomery (one of his early influences) and the super-successful George Benson. On both *Stepping Out* and *Passion* he collaborated with keyboardist Ron Satterfield and drummer Duncan Moore, with whom he has played for the past ten years.

He's very satisfied with his first two solo albums. In 1993 he released a third, *Keeping the Faith.* This time Laury has a whole new outlook on his life and career. "I take things day-by-day and not looking way ahead down the pike," he says. "My career to me has now taken a back seat. When I was on my deathbed, I came to the realization that careers and success and all the things that we work so hard for all our lives and spend all our time and energy on are really not important." He now wants to use his music as a vehicle to give people hope. "A lot of people don't create anything. All they do is generate money. We're here to help other people. I believe that the most important thing in your life is your relationship with Jesus Christ and everything else is secondary," he says.

Nick Reynolds
Guitarist for the Kingston Trio

Nick Reynolds was a founding member of the acclaimed Kingston Trio, one of the most successful and top-selling musical groups of the late 1950's and early 1960's. He achieved fame and fortune with them only to walk away when the Beatles brought the British Invasion to America. Thirty years later, he's back, touring with the Trio again, enjoying it more than ever and making more money than he did when they were at the height of their popularity.

Their welcome blend of calypso and folk music paved the way for Peter, Paul and Mary, Bob Dylan, Joan Baez, Judy Collins and John Denver. Looking back, Reynolds' proudest achievement is his ability to help other musicians. "If the Kingston Trio was able to get one person to pick up the guitar and start playing, that is the most important thing in the world. We've done that for hundreds of great musicians – Lindsey Buckingham of Fleetwood Mac, for one. People like that never would have picked up a guitar [if it weren't for us]."

Oddly enough, Nick Reynolds started out with an extreme fear of performing before a live audience. He was born nervous and suffered from acute stage fright. He still has to find courage within himself to face an audience now that he and the Kingston Trio are on the road more than half the year, playing before audiences as large as 5,000, fans of all ages who come to hear their enduring hits, "Tom Dooley,"

"Scotch and Soda" and "Greenback Dollars."

A San Diego native and graduate of Coronado High School, Reynolds' roots run deep in Coronado. His grandmother settled there in the 1800's. He currently lives a block and a half from his mother, Jane, and only two blocks from his sister. His three children and countless relatives all live nearby, not to mention his nephew, Joey Harris of the Beat Farmers. Reynolds is proud of Harris' fame and remembers teaching him his first chords on the ukulele. Reynolds' father, a captain in the Navy and a great guitar player, taught all the Reynolds kids songs he learned from all over the world.

Although he has fond memories of his years growing up in Coronado, where he hung out at the beach, body-surfed, visited Tijuana, went skin-diving in Mexico and to Oscar's Drive-In in Loma Portal, Reynolds left his hometown for fame and fortune and didn't return for nearly thirty years. He left to attend the University of Arizona but dropped out to become a door-to-door salesman for Fuller Brush. After that he enrolled at Menlo College, where he met Bobby Shane and began the relationship that changed his life forever. Both were trouble-makers and poor students. They became instant friends. Reynolds recalls, "He was asleep at the back of the class, so I had to meet him."

The two started playing together, then added Dave Guard from Stanford University to complete their group. They performed regularly in the San Francisco Bay area as Dave Guard and the Calypsonians. Reynolds went on to earn a degree in Business Administration in 1957, all the while enjoying the group's modest success. "We said, 'Let's give it a try for six months. Otherwise I'll come back to Coronado and go into the hotel business with a friend of mine,'" Reynolds remembers.

Frank Werber, a San Francisco publicist, heard them play and offered to manage the group. He sent them to a vocal coach and helped them choose a name. They opted for the calypso flavor of the Kingston Trio. They took great pains to develop both their music and their clean-cut, collegiate image. All wore grey flannel pants, striped shirts and crewcuts. "Our lucky break was getting to audition and start playing at a little club called the Purple Onion. All of a sudden we were the darlings of San Francisco. For some reason, we packed 'em in every night. It all just sort of happened," says Reynolds.

They first heard "Tom Dooley" being performed by someone else auditioning for the club, liked it and included it on their debut album. The song was given constant airplay by DJ's all over the country, and Capitol Records released it as a single. That was all it took to launch the Kingston Trio as superstars of folk music. In 1958, "Tom Dooley" was number one for eighteen weeks, selling over a million copies. Reynolds says, "That was the only hit song we ever had, and we've been going strong for thirty years off one single record."

Their first album was number one on the charts for 195 weeks. Fourteen of their albums made it to the Top Ten and earned them a Grammy. In their early twenties, they signed a long-term deal with Capitol Records that made them very wealthy. At the peak of their popularity, their earnings were estimated at a million dollars per year and by 1965 they had sold eighteen million records in twenty-eight albums. "It got to be big business, and I hated it," says Reynolds. "That's why I got out in 1967." He sold his interest in the group and became a rancher in Oregon, where he lived with his wife and three children.

In 1987, Reynolds decided to move back to Coronado, after twenty years in Oregon. On his return, he played and sang with another San Diego native, John Stewart, who replaced Dave Guard in the Trio in 1961. They recorded an album together, calling it *The Revenge of the Budgie.* "Budgie" is Reynolds' nickname because of his height – he was always known as "the short one" in the Trio. He doesn't consider being short a hindrance, saying "being small gets you through crowds faster." Playing with Stewart and managing Bula's restaurant in Coronado, Reynolds didn't give much thought to rejoining the Trio until Bobby Shane approached him in 1988.

The reconstituted Trio consists of Shane, Reynolds and George Grove, the newest and youngest member by fifteen years. They perform thirty-five weeks out of the year and are enjoying immense success. "It's so nice to go out with the boys now," smiles Reynolds. "We go out on the road and have a great time doing what we love. There is a tremendous revival of this type of music. People are crazy about it. All I have to do now is carry my guitar to the cab, then go to the airport and play the next night. That's success to me."

At fifty-eight, Reynolds has no plans to retire soon, and doesn't think retirement is necessary if you're doing something you enjoy. Why would anyone retire if they're making more now and working less?

"Success is peace of mind and a feeling of well-being within yourself," Reynolds says. "I have that now."

Peter Sprague
Jazz Guitar Virtuoso

Peter Sprague is one of the premier jazz guitarists in the country. His virtuosity has been documented by jazz experts such as Leonard Feather, who calls Sprague "one of the emergent great guitarists." Sprague studied with notable guitarist Pat Metheny and has played with jazz greats Chick Corea, Al Jarreau, Joe Pass, Hubert Laws, Alphonse Mouzon and Stanley Clarke, as well as San Diego's elite jazz performers Charles McPherson, Kevyn Lettau, Nathan East and Bob Magnusson. Sprague has recorded several records of his own and is currently working on the follow-up to his 1985 release, *Na Pali Coast,* which reached number seven on the jazz charts. He taught music at the Musicians Institute in Los Angeles, worked on the film score for *The Cat Chasers,* starring Kelly McGillis and Peter Weller, published seven of his own books and transcribed music books for Chick Corea.

Sprague, now thirty-six, acquired his taste for jazz by listening to his father's records while growing up in Del Mar. His brother, Tripp, plays the saxophone. His father, Dr. Hall Tripp Sprague, a psychologist and author, was also a pretty decent drummer. Sprague took up guitar when he was twelve and, by the time he was fifteen, he spent all his time working to master the instrument. "When I first started getting into music, I just developed a strong sense of discipline. I was disciplined in my practicing and I practiced incessantly. When I went away to music school at Interlochen Arts Academy, I sort of got this informal award for the person who practiced the most. This is a big-time academy with people from all around the world. I was used to being one of the better guitarists, but when I got there I was nothing special. At the same time, I saw a lot of these people just sort of blow their God-given talents. Here are these people who have more than I do and they're not utilizing it. It was really an eye-opener. I decided I have to utilize what I have to my best, and I somehow started developing all this discipline and really practiced," Sprague says modestly.

All that practice paid off when he returned to Del Mar and started building a reputation as a whiz kid and one of the hottest young players around, noted for his impeccable technique and major league chops. He remains loyal to his jazz roots and chooses to live in his hometown of Del Mar rather than move to Los Angeles, despite the fact that he remains in relative obscurity here. But Sprague is more than happy with his lifestyle and musical career. "I've done very well, and things are still on the up-and-up for me," he says. "I'm in the process of working on a new record, so it's not as if things have reached their peak and that's it. A lot of my friends are much more famous, but they don't have the same life that I get to have. I live right near the ocean, and I can virtually have my schedule any way I want it." Recently married, he prefers running his career from his home.

Sprague has hustled to reach his level of success, and one of his proudest accomplishments is having played with his childhood hero, Chick Corea. "I thought it would be really amazing if one day I could play with Chick Corea, which was a dream that started when I was a young kid," Sprague admits. "So I just sort of cultivated it. I'd write him a letter and he'd write me back. Every time he came to town, I'd go see him. When I got my own record deal, I recorded some of his songs; I sent him the record and said, 'Will you write a little comment for the liner notes?' That got him to hear how I could play. Then every time he came to town we'd meet. Finally, it came down to where he was looking for a guitar player – and he hired me. That started out as such a small, impossible thing, and it ended up possible."

Sprague chooses when and with whom he wants to work. And, because he's financially free, he doesn't have to sell out to anyone. "When I was young, I said I want to play jazz and to make a great amount of money on jazz," he says ruefully. "I figure I probably will never do it." Yet he has. Sprague owns a beautiful home in Del Mar, has money in the bank and lives virtually debt-free. Because he's carved out such a niche for himself in jazz music, he's always guaranteed a certain amount of work. Recently suffering from tendinitis in one of his fingers, he was able to take six months off from playing and recording without having to worry about generating any income.

Sprague became financially independent by living with a low overhead. He started out living very simply, renting a garage for $150 a month and saving toward the purchase of a small home in Del Mar. He put as much money as he could into the home, keeping his monthly payments low. By being careful, he saved enough money to purchase another home worth nearly half a million dollars.

The most common misconception about musicians is that they live self-destructive, wild lifestyles. Sprague's way of life can only be described as natural. He's a vegetarian, into yoga, meditation, surfing and running. He keeps himself in shape, both mentally and physically. He's also a responsible, organized and professional person who takes the business of music very seriously. Even so, he's always searching for the perfect balance between work and the freedom to enjoy life. "I think the flow of the world will take you far from [enjoying life] if you go with it," he says seriously. "You can end up watching television way too much, for instance, or you can let your health go bad. The flow of getting old takes you in those directions, and you have to step in and say, 'Wait, what if I, instead of watching TV, went and studied this, or what if I went out and heard some music or went to a play or even just went outside and checked out the stars?' It's those kinds of things that you have to put effort into, not going with how the world takes you as a grown-up."

Sprague sets goals to help dictate the best use of his time. He makes a list of all the things he wants to accomplish, then maps out how much time each will take. In this way, he's able to work on a number of projects at the same time without stressing out. He suggests that just getting the ball rolling on any project makes it easier to complete. His goals for the future include streamlining his life, finding time to do the things he enjoys most, recording one album a year and touring part-time, hitting all the major jazz festivals. Knowing how Peter Sprague operates, there's no doubt he'll do it all.

Briefs

Peter Allen (?? - 1992)

Pianist, singer and songwriter Peter Allen was born in Australia but lived in Leucadia the last fifteen years of his life. He's best known for the hits "I Honestly Love You" sung by Olivia Newton-John, "Don't Cry Out Loud" sung by Melissa Manchester and the Academy Award-winning "Arthur's Theme" sung by Christopher Cross in the film *Arthur,* which co-starred Allen's ex-wife, Liza Minelli.

A.J. Croce

Son of the late Jim Croce and Ingrid Croce, a pioneering entrepreneur of the Gaslamp Quarter in downtown San Diego, the 21-year-old singer-pianist has already made a name for himself. He's on the verge of national stardom, signing a record deal under the guidance of his manager, Kenny Weisseberg of Humphrey's Concerts-by-the-Bay fame. Although his father was a famous folksinger, A.J.'s forte is blues and jazz. The family moved to Point Loma in 1973, when A.J. was a toddler – the same year his father was killed in a plane crash. Since then, Ingrid opened Croce's Jazz Bar, Croce's Top Hat, Ingrid's Cantina and Croce's Restaurant, keeping Jim Croce's name and memory alive while giving her son a place to learn the business and find his own place in it.

Bob Crosby

This La Jolla resident has been the jazz bandleader of the Bobcats since 1935, although his brother Bing was the most famous member of the family. Still, Bob didn't do too badly with the band, and he also had his own daytime radio and television shows. Crosby and his wife, June (a noted author and columnist) settled in La Jolla in 1969.

Fattburger

This chart-topping jazz/pop band has been a fixture in San Diego for years. With numerous albums to its credit, the band is also nationally recognized, reaching the top of the contemporary-jazz charts and selling thousands of records over the years. Their 1992 release is entitled *On A Roll.*

Rosie Flores

During the 1970's and early 1980's, Flores played the local club scene, singing traditional country music with various bands, including the highly-regarded Rosie and the Screamers. A San Diego resident since her teens, Flores left San Diego for Los Angeles, where she eventually began a solo recording career.

Hollis Gentry

This San Diego-based saxophonist has performed with such nationally-regarded artists as Al Jarreau, Larry Carlton, Joe Sample and Stanley Clarke, just to name a few. His own band, Hollis Gentry's Neon, can be seen locally, or you can pick up their album. While Gentry is an accomplished and versatile musician, he's well-educated as well, earning both his Bachelor's and Master's degrees from the University of California at San Diego. He was honored as UCSD's Alumnus of the Year in 1991.

Sam Hinton

Although Hinton is best known around the world as a folksinger, many San Diegans remember him as curator of the Aquarium Museum at Scripps Institute of Oceanography from 1945 to 1964. The marine biologist also taught classes in folklore and has written books on the ocean and its creatures.

Iron Butterfly

This San Diego progressive-rock band scored big with their Top Ten hit "In-A-Gadda-Da-Vida," selling more than a million records in 1968.

Frankie Laine

The famous gold-record singer and his wife of over 40 years (former actress Nan Gray) have called Point Loma home since 1968. His biggest hits include "Rawhide," "Mule Train," "That's My Desire," "Moonlight Gambler," "High Noon" and "Jezebel." He has sold literally millions of

records, producing twenty-one gold records, becoming an internation-
ally-loved star and a very wealthy man. But there was a time when he
didn't have a dime to his name. He slept in Central Park and hotel
lobbies in New York while trying to make it as a singer. During the
Depression, Laine became a marathon dance champion, which was a
hard way to earn a little extra money. When the craze died out, he was
back to the daily struggle to make a living as a singer, hitchhiking from
gig to gig, sometimes making as little as $5 a week. In the mid-1940's,
he headed for Hollywood, where his diligence finally paid off with the
success of "That's My Desire" in 1946. He never forgot the hard times
he went through, however, and today helps the homeless with his Old
Shoes charity campaign.

Kevyn Lettau

Raised in Del Mar, Lettau paid her dues singing in San Diego clubs
before recording her debut album, *Braziljazz* with Peter Sprague and
her husband Michael Shapiro. She is well on her way to becoming a
highly successful jazz-pop vocalist. Her latest release, *Simple Life,* was
produced by Michael Shapiro and Marcel East.

Bob Magnusson

Along with drummer Jim Plank and pianist Mike Wofford, bassist
Bob Magnusson is one of San Diego's most accomplished jazz musicians. He has worked with some of the biggest names in jazz, including
Sarah Vaughan, Buddy Rich and Art Pepper. He also name-drops a few
pop credits as well – Neil Diamond, Linda Ronstadt and Bonnie Raitt.

Barbara Mandrell

The country music superstar, born on Christmas Day in Houston,
doesn't really qualify under the definition of "San Diegan," but she did
live here briefly, winning the Miss Oceanside beauty pageant. What
makes hers such an extraordinary success story is her longevity – thirty
years in the business – and versatility – she is proficient on a number of
instruments, in both pop and country music venues, and acting in
commercials and film. She's been dubbed "the human dynamo" because she maintains an incredibly busy career schedule without neglecting her husband of twenty-five years, an ex-Navy pilot, and their

three children. On September 11, 1984, Mandrell barely survived a head-on car crash. Amazingly, minutes before the crash she asked her children to buckle up. Amazing because she'd never been a seatbelt user before that fateful day. She came back from her injuries to resume her career and lives her goal of "always reach a little higher."

Mojo Nixon

Some of the most unusual songs ever recorded have made this outrageous singer-humorist popular. These ditties include "Debbie Gibson is Pregnant with My Two-Headed Love Child," "Elvis Is Everywhere" and "Don Henley Must Die." He was onstage with the ex-Eagle performing the latter song in Austin, Texas in 1992 when Henley joined him in the chorus: "Don Henley must die/Don't let him get back together with Glenn Frey."

Gary Puckett and The Union Gap Band

This group scored some big hits during the late 1960's, including "Woman, Woman," "Young Girl," "Lady Willpower," "Over You" and "This Girl Is A Woman." During the height of their popularity, they sold millions of records a year, played in sold-out arenas across the country and collected substantial royalties for their efforts. It all started in San Diego when Puckett formed the band with fellow locals Dwight Bement, Gary Withem, Paul Whitbread and Canadian-born Kerry Chater in 1967. Dressed in Union-soldier outfits, they were finally signed to a record deal after relentless trips to Los Angeles peddling their demo tapes. And the rest, as they say, is history.

Ratt

Ratt, a very successful hard-rock band, at one time featured three San Diegans. Native son Steven Pearcy played in various bands around San Diego, one of which was called Mickey Ratt, before heading to Los Angeles in his early twenties. He founded Ratt and became its lead singer. Guitarist Robbin Crosby, another San Diego native who'd been in bands playing at parties and dances all over town, followed Pearcy to L.A. Lead guitarist Warren De Martini left San Diego to join Pearcy and Crosby. He and Crosby had known each other since they were kids. Before the band released their debut album, *Out of the Cellar,* which sold more than three million copies and was on the charts for fifty-six weeks in 1984, the frustrated rockers struggled to make a name for themselves. People close to them told them they'd never make it. Pearcy told *Seventeen* [June 1987], "In the beginning [early 1980's] we could barely support ourselves. We wore things we'd made or bought with no money to speak of. What we had, we spent on equipment, flyers — we made our own t-shirts, stickers, buttons. Anything to get the name around." Crosby added, "We were disgustingly poor, playing and playing and playing around the Hollywood clubs and not getting paid. We couldn't get around to rehearse because we didn't have gas money." Their persistence paid off — they became a supergroup when their debut album and a single called "Round and Round" launched them into the limelight.

Roger Reynolds

This UCSD Music professor/composer won the 1989 Pulitzer Prize for his composition "Whispers Out Of Time," a six-movement, twenty-five-minute work for string orchestra.

Gustavo Romero

This brilliant pianist from Chula Vista received his early musical training in San Diego before leaving for New York at the age of fourteen to study at Juilliard. At the tender age of six, he taught himself musical notation from the *Encyclopedia Britannica*. At nine, he taught himself to play Chopin's "Ballade in G Minor." At thirteen, he dazzled the audience as a soloist with the San Diego Symphony, performing on only a few hours' notice when a scheduled guest artist fell ill. At fourteen, he first appeared as a soloist with the New York Philharmonic. Now twenty-seven, Romero has been all over the world, performing in Paris, Milan, Brussels and Zurich. Yet, despite his demanding schedule, he still makes San Diego a regular part of his itinerary.

Jack Tempchin

This popular songwriter and long-time North County resident has written major hits for the Eagles ("Peaceful Easy Feeling" and "Already Gone"), Glenn Frey ("You Belong to the City") and Johnny Rivers ("Slow Dancing"). He collaborated with Frey on "Smuggler's Blues" and "The Heat is On," recently contributing to eleven songs on Frey's new album, *Strange Weather*. Tempchin's own recording career includes solo albums, and he was the opening act for Frey's San Diego shows.

Earl Thomas

This San Diego blues man can be heard at local clubs belting out his own brand of the blues. His debut album, *Blues... Not Blues,* which includes the song "The Way She Shakes That Thang," showcases this fine young singer's soulful talents.

Eddie Vedder

This San Diego singer and long-time surfer is now the frontman for the Seattle-based band Pearl Jam. The former Bacchanal roadie can be seen on MTV and performing live with Pearl Jam, which has sold over two million records to date.

Tom Waits

Singer-songwriter-actor Waits was once an honors student at Chula Vista's Hilltop High School. While there, he was a member of the Systems, a soul group that performed in local folk clubs. Later he headed for Los Angeles, where he became a piano bar drifter, playing in dive bars and sleeping in derelict hotels. His songs often reflect this side of life and the characters he met in these unsavory places. His debut album, *Closing Time,* received critical acclaim, but few sales. Waits' first success as a songwriter came when the Eagles recorded "Ol' 55" for their album *On The Border.* His biggest single success was in 1990, when Rod Stewart recorded "Downtown Train," which reached number two on the U.S. charts. Waits' first acting job was a bit part in Sylvester Stallone's *Paradise Alley.* At the time, Waits was quoted as saying, "I'm so broke I can't even pay attention." But his income and his star began to rise during the 1980's. He worked on the soundtrack to Francis Ford Coppola's *One From The Heart* for over a year, receiving an Oscar nomination for his efforts. He co-wrote the musical *Frank's Wild Years* with his wife, Kathleen Brennan. It opened in Chicago and later moved to New York. His acting career moved up from bit parts to character roles in important films, including *The Outsiders, Rumblefish,*

Ironweed, Shakedown, Cold Feet and the part of Renfield in *Bram Stoker's Dracula*. His many credits as a musician include singing the title theme to the hit movie *Sea of Love* in 1989. He collaborated with Point Loma High School music teacher Francis Thumm on the music for the film *Night On Earth,* released in 1992. Known for his gravelly voice, he won a multi-million-dollar suit against a potato chip company for using a "sound-alike" in their ads. "Now by law I have what I always felt I had," he says, "...a distinctive voice."

Frank Zappa

This avant-garde musician, composer, lyricist, record producer and entrepreneur has been called a musical genius. He's been categorized as a pop musician, with songs like "Don't Eat the Yellow Snow," "Dancin' Fool" and "Valley Girls" (which featured the voice of his daughter, Moon Unit). His symphonic, chamber and ballet compositions have been performed by a number of outstanding orchestras and ensembles. His music is hard to categorize, because he blends facets of jazz, rock, classical and blues to create his own unique sound. Born on December 21, 1940 in Baltimore, Maryland, Zappa's family relocated to San Diego, where he attended Grossmont High School as a freshman and Mission Bay High School as a sophomore. His family eventually settled in Lancaster, California, where Zappa finished high school. As a teenager, he taught himself to play drums and electric guitar and began to write music. His early influences include Howlin' Wolf, Muddy Waters and Lightnin' Slim. After graduation, he took on odd jobs, working as a greeting card designer, ad writer, window dresser and encyclopedia salesman while playing in various bands around Los Angeles. He earned $1500 for scoring the movie *Run Home Slow.* He used that money to set up his own recording studio. In the mid-1960's, his signature band, the Mothers of Invention, released *Freak Out* – and his career was assured. He has such a loyal following that his mail order company, BarfkoSwill, sells a million dollars a year worth of Zappa merchandise. The

Entertainment

Chapter 3: Celebrities

Joan Embery

Ted Giannoulas

Steve Kelley

Regis Philbin

Briefs

Frank Capra

Art Linkletter · Des McAnuff

The Nicklins · Craig Noel

Orville Redenbacher

Stephanie Seymour

Joan Embery
Goodwill Ambassador, San Diego Zoo

As Goodwill Ambassador for the world-famous San Diego Zoo, Joan Embery has achieved international celebrity. She's introduced her furred and feathered friends to millions of viewers on various television shows, most notably *The Tonight Show*. She has appeared with Johnny Carson roughly seventy times since 1970, bringing with her over 300 unique animals who call the Zoo and Wild Animal Park home. In her most memorable Carson show, she brought a marmoset with her. The small South American tree-dweller jumped out of her hand and onto a startled Carson's arm, climbing up his shoulder to perch on his head. After wrapping its tail around Carson's ears to the delight of millions of viewers, the animal proceeded to mark its territory right there.

Admittedly her own toughest critic, Embery has built a successful career around her love of animals, and she works hard to generate interest in saving endangered species. Still, she downplays her own success. "I have fairly high goals for myself," she admits. "There are a lot of things I'd like to do better than I do. Some people evaluate success by what they've done. I evaluate it by what I'd like to do."

Anybody looking at Embery's career would see nothing but immense success. She and her animal friends have appeared on almost every major television talk show, including *David Letterman, Merv Griffin, Dinah Shore* and *Steve Allen*. Embery was a regular guest on *PM Magazine* and hosted two syndicated series of her own, *Animal Express* and *Animals of Africa*. She's guest-starred on *Newhart* and *Alf* and has appeared on various game shows. *Saturday Night Live* and *In Living Color* have even built comedy skits around her character. She's written three books, including an autobiography, *My Wild World*. Embery is known internationally for her dedication to educating and entertaining the public while helping the cause of animals.

It all started for this San Diego native and graduate of Crawford High School when she began working in the Children's Zoo and Animal Nursery in the late 1960's. While at San Diego State University, the

Joan Embery

Photo by Ron Garrison
Reprinted with the permission of the Zoological Society of San Diego

attractive and congenial Embery was given the opportunity to repre-sent the Zoo. Her duties included handling the animals, making televi-sion and radio appearances and public speaking engagements.

"Most of what I've learned, I learned by doing. From the begin-ning, it's been trial and error, sink or swim. There weren't a lot of people to teach me what to do," Embery remembers. "It's a unique field, and I didn't have anybody really preceding me. Nobody even defined what it is I do!"

Embery learned as much as she could about the Zoo, worked

closely with often-unpredictable animals and went back to school to learn how to get up in front of a group of people while being totally terrified. "It started out where I had more time to learn and study to keep up to speed," Embery says. "But as things have progressed, the treadmill [I'm on] seems to be going faster and faster. I've had to learn how to delegate and how to organize." Her work keeps her so busy, in fact, that she hasn't had a real vacation in over five years.

When she does have time, Embery rides show horses, although she finds it hard to keep up with the competition circuit. She receives thousands of letters every year from people who say they'd give anything to do what she does, but she'd like these same people to know just how hard her job really is. "People think, oh, she takes baby animals on TV, wouldn't it be fun? They think I sit and handle wild animals all day. I don't do that at all. I spend half of my time on the phone or I'm on planes flying all over the country, coordinating people and animals, transportation, security, liability... it's unbelievable." To be on the air for five minutes requires a sixteen-hour day and two days of preparation before that, and Embery only has one full-time assistant to help.

Home is a 50-acre ranch in Lakeside where she and her rancher/ artist husband, Duane Pillsbury, maintain their own mini-zoo of over thirty different species. Embery's husband, a former real estate broker and college professor who retired to concentrate on his artwork, has become involved in her career and offers some assistance.

Through it all, she keeps a smile on her face, collecting wonderful anecdotes and recounting them with style and humor. One such story occurred on her way to Los Angeles with a penguin. She stopped in San Juan Capistrano to escape the scorching heat and went into a hotel with one of her animal handlers. She asked the clerk at the front desk if they could rent an air-conditioned room for an hour. He huffily said they didn't rent rooms by the hour. Embery explained that she needed to keep a penguin cool while they grabbed a bite to eat. The disbelieving clerk agreed to let them have the room for free if they could show him a penguin. Little did he know that he was talking to a modern-day Dr. Doolittle. She produced the penguin and got the room, only to have the rowdy bird semi-trash it.

All in a day's work for Joan Embery.

Ted Giannoulas
The Famous Chicken

San Diego has many indigenous birds – seagulls, pelicans and gnatcatchers – but the rarest bird of all is the famous Chicken, also known as the San Diego Chicken. *The* because there's only one! Millions have seen this high-flying, zany and lovable bird in stadiums and arenas across the country. Ted Giannoulas is the most acclaimed man-in-a-chicken-suit ever. A crowd-pleasing comedian with a hilarious sense of timing, he has brightened sporting events and brought laughter to children and adults alike for more than eighteen years.

What began as a one-week radio promotion for KGB turned into a unique and successful career for Giannoulas, who performs over 250 days a year as the famous Chicken, mostly at sporting events. He has also made countless movie and television appearances, including a five-year stint on the Emmy Award-winning *Baseball Bunch* hosted by Johnny Bench.

This Hoover High School grad went to San Diego State University, intending to pursue a career in journalism. In March of 1974 he was hanging out at the campus radio station (KCR) with several friends when a representative of KGB radio walked in looking for someone – anyone – willing to give up their Easter break to wear a chicken suit and hand out candy eggs at the zoo. At five-foot-four and a hundred and forty pounds, Giannoulas was the right size for the rented costume, and the job was his.

Originally, he was paid chickenfeed (!) and didn't get much notice. But after he broke out of his shell and added some comic spirit to his routine, things began to fall into place. Giannoulas tried not to act like a human dressed like a chicken – but rather like a chicken trying to be human. The strategy worked, and the one-week stint turned into a five-year stretch with KGB, where he became part of the most successful promotion in radio history.

Eventually, Giannoulas' career ambitions conflicted with the management's policies, and a much-ballyhooed flap ensued. It took the

California Supreme Court to declare him a free agent before he was able to expand his Chicken activities. June 1979 marked a new beginning. In an elaborate ceremony, complete with Highway Patrol motorcade into the sold-out stadium before a Padre game, the Chicken hatched out of a gigantic egg to debut his new, redesigned costume.

Since then, he's become his own boss, a local legend and the world's funniest and rarest of birds. He gets away with things in his chicken suit that would otherwise get him arrested. He's been known to take a baby under his wing – then into his beak. But then, crazy things are expected of the Chicken. He taunts the opposing team, rousts the umpire after a controversial call and mimics the players, all in good fun.

One of the reasons for Giannoulas' success is his old-fashioned work ethic. He made plenty of sacrifices to reach his goals, both personal and professional. His reward is the laughter of the crowd each night and being able to earn a living doing something he truly enjoys. And the pay has gotten a lot better. Although it's hard work, involving months of traveling with little or no leisure, to him it's still not a job. He's having the time of his life!

Steve Kelley
Editorial Cartoonist/Comedian/Actor

As the editorial cartoonist for *The San Diego Union-Tribune,* Steve Kelley has entertained and outraged San Diegans for a decade. His work regularly appears in more than a thousand newspapers around the country and is frequently published in national news magazines, including *Time* and *Newsweek.*

He became known locally when he drew his infamous Uvaldo Martinez cartoon, depicting the ex-councilman as the "Freeload Bandito" at a time when Martinez was being investigated for city credit card abuse. "That cartoon sort of put me on the map locally," Kelley says. "People began to realize that a lot of the savage cartoons running on the editorial page were drawn by a local guy."

Kelley is also making a name for himself on the stand-up comedy circuit. After paying his dues as a popular amateur night regular in San

Diego, he took his act to television, making several successful appearances on *The Pat Sajak Show,* quickly followed by equally successful appearances on *The Tonight Show* with both Johnny Carson and Jay Leno. To improve his comedy technique, Kelley took acting lessons, which led to a bit part on the sitcom *WKRP in Cincinnati.* "It wasn't exactly a demanding role. I played a guy in an audience who asks a question. I've faced tougher acting challenges calling in sick for work," he cracks. Still, with his talent and drive to succeed, nothing seems impossible. "I always wanted to be good at what I did. It sounds funny, but I figured that whatever I decided to do for a living, I would succeed at it. The alternative never really crossed my mind," Kelley says.

Born into an upper-middle-class family in Richmond, Virginia, Kelley lost his father, an attorney, in a plane crash in 1969. His mother, a self-made real estate businesswoman, moved her three sons to private school, which Kelley attended from the fifth grade through high school graduation. At Dartmouth College, he drew cartoons for the two major newspapers on campus. In the middle of his senior year, he sent samples of his work to two metropolitan newspapers that were looking for cartoonists, *The Omaha World Herald* and *The San Diego Union.* When both offered him jobs, he chose to come to San Diego. "Not a tough choice there," Kelley grins. "I flipped a coin and it came up Omaha. So I flipped it again."

Kelley entered the field in 1981 as one of the youngest political cartoonists in the country. Obviously unseasoned, his priority was to develop as quickly as he could. To sharpen his skills, he asked to do six cartoons a week instead of the usual five. "I was always success-oriented and relentlessly driven," Kelley says. "Of course, it helped that I was doing something for which I had some natural talent, and for which there is not a whole lot of competition. There are only two hundred full-time political cartoonists in the entire country."

Kelley has no plans to stop drawing cartoons, no matter what happens with his other career interests. "I find comedy fulfilling in the short run and newspaper work satisfying in the long run," he explains. "The first time I ever tried stand-up, a heckler shouted, 'Don't quit your day job!' I think it was pretty good advice. Plus, I'm far too practical to quit the newspaper. Comedy's great, but there's no dental plan."

In both careers, having a thick skin is a requisite. "I hope people understand that the vicious stuff I do in the newspaper is simply my job. Sure, it's often insensitive, but insensitive happens to be what I do for a living," Kelley says. In contrast, his stand-up routine is inoffensive humor about current events and everyday goings-on. He finds it challenging to get people to laugh without resorting to profanity, bathroom humor or ethnic slurs.

Kelley began his stand-up career when another comedian started incorporating some of Kelley's cartoon captions into his act. After offering to write jokes for the man, Kelley let himself be talked into appearing on amateur night the following week. Although his start was shaky, he developed quickly and soon found himself performing at clubs around the country, sometimes drawing his cartoon in a hotel room by day and sending it by Federal Express to San Diego.

Kelley attributes much of his success quite simply to setting goals for himself. "I wanted to set our high school record [in the pole vault]," he says by way of example. "and I worked at it until I did. When I got to Dartmouth, my big goal was to jump fifteen feet, which I did my senior year. Then I figured, hell, the college record is only six inches more, so I went after that and got it. When I got to the *Union,* all I could think about was getting published in *Newsweek.* That happens often now. When I started stand-up, like every other comedian, I wanted someday to appear on the *Tonight Show...* I kept working toward that and it happened. You just have to set optimistic goals, but never anything completely out of reach. Then you work your tail off. I don't think the formula for success ever really changes."

Some might say he was just lucky, that he was in the right place at the right time. Kelley doesn't deny that, but he also believes you make your own luck. "I think luck is to a certain degree a function of determination. I think if you work hard enough at something, you'll end up getting a few breaks along the way," he says.

Although he makes a steady living at what he does, Kelley is quick to point out that money is rarely analogous to success. "Certain professions simply come with higher salaries attached to them, and some people are in them and some people aren't," he says. "That doesn't mean that you have to make a six-figure income to be a success, or that there can't be doctors or lawyers or professional hockey players who are failures."

Regis Philbin
National Talk Show Host

Regis Philbin is a household name to millions across the nation who tune in daily to the syndicated morning television talk show, *Live with Regis and Kathie Lee.* He's so well-known that Dana Carvey of *Saturday Night Live* does a hilarious take-off of him. He's considered one of San Diego's first big-time television stars, now celebrating his thirty-first year as a talk show host.

A native New Yorker from the Bronx, Regis Francis Xavier Philbin is the eldest son in a strict Catholic family. At an early age, he knew that he wanted to be on television like his idol, Jack Paar. He graduated from Notre Dame in 1953 with a degree in sociology and then enlisted in the Navy, which is how he came to San Diego. Out of the Navy, he worked as an NBC page on Steve Allen's *Tonight* program, as a stage-hand, a radio news reporter on KSON in San Diego, a feature reporter and substitute news anchor on Channel 8 and as a very popular anchor-man on Channel 10. In 1961, when Philbin was thirty years old, *The Regis Philbin Show* debuted on Channel 10, quickly becoming a favorite local late-night show. Its format set a precedent with its spontaneity and lack of scripting – characteristics still evident on his show today.

With his celebrity status firmly established in San Diego, Philbin set off to make it big in Hollywood. He took over Steve Allen's show at Westinghouse, but only lasted four months. He had to watch Merv Griffin follow in his footsteps, becoming a billionaire with *The Merv Griffin Show.* Then Joey Bishop got a show, and Philbin spent three years as his sidekick, taking the brunt of many of Bishop's jokes. When Bishop failed, NBC gave Philbin a shot at his own show, which was canceled despite his witty and charming approach to hosting. It is Philbin's unique ability to poke fun at his guests and get away with it that makes him so likable and fun to watch.

"Reege," as he's affectionately called by his co-host, Kathie Lee Gifford, hosted nearly a dozen talk shows between 1970 and 1993, but none was as successful as *Live with Regis and Kathie Lee.* The chemistry between Philbin and Gifford is palpable. They go on unrehearsed to keep it fresh, and the first fifteen minutes are unscripted, leaving the door open for anything to happen. That's the way Philbin likes it. He has succeeded in the world of television because of hard work and persistence. He never gave up his dream. Between television jobs, he took work as a truck driver to get by. He's energetic, excitable, sometimes loud – but he's never phony. He's a professional who always makes his very difficult job look easy.

Philbin and his wife, Joy, who co-hosts with him when Gifford is off, met when he was on *The Joey Bishop Show.* They have two teenage daughters and currently live in New York. The man with a funny name has come a long way since winning the Point Loma Optimists Club's "Mr. Success" award in 1965.

Briefs

Frank Capra (1897-1991)

This legendary filmmaker was best known for his feel-good movies, including *Mr. Deeds Goes to Town* and *Mr. Smith Goes to Washington*. Both of these 1930's films are Oscar winners. The 1947 *It's A Wonderful Life* can be seen on television every year at Christmastime. His inspirational pictures still have wide appeal, showing that the common man can use his God-given resources to overcome adversity. Capra felt that movies should be a positive expression of hope, love, mercy, justice and charity. An immigrant, his early life was marked by poverty. He grew up in Los Angeles' poor Little Sicily area along with thirteen siblings. To help the family, he sold newspapers and picked fruit. He paid his own way through college, only to graduate and find there weren't any jobs. He survived unemployment and the Depression by taking any odd job he could find before finding his niche as a motion picture director. He met his wife Lucille at the Hotel Del Coronado, and his children grew up and went to school in the Fallbrook area. He purchased the Red Mountain Ranch in 1939 and lived there until 1972, when he moved to the desert for his wife's health. The famous director's 1972 autobiography is titled, *The Name Above the Title*.

Art Linkletter

He began a successful broadcasting career spanning nearly half a century as a radio announcer at KGB while still a senior at San Diego State University. An English and psychology major in college, Linkletter was also an outstanding athlete. He hit it big with the shows *People Are Funny* and *Life with Linkletter*. He also wrote a number of books, one of which — *Kids Say The Darndest Things* — became a best-seller. An excellent interviewer, much of his success came as a result of his skills as an effective listener who allowed his guests to become the stars of his shows. Born in 1912, he was deserted as an infant by his natural parents and adopted by the Linkletter family. His own daughter died a drug-related death in 1969. A motivational speaker, he travels from coast to coast delivering his message of hope, telling people how to make the best out of whatever setbacks life may deal you. His autobiography is aptly titled, *Confessions of a Happy Man.*

Des McAnuff

The brilliant and talented artistic director of the La Jolla Playhouse has made quite an impact on San Diego theater since he arrived from New York in the early 1980's. An award-winning director, he combines an immense talent with hard work and a drive to succeed. Of course, it doesn't hurt to make your hobby a career as McAnuff has. His passion for his work is very evident. In 1992, he scored a smash hit with an adaptation of The Who's 1969 rock opera *Tommy,* directing and working with original Who member Peter Townshend on the script.

The Nicklins

Chuck, Flip and Terry share not only a love for the ocean but a thriving business as well. The three are partners in the Diving Locker, one of San Diego's oldest dive shops. Chuck Nicklin, father of Flip and Terry, is a highly-regarded underwater cinematographer whose credits include camera work on some of the best underwater films of all time. Flip is a natural history photographer who travels the globe in search of the ultimate underwater shots of marine life, including killer whales, sharks, penguins and dolphins. His work has frequently appeared in *National Geographic.* Terry, who has been scuba diving off the San Diego coast since he was a kid, prefers to stay home and take care of the everyday running of the business. An avid diver, he remains optimistic about the future of San Diego's greatest natural resource – the ocean. "There are all kinds of things that are positive," he says. "In the late 1960's and 1970's, there was no kelp. Everybody thought that the kelp was dead and gone forever... that we polluted San Diego to the point that there would never be kelp beds again. Yet now we have beautiful kelp beds. I think the underwater park the city created in La Jolla is very progressive and will make for a much more interesting and long-lived environment underwater for San Diego."

Craig Noel

This icon of local theater has spent much of his life in San Diego and almost a decade at the Old Globe. Born in New Mexico in 1915, he moved to San Diego with his family. He attended Jefferson Elementary School, Roosevelt Junior High, San Diego High School and San Diego State University. He joined the Old Globe right out of high school and maintained his interest in that venerable institution, except for a time during World War II when the Navy used the theater as a hospital facility. Noel directed movies in Hollywood for a time, working with Marilyn Monroe, among others. He returned to the Globe in the late 1940's and turned it into a big success, despite major setbacks — including two fires. At seventy-seven, he is still involved with his beloved theater.

Orville Redenbacher

The Popcorn King has called Coronado home for the past fifteen years. Although he still travels the globe promoting the popcorn he invented years ago, he sold his popcorn interests in the late 1970's. He also enjoys spending time in his high-rise Coronado Shores condominium overlooking the ocean. Redenbacher is a national celebrity, known for his many public appearances and television commercials, sometimes appearing with his grandson, Gary, to promote his light and fluffy gourmet popcorn.

Stephanie Seymour

You may have seen this former Poway High School student and current "super-model" on the covers of *Vogue, Mademoiselle* and *Cosmopolitan.* Surely you've seen the gorgeous, five-foot ten-inch Seymour featured in *Sports Illustrated's* swimsuit issue. It all started when she was a teenager growing up in Poway. She entered a magazine competition called "The Look of the Year." She finished in the top ten and got a modeling contract. She modeled briefly in the San Diego area before moving to New York, launching a very successful modeling career in 1985.

Entertainment

Chapter 4: Writers

Jeanne Jones

Natasha Josefowitz

Richard Louv

Max Miller

Joan Oppenheimer

Anthony Robbins

Dr. Seuss (Theodor Geisel)

Brian Tracy

Briefs

Greg Bear · Dr. Kenneth Blanchard
Raymond Chandler · Cameron Crowe
Raymond Feist · Spencer Johnson
Anita Loos · Dr. Carl Rogers
Victor Villaseñor
Robert Wade · Dr. Denis Waitley
Sherley Day-Williams

Jeanne Jones
International Cookbook Author and Diet Consultant

Jeanne Jones has literally defined the meaning of lighter, low-fat cooking. Her first cookbook, *The Calculating Cook,* was published in 1971, and ever since she's been a supreme guru of healthy eating. With more and more people wanting to learn how to eat right, Jeanne has become a respected authority who is involved in almost every facet of the field she helped create. Twenty years ago, people didn't even know what she was talking about. She described saturated fats and how it's possible to eat foods that taste good and are good for you. It was a real education for most people. "Now that's all you hear every time you turn around – and it feels wonderful!" Jones exclaims. "When I started out, I believed that by writing very commonsense, straightforward books telling people how they could look better, feel better and probably live longer, I was really offering a great service. Only I didn't realize that not a lot of people were willing to listen at that point. There were a few."

Today, millions of people are interested in what this La Jolla resident has to say. Two decades after writing her first book, she's still spreading the word. "People have always kidded me because I have a religious zeal about nutrition," she says. Her syndicated column *Cook It Light* is carried by over 350 newspapers and read by over thirty million people worldwide. As a respected food consultant, her client list includes Jenny Craig Weight Loss Centers, The Golden Door, Four Seasons Hotels and La Valencia in La Jolla. She also keeps a busy lecture schedule, with stops in Europe and Asia as well as across the United States. She appears frequently on Channel 10's *Inside San Diego* and has authored twenty-two books so far. Her latest, *Eating Smart,* was released in 1992.

Born Jeanne Castendyck in Los Angeles and raised in Newport Beach, Jones grew up with the proverbial silver spoon in her mouth. She learned to cook with it. While her father, the largest manufacturer of concrete mixers in the world, was off traveling with her mother,

Jones embarked on her own adventures in their home kitchen, staffed by an expert European chef. By the time she entered high school, she was an accomplished chef herself. Oddly enough, Jones chose fashion design as a career after attending Northwestern University. She and her husband, a physician, traveled extensively, taking cooking classes in Europe and the Orient. They loved to entertain with beautiful, black-tie dinners, replete with all the rich and fattening sauces they'd discovered on their travels. This high-fat diet may have caused her husband's death at the age of forty-one, only two years after their wedding. Weeks later, Jones learned that she had diabetes.

Jones and her two sons moved to Mexico City, where she studied nutrition and amassed enough information about cooking for diabetics to fill a book. So that's exactly what she did. Her first book led her to work with the Diabetes Association, where she discovered that diabetics often die from coronary complications. She promptly researched and wrote *Diet for a Happy Heart: Recipes Low in Cholesterol and Saturated Fats*. In this way, she turned two devastating blows – her husband's death and her own health problems – into positive, energizing life changes. "If you really believe that you can make the best of any situation," she says, "then no matter how bad it is there is only one way out. And that's up."

Other books on specific health problems followed, but after writing for people already on restricted diets, her work went to a whole new level. She realized that many of these people could have avoided restricted diets in the first place, and she began writing books for healthy people who wanted to stay healthy. She teaches the benefits of a good, commonsense, low-fat diet. She says if you drink six to eight glasses of water a day, increase your complex carbohydrates, decrease animal protein, limit fats, salts and sugars and use moderation with alcohol and sweets, you'll find out how much better you can look and feel. "How do you feel today?" she asks. "If you don't feel terrific, there's something wrong – and it's probably that you aren't eating right or aren't getting enough exercise."

People today who are concerned with their health are watching their weight and their wallets, too. "Eating properly costs less money, and you can exercise by getting out and going for a real good walk every morning," Jones points out. "You don't have to join a fancy gym.

You don't have to buy expensive food. It's the only thing in today's economy where less money can actually buy you a better life."

Who has the time or energy after a hard day at the office to think about exercise or preparing healthy dishes when fast food and a relaxing night in front of the television sound better? "How important is it to you?" she asks. "Once you start doing it — and here's the real kicker — once you really start getting adequate amounts of exercise and start eating a reasonable, healthy diet, you're going to feel so much better that it becomes addictive. And yes, you'll fall off, because as human beings we have choice, and because we have choice we often make the wrong choices. But if you stay out too late too much, drink too much and don't exercise, you don't feel good. And when you know what it's like to feel terrific, you're not going to permanently give it up." Jones lives by the advice she gives in her books and goes to an exercise class every morning at 6:00 a.m.

San Diegans are healthier than many people Jones talks to across the country. She attributes it in part to the warm climate. A San Diegan herself, she has lived in La Jolla since 1971. "I think La Jolla is one of the prettiest places in the country. I realized I could live anyplace in the world I wanted, and I wanted to stay in San Diego. Every time the plane is coming back and I come in over that beautiful coastline, I think, 'Boy, am I lucky this is my home.'"

Luck had very little to do with Jones' success. Hard work, enthusiasm and having a vision and a purpose has brought her to the lifestyle she projected for herself years ago. She's financially rewarded for her labor, and she can take comfort in the fact that she has helped so many others live a better life as well. That's what success is all about.

Natasha Josefowitz
Author/Lecturer/Syndicated Columnist

Natasha Josefowitz has had a tremendous impact on an extraordinary number of people. She is an inspiration to all that it's never too late to try anything, to change your life. Through her books, lectures, radio and television appearances and nationally-syndicated columns, she is "empowering women and enlightening men" on ageism, sexism and racism. Her whole life has been spent helping people of all kinds. In New York, she went into Harlem, a predominantly poor black area, volunteering her time and instituting her own plan of finding mothers for abandoned babies. In the process, she was able to change the adoption system for the better.

Josefowitz was born in Paris and lived there until her Russian Jewish family came to the United States in 1939. She went to college, married and raised two children before returning to Columbia University at thirty-six. At that time, Columbia didn't admit students older than thirty-six, but she changed their minds. After receiving her Master's in Social Work from Columbia at the age of forty, she went back to Europe, to the University of Lausanne, to get her Ph.D. by the time she was fifty.

Josefowitz returned the United States to teach in the business school at the University of New Hampshire, where she asked to teach a course called "Women in Management." Trying to gather background material for the course, she realized there was none to be found. So she decided to write about the subject herself. She wrote the class materials each week and had her secretary type them up and hand them out to the students. Her secretary talked to a publisher's representative who was scouting for academic material and Josefowitz was discovered. She signed on to write a book based on her class materials, which turned into *Paths to Power: A Woman's Guide from First Job to Top Executive.* Her secretary was so inspired that she quit her position to further her own career.

Paths to Power was the only book of its kind in 1980 and enjoyed huge success. Suddenly, Josefowitz was in demand as a lecturer. She overcame her fear of public speaking and addressed groups all across the country, opening and closing with "little kernels of truth," her own poetic words of wisdom. Interest was so great in these verses that Josefowitz self-published a book of her poems. In 1982, she sold seven thousand copies of *In A Nutshell,* feminine/feminist verse. Warner Books showed interest in her poetry, and Josefowitz collaborated with renowned artist Françoise Gilot (wife of Jonas Salk), who did the illustrations for *Is This Where I Was Going?* published by Warner in 1983.

Some of her best-selling humorous verse includes a book of

children's poetry, *100 Scoops of Ice Cream.* Her work has been trans-lated into a dozen languages.

Josefowitz didn't neglect her prose, however, and rapidly became a nationally-recognized authority on women and work. Her articles have appeared in *The Harvard Business Review, Psychology Today, Ms. Magazine* and *The Los Angeles Times.* She has guested on *The Dr. Ruth Show, Larry King* and almost every morning television talk show in America. She had her own weekly segment on public radio and appeared monthly on Channel 8's *SunUp San Diego* until it went off the air. Her second book on management, *You're The Boss,* deals with minorities in the workplace. She also co-wrote *Fitting In* with her second husband, Herman Gadon. It deals with being new on the job.

For Natasha Josefowitz, life really did begin at forty. And it's contin-ued to get better and better. Now in her mid-sixties, this San Diego resident is an inspiration to everyone, proving it's never too late to accomplish anything!

Richard Louv
Award-Winning Author and Columnist

For three years, Richard Louv traveled the country interviewing over three thousand children, parents, grandparents and teachers for his highly-acclaimed second book, *Childhood's Future,* published by Houghton Mifflin and now in paperback from Anchor Books. Louv explores the problems facing America's children and families while offering insightful recommendations on how to correct these ills. *Publisher's Weekly* called it, "A compassionate, comprehensive view of modern American family life." *Kirkus Reviews* further describes *Childhood's Future* as, "An illuminating and motivating how-to for families of the 1990's." Louv is also an award-winning columnist for the *San Diego Union-Tribune* and author of *America II,* released in 1984, a book which focuses on social and political trends.

Now forty-three, Louv remembers his mother's words to him as a young child. "I had a very strong mother, and if there is one thing she taught me, it was to never quit." The people he wished to emulate while growing up were politicians and writers. He mentions Robert

Kennedy and John Steinbeck as his two most influential role models. He chose to become a writer, earning his degree from William Allen White School of Journalism at the University of Kansas. Before becoming a writer, he was director of Project Concern's OPTION program, recruiting and placing medical professionals in areas of need. His work took him to the hard-core, poverty-stricken areas of Third World countries, but in all of his travels he was never as moved as he was while interviewing inner-city children during his more recent journey across the United States.

"The single most defining characteristic of kids today is that so many of them receive so little positive adult contact from their parents or anybody else," he says. "I don't think the problem with kids is the kids. The problem is with the adults." He backs up these statements with dozens of disturbing stories. A twelfth grader describing his upbringing says, "My mom works and my dad works, and I kind of raised myself. So my parents really didn't have to worry about parenting." What surprised Louv most was the compassion the kids showed toward their parents, despite the anger they felt about the uncertain future their parents have left them.

In the 1970's, Louv was a contributing editor for *San Diego Magazine* and wrote for the *Reader* and the *San Diego Union.* He was also a contributing editor for *Human Behavior Magazine.* Since 1984, he has had a regular column in the *San Diego Union-Tribune* that also appears in newspapers across the country. Recently, he became a contributing editor and columnist for *Parents Magazine.* He focuses mainly on family issues, the environment, technology, personal and public ethics, grass-roots politics and on the kind of people we are becoming. "I'm most comfortable writing about people with few outward signs of power, but whose inner strength is often inspiring," he says.

When Richard Louv speaks of success, he's not talking about book sales or television appearances, but rather about something that has the feel of truth about it, not only for himself but for others as well. He has appeared on *The Today Show, Donahue,* Bill Moyers' PBS series *Listening to America* and many other television and radio programs. His work has won him many awards, and his book has been featured and praised by countless publications. Judy Woodruff of the *MacNeil/*

Lehrer News Hour says of *Childhood's Future,* "I am recommending it to every parent and prospective parent I know – as well as a few policy makers."

Louv and his wife, Kathy, a nurse practitioner, have two young boys, Jason (class of 2000) and Matthew (class of 2006).

Max Miller
Author/Journalist

Max Miller truly loved San Diego and, through his writing, became one of the area's best publicists. No one captured the character of the area better than Miller when he painted San Diego as a sleepy little town, a virtually unknown paradise just waiting to be discovered. He wrote nearly a book a year from his beautiful La Jolla home until his death in 1967. Although some of his later books were more factual, he was more of an artist than a historian, combining history with legend. This long-time newspaperman, author, sportsman, traveler and ocean enthusiast walked the San Diego waterfront and the beaches of La Jolla, went for daily swims in the Pacific and dove for abalone off the coast as he tried to personally experience the places and events he wrote about. In the opening paragraph of his immensely successful first book, *I Cover the Waterfront,* he writes, "I have been here so long that even the seagulls must recognize me. They pass the word along from generation to generation..."

Miller was born February 9, 1899 in Traverse City, Michigan, but he grew up in Everett, Washington, where he was a voracious reader. He set his sights on becoming a journalist, and worked as editor of the University of Washington's newspaper. His Husky dog was mascot of his fraternity, which suggested the name for the school's mascot, and they're known as the "Huskies" to this day. When he graduated, he left without ever picking up his diploma, not receiving it until 1963, when he opted to have it sent to him by mail. He went to Seattle, Montana and Australia pursuing a career in journalism. An aborigine hit him in the hip with a spear when he was on assignment in the Solomon Islands.

Still in his teens, Miller was a signalman aboard a submarine chaser

Max Miller, circa 1934   *San Diego Historical Society, Union-Tribune Collection*

in the Caribbean. The year was 1916. He fell overboard and had to tread water for nearly two hours before being rescued. He never lost his love of swimming – or his dedication to the Navy. In 1942 he served as a Navy commander and returned to serve during the Korean conflict.

In 1924, the young reporter came to San Diego, broke but eager. He worked as an office boy and reporter for the old *San Diego Sun* working his way up to earning fifty dollars a week covering the waterfront. This is the assignment that eventually made him both rich and famous. He gave up day-by-day reporting when his first book, *I Cover the Waterfront,* became a success. It was made into a movie starring Claudette Colbert and Ben Lyon, and a popular song followed.

Over the next thirty years, Miller devoted his time to writing books, magazine articles and newspaper features. He sold portions of *I Cover the Waterfront* to other publications, using the proceeds to purchase an oceanfront La Jolla estate, where he lived with his wife of forty years and wrote his twenty-six other books. His only other bestselling book was his last, *Holladay Street* (1932), which sold over a quarter of a million copies in hardback.

Living in La Jolla, Miller was one of the principal promoters of the La Jolla Rough Water Swim, competing in the event for nearly thirty years and happily coming in dead last every time. He made sure everyone else finished before him. This "last man to finish" plot definitely delighted him, but it in no way signified his life's plan. In the hearts of true San Diegans, Max Miller will always be number one.

Joan Oppenheimer
Author

Joan Oppenheimer of Chula Vista is best known as the author of young adult books. Of her twenty popular titles, three have been made into ABC After School Specials, resulting in two Emmy Awards. Her concern over the increasing drug problem in our country triggered her first book and, since then, she has tackled tough issues such as broken homes, alcohol abuse, foster homes and the pain and confusion of being a teenager. Much of her success comes from the fact that her young readers appreciate her honest and realistic approach to these troubling subjects. "They say writing for children is the most difficult writing of all. If you're successful at it, it means that you've succeeded in not preaching," she says.

Oppenheimer is well-respected in her field not only for the marketability of her books, but also for her ability to really help teenagers cope with their problems. She loves the fact that her young readers take the time to write to thank her and tell her exactly what they thought of her books and characters. "It's very moving when you think there are problem kids somewhere in the country who've never met you, will never meet you and you have communicated through a book."

Joan knew by the age of nine that she would be an author one day. Born January 25, 1925 on a wheat ranch in Ellendale, North Dakota, she grew up in the country, far from other families, with "three sisters who hated me." Her childhood was very lonely, so she created imaginary friends and filled notebooks with her own stories to amuse herself. Still, while her childhood wasn't exactly a happy one, she never had to deal with the kinds of problems she covers in her books today. "Think about the childhoods of many kids nowadays and the things that they face," she says. "It's one reason I went into writing for teenagers − because of all the dangers they face that didn't exist when I was a kid." But human emotions don't change, and those feelings form the basis for her stories. She just researches the rest to keep up-to-date.

Oppenheimer worked as a voucher clerk for the FBI in Chicago from 1943 to 1945. "Nobody else knew what I was doing or where I would be at any given hour of the day. A dream job," she says. It was fascinating and demanding at the same time. The only holiday she had off in two years was Christmas Day. While with the FBI, Oppenheimer learned many things that are only now becoming public knowledge. She remembers seeing J. Edgar Hoover when he was head of the organization. "He was a fanatic. If you wore the wrong kind of tie he'd send you to Boise, Idaho. I saw him a couple of times when he came through the Chicago office," she says. "I remember his eyes. He had the eyes of a fanatic."

Oppenheimer made sure she raised her family before becoming a professional writer. She was in her mid-thirties and her youngest was in kindergarten before she even took a course in short story writing. "I always had the feeling that I had a little talent, but I didn't know if I could work with that little talent. I'd been writing for years with no technical training," she confesses. In that class, she wrote a short story about a couple adopting a small boy, which she sold to *Redbook* magazine. The story was picked up by *The Loretta Young Show* and aired on television. She wrote thirty more stories before making a second sale. After years of writing short stories, she switched to books, where she has made a name for herself. "I'm very proud of all my books. In each book there were certain things I had to say," Oppenheimer says. "They're like your children. There are certainly a lot of parallels between the gestation of a child and the gestation of a book."

Over the years, Oppenheimer has found writing both challenging and rewarding. It's always been hard work, requiring discipline and commitment. She gives a lot of credit to her husband for his constant and continuing support. "So many marriages and relationships break up because when a writer is committed a partner can be threatened and jealous of the time involved in writing. It can be a big problem," she says. Oppenheimer maintains that as a writer you need at least one person who believes in you and your work.

Oppenheimer has taught at UC San Diego and Southwestern College in Chula Vista. "I realized that someday I wanted to teach, because if one class could do it for me, it could do it for a lot of other people," she says. "I never took enough college to pick up a piece of paper, and I remember my son saying, 'You should really finish and get your degree, and then you can teach at Southwestern.' I said, 'I'll be teaching at Southwestern and I won't have to take math or anything I don't want to.' And that's exactly what happened. They came after me."

Today, Oppenheimer is working on adult mysteries, trying to break into an entirely different field. She has two adult mysteries to her credit and, with her track record, you can be sure that her new book will appear on the best seller list. "Can I be that lucky twice?" she asks.

Anthony Robbins
Entrepreneur/Author/Speaker

Anthony Robbins' rise to success is the inspiring, rags-to-riches story of an unhappy, overweight young man who went from living in the back of his Volkswagen Bug and buying his clothes at thrift stores to building a multi-million-dollar empire with only a high school diploma. He first received recognition for his famous "fire walk," where people paid to walk barefoot across a bed of burning coals. Robbins helped turn peoples' fears into power as they realized their own

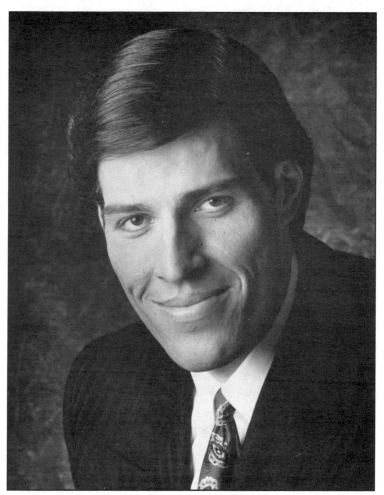

Anthony Robbins   *Photo by Bil Timmerman*

potential. They came from all over the country to see this charismatic kid, and he changed their lives with his standing-room-only seminars. In an effort to reach even more people, he published *Unlimited Power,* which sold over a million copies. His second book, *Awaken the Giant Within,* was released in late 1991 and also hit the best-seller list. If you're not one of the over eight million people who have attended one of his seminars, chances are you have at least seen his "infomercial" on television. The half-hour spot has been on the air every thirty minutes, twenty-four hours a day non-stop somewhere in the United States since

1989 and has been seen by an estimated one hundred million viewers. Many famous and successful people enthusiastically praise and use Robbins' powerful tools for self-change, personal achievement and success. Actors Martin Sheen and LeVar Burton and best-selling authors Kenneth Blanchard *(One Minute Manager)*, Charles Givens *(Wealth Without Risk)* and Dr. Barbara De Angelis *(Making Love All The Time)* support him, as well as Pat Riley, NBC Coach of the Decade, Peter Guber, head of Sony Entertainment and other Fortune 500 companies, which use him as a consultant. Anthony Robbins has certainly made his mark as a leader in the field of personal development.

He started his first company, Robbins Research Institute, in 1983 with only a thousand dollars. Today, he runs nine corporations grossing an estimated fifty million dollars a year. His companies include three that are seminar-oriented, including a video-based franchise, a television production company that produces infomercials for himself and clients like Cathy Smith (who has a series of exercise videos), a management company for medical professionals that assists in the administration of their practices, a corporate training firm, an insurance brokerage, an investment advisory firm and a finance company. He's also the proud owner of Namale Plantation Resort, a 121-acre resort in the Fiji Islands that accommodates only twenty people at a time. "I bought Namale because I love to see people get turned on and get excited about life again," Robbins says, "and Fiji does it."

A reluctant San Diegan at first, Robbins now resides with wife Becky and children in a castle built in 1924 on three acres in Del Mar, overlooking the Pacific on one side and the racetrack on the other. A native of Glendora, California, he used to think the pace of San Diego was too slow for him. Now he sings the praises of his adopted hometown and its people. "Because of my business, I could live anywhere in the world. I want to live and I choose to live here," he says. Besides, the hustle and bustle of Los Angeles is only thirty-eight minutes away in the helicopter he pilots himself. His businesses are based here as well.

After many years of struggle, Robbins is able to surround himself with luxury while helping to better the lives of others. His story is truly inspirational. He got his first taste for being an entrepreneur as a kid growing up in a poor neighborhood in Los Angeles. As the oldest of three, he learned responsibility and leadership when his mother kicked his father out of their home, making Robbins "the man of the house." "I was responsible for fixing the house, and it seemed like it was always breaking down. At the local hardware store they had a book called *H.E.L.P. (Home Emergencies Ladies Packette)*, and I used it to help me with repairs because it was so simple. I believed in this book. So I borrowed a friend's bike and I rode down there with ten dollars in my pocket, and these books were marked down to twenty-nine cents. They had two dollars and ninety-five cents marked on the cover. I bought all the books they had," he remembers. He sold the books door-to-door for a dollar each until he had enough money to ride the bike five miles to load up on food at a smorgasbord.

Still in high school, he took a telemarketing job for a local paper and started putting his gift for gab to work for him. "The first day I was there I broke the record for sales," he says. "The second day, I broke my own record and the third day I quit." As a senior at Glendora High School (Class of 1978), he was elected class president. He was always a student of human development, reading everything he could get his hands on about the subject. "I've always loved learning, and I also loved to share something I learned and see somebody light up," Robbins says. "It's what I still love to do." He wanted to help change peoples' lives even then, and found power in being able to help people. He was known as Mr. Solution, and other students asked for his advice and believed in him.

Robbins' mother sent him packing after graduation, despite the fact that he had nowhere to go. He lived in his car and earned $140 a week as a janitor. "It was one of the best things that ever happened to me," Robbins says, "because I had these visions of what I thought I might be able to do in my life, and now I had to really apply what I'd learned. Once she said, 'You're outta here,' I thought, 'Okay, now I'm on my own.' And I had to figure out what I wanted to do." Six months later, he attended a seminar by Jim Rohn, who inspired him so much he decided to go to work for him.

While figuring out a way to meet Jim Rohn and convince him to give him a job, Robbins answered an ad in the local paper that said you could make five hundred dollars a week as a manager in training. "I figured I was management material, and they said the key words, 'no experience necessary.'" Robbins says. It turned out the "management" job was a sales job selling musical cassette collections door-to-door. Using his enthusiasm and energy, he did very well. While selling cassettes to a man in Orange County, the customer told him he was the best salesman he'd ever seen and that he should start selling people on what they are capable of, because he could move people to action. "I think he also wanted to just get me out of his house," Robbins says ruefully. The man also told him he knew Jim Rohn and would be happy to introduce him personally if Robbins would meet him at Rohn's next seminar.

"I went down to South Coast Plaza Hotel in my 1968 Volkswagen Baja Bug," Robbins remembers. "I was wearing a two-piece leisure suit I got from the thrift store, open collar, long hair, acne-faced... I pulled up to the valet, and my engine exploded. I went in and told them I was there to see Jim Rohn personally. They treated me like, 'Who the hell do you think you are, you pimply-faced kid?' I kept asking for the guy who was supposed to meet me there and nobody knew who he was." It turned out the guy had duped Robbins. He'd only *attended* a Jim Rohn seminar and didn't know him any better than Robbins did at that point. Not one to give up, Robbins talked his way in, managed to meet Rohn and convinced him to give him a job. The only catch was that he had to invest twelve hundred dollars in Rohn's products and attend a two-day seminar. It was a big catch, but Robbins set about getting a loan for the money. Bank after bank turned him down, but he persisted until he got the money. "I went to the two-day seminar and probably got more out of it than anybody else because I figured every word was worth about twenty-two cents and I had to get every ounce out of this thing. To the other people, their twelve hundred dollars was no big deal, but to me twelve hundred dollars was a new car."

Robbins became Rohn's best salesman in the nation almost overnight, but the bottom fell out when a number of his clients dropped out or failed to pay. Robbins hung in there and, at nineteen, was offered the chance to open up Los Angeles in a new plan called Phase II. He'd have his own office and a staff of thirty to help him. Robbins opened an office in Beverly Hills and politely asked Rohn when he'd get the money to get started. Rohn told him, "You already have it" — meaning that Robbins had to come up with the money to rent the hotel and fill it with people. In return for this investment, he would become

Rohn's partner and get half the take. "I didn't want to turn him down," says Robbins, "so I had to figure out a way to make it work. I learned how to speak to every human being on earth in groups doing three speeches a day. I learned how to move an audience to action, not just to be inspired and clap their hands. I believed so much in it, I began to build my company out of that. I built a team and I began putting on other seminars."

By the time he was twenty-one, he was a very successful promoter in terms of the size of the seminars he produced. He was financially successful as well, but he had a hard time dealing with his success. "Whenever money wasn't in my life, that equaled pain. And all of a sudden I had it – and it equaled pain." Robbins remembers. "I tried to sabotage it." Marilyn and Harvey Diamond, authors of *Fit For Life,* came to Robbins for help in marketing their health seminars to businesspeople. He became partners and friends with them, but when they had a falling out he ended up with a company which was sinking fast and ultimately left him flat broke. He was angry, frustrated over the break-up and the fact that he would have to start all over again from nothing. Robbins began "eating like a pig" and gained thirty-eight pounds. He took up residence in a tiny apartment that he describes as "a hell-hole," washing his dishes in the bathtub.

He hit bottom, and he decided to fight. He remembers clearly going to the beach and making a list of everything in his life that he was disgusted with. He could no longer abide his poor eating habits, he would not settle for an unhappy relationship, he hated his financial situation. He started pulling himself together, first on the physical side, with a sixteen-day fast. "My belief to this day is if you want to change your life, the first place to start is in the physical area," he says. This gave him the energy and vitality to work on the other problems. He learned as much as he could about the seminars the Diamonds presented and began doing them himself. He ended his unhappy relationship. "It was like this radical, unbelievable level of determination," Robbins says. "I made the decision that I was going to do this, and from there, things started to go like crazy."

Robbins began studying neurolinguistics and was asked to give his first seminar on the subject in Vancouver, Canada. He took on challenges that changed peoples' lives and helped them overcome their fears and phobias. About this time, he learned the fire walk. "I became this wonderboy, and they started writing me up in newspapers and magazines. *Life* covered me twice in two years. I was getting unbelievable media coverage. I was covered in nineteen different countries," he says. One of his first fire walks brought news crews from ABC, CBS *Nightly News with Dan Rather* and *Eye on L.A.* out to report on the extraordinary Anthony Robbins. Then he was subjected to an onslaught of negative coverage, accusing him of controlling the minds of some of the most influential people in the country. He overcame the bad publicity – changing the term *motivational guru* to *success coach* – and the bad rap he got for the fire walks.

"There is nothing metaphysical about this [the fire walk]," he says. "The only thing stopping you is your belief, and your belief says you can't do this and you don't know how. Fire walking isn't going to change your life. What's going to change your life is learning how to take action in spite of fear. The fire is a metaphor for the fire of your life, the fire of a relationship or the fire of our fear of rejection or whatever it is you are trying to deal with in life that keeps you from really using all your capacity, all your ability and all your skill. I'm here to remind you of what's already inside of you."

Robbins made local headlines when he purchased his Del Mar castle from local developer and attorney Sandor Shapery. He first saw the property when he leased it for a New Year's Eve world record fire walk in 1984. He had just met his wife-to-be at one of his seminars and was on the road ninety percent of the time. The castle desperately needed an overhaul, but Robbins saw its potential and readily accepted Shapery's lease offer after the fire walk. "I wanted to create a place where I'm going to stay and build a family," Robbins says. "That was my whole goal, and when I saw the castle, I said, 'This is it. I'm going to make this happen.'"

He wasn't making nearly enough to afford the rent and upkeep, but – despite the fact that he lacked furniture and dishes – he leased it anyway. Now he admits that, when he heard the price, his initial reaction was, "Oh my God, I was looking for a place one-sixth of that."

His new address was a big move up. "When I set those standards that day on the beach, I moved within a month and a half from my hell-hole in Venice to Marina Del Rey. It was a major jump to cross over

Washington Boulevard, and I was trying to decide between two apartments. One was like six hundred bucks – my share because I had a roommate – and the other was five hundred and fifty dollars. I went for the big money one. I moved from that to here. That gives you an idea of how big a jump it was." He eventually purchased the eight thousand square-foot castle outright. "Sandy finally said, 'Give me every penny you have as downpayment within twenty-four hours, and the house is yours,'" says Robbins.

When he was twenty-five, Robbins wrote his first book, and his career took off once again. "I wrote the book and nobody had any clue how well it was going to do," he remembers. *Unlimited Power* became a national best-seller, published in thirteen languages and selling nearly a million copies. Robbins' income soared from forty thousand dollars a year in 1983 to a million dollars in 1985. In 1989, he began selling audio cassettes with his now-famous infomercial hosted by NFL football great Fran Tarkenton. Since then he's sold an estimated ten million cassettes, earning nearly seventy-eight million dollars.

Robbins regularly gives to causes in San Diego and across the country, particularly through his "Basket Brigade," which distributes food to the needy at Thanksgiving. "When I was eleven years old, we had a Thanksgiving with no money and no food, and somebody knocked on the door and they had this big box of food. My dad didn't want to take it, and the guy said, 'I'm just the delivery person.' [It was] perfect, because he wasn't insulting and my dad had to take it. I think that shaped a lot of my values, because I was so moved by it that I promised myself that one day I would do the same for somebody else."

Robbins also helped build a new gym for the local YMCA, and last Christmas he dressed up like Santa Claus to distribute gifts at a very special school in Clairemont. He pays the entire annual food budget of a local, non-profit organization that feeds and provides other services to the homeless in North County. He was so touched by a fifth grade class in Houston that he made a pledge to pay the college tuition of any class member who maintains at least a "B" average, stays away from drugs and donates a minimum of 25 hours a year for charity. He's putting money away now to honor that commitment when the time comes.

With his busy schedule, Robbins finds it a constant struggle to find the time to enjoy all he has worked so hard to achieve. "I have nine companies now, and I'm spinning all these plates, doing my seminars, writing, trying to be the best dad I can be and a great husband. I recently found myself getting a bit burned out," he admits. "I run in cycles, although I keep saying I'm going to cut my schedule back and I do. I used to spend about two hundred and seventy-five days on the road doing seminars." He relaxes by going to the resort in Fiji, cruising above the traffic in his helicopter or going river rafting with the movers and shakers of Hollywood and the sports world. Robbins' newest passion is for the "sport of kings." "I always thought polo was this elitist and stuffy sport," he says. "There is nothing in terms of a sport that is as intense or exciting. Polo is my passion, and I think everyone needs to find a passion that is outside of their normal reality and is total fun. I think that is one of the ways to keep your life balanced."

At thirty-two, Anthony Robbins walks his talk. He's the inspiration for millions of people to strive for constant and never-ending improvement. He took control of his destiny and made himself into a walking testimony of what is possible.

Dr. Seuss aka Theodor Geisel
Author

By making reading fun instead of a chore, Dr. Seuss (Theodor Geisel) helped millions of children to read and love it. In his over forty-five books, the author, illustrator and master of rhyme used bizarre creatures and entertaining verse to take the world of children's books by storm, selling more than two hundred million copies in twenty languages. Of the ten best-selling hardcover children's books of all time, four were written by Geisel: *The Cat in the Hat, Green Eggs and Ham, One Fish, Two Fish, Red Fish, Blue Fish* and *Hop on Pop.* In 1984 he was awarded a special Pulitzer Prize for his total body of work.

Originally, Geisel wanted to write serious novels, and in 1939 he published *The Seven Lady Godivas.* It was a flop. He didn't give up — he just changed direction and ended up pleasing millions of kids. His first children's book, *And to Think That I Saw It on Mulberry Street,* became a best-seller.

Theodor Seuss Geisel was born in Springfield, Massachusetts in 1904. He began sketching animals on visits to the local zoo with his father, whose job was running it. Geisel was quoted as saying, "I've always drawn, but I never learned how." After graduating from Dartmouth in 1925, he went on to study at the Lincoln College of Oxford University for a year. He traveled through Europe for a year and returned to New York to make a living selling cartoons to magazines and working in advertising. His ad work included a campaign for an insecticide called "Flit." His bug cartoons and the slogan, "Quick, Henry! The Flit!" were used for over fifteen years.

Geisel was in his forties when he joined the Army, serving from 1943 to 1946 and making two Oscar-winning documentaries, *Hitler Lives* and *Design for Death.* He won a third Oscar for a 1951 animated cartoon called *Gerald McBoing-Boing.* Much later, he received two Emmy Awards for the animated television specials *Halloween is Grinch Night* (1977) and *The Grinch Grinches the Cat in the Hat* (1982). He has delighted kids with other television specials, including the annual Christmas show, *How the Grinch Stole Christmas* and perennial favorite, *Horton Hears a Who.*

A resident of La Jolla since 1948, Geisel supported countless civic and charitable causes, working to improve the environment. He had no children of his own, although he had stepchildren from his second wife, Audrey Stone Geisel. He died at home on September 24, 1991 at the age of 87. Nevertheless, he lives on as someone who brought smiles to the faces of generation after generation of kids, teaching them to read and subtly educating them about the environment, tolerance and peace.

Brian Tracy
Speaker/Author

Brian Tracy is in the business of helping others. As a best-selling author/narrator of audio and video training programs and a professional speaker, he helps thousands of people each year reach their full potential. In his tapes and seminars, he tackles the subjects of developing leadership skills, increasing self-esteem, managing your time, selling effectively and achieving personal goals. "My mission is to help other people become successful," he says. "The toughest hurdle that anyone has to get over on the road to success, including myself, is the ability to discipline yourself to do the things necessary to achieve the things you want. I had to spend thousands of hours studying and learning about the various businesses I wanted to be successful in. I then had to spend many hours every working day, starting as early as five in the morning and finishing at midnight, month after month and year after year, to finally break out of the pack and begin to move ahead. The ability to delay gratification is always the biggest single challenge on the road to success." Personally, he has had immense success in a number of fields. He built and managed or consulted for more than three hundred businesses, large and small. He also knows what it's like to struggle. He's seen his share of hard times.

Born January 5, 1944 in Edmonton, Alberta, Brian Tracy grew up poor. "My childhood was unhappy because I had unhappy parents — not an unusual experience. My childhood was helpful in that it was an incredible learning experience with regard to people, and which my family is now benefiting from every single day," Tracy says. "The most important thing to learn in life with regard to what has happened to you is that it is not where you're coming from, but where you're going that matters most." It's not surprising that, even with his many suc- cesses, he says, "My proudest accomplishment is easy. It is to have met and married my wife, Barbara, and to have four beautiful, healthy children who are raised in a home surrounded by love, praise and positive encouragement."

Tracy worked as a construction worker, factory worker, deckhand and farm laborer. When he made the decision to switch from manual labor to sales, he didn't find the going much easier. "I started making my living cold-calling on the streets long ago. I remember the feelings of frustration. I know what it's like to be rejected," he says. He went deeply into debt, finally asking himself why some people are more successful than others. He began studying successful people. He ana- lyzed his own shortcomings and came up with a strategy that eventu- ally made him successful and wealthy. At twenty-five, he built a ninety- five person sales force covering six countries, doing more than a million dollars in sales each month. Tracy also started an automobile import company and built it from nothing to twenty-five million dollars in sales in less than three years. He served as the chief operating officer for a real estate development company with $256 million in assets and seventy-five million dollars in annual sales and was successful in sales, marketing and investments before going into training and management consulting. He began sharing his ideas in talks and seminars, becoming one of the best-selling authors of audio and video cassette learning programs in the country. Tracy travels widely in the United States, Canada and Australia, addressing thousands of people each year. He's considered a leading authority on the development of human potential and personal and professional effectiveness. He's living proof that you can become anything you want in life if you clearly define it and then learn how to accomplish it.

In his audio and video training programs, Tracy's advice is both valuable and practical. In *The Psychology of Success,* he points out that some of the basic qualities successful people share are purpose, persistence, courage, creativity, excellence and integrity. In *The Universal Laws of Success and Achievement,* he points to "the First Law of Success," from which all others flow: "If you want something good to happen, find out what action causes it and take that action. If there is something bad happening, find out what action it results from and stop or prevent it." It seems simple, but sometimes the simplest ideas are overlooked. "Many people think that they need some sort of breakthrough idea, something revolutionary to climb higher on the ladder of success. However, as any seasoned professional would agree, the most effective ideas are simple," Tracy says.

Tracy repeatedly refers to goal-setting as the "master skill" of success. Success is often based on your ability to set personal and organizational goals and formulate effective plans of action to accomplish these goals. "If you don't set goals for yourself, you're doomed to work to achieve the goals of someone else," he warns. In *Getting Rich in America* he points out that owning your own business is the fastest way to become wealthy in America. He advises opening a savings account and putting away ten percent of everything you earn to build a cash reserve. He urges his pupils to become debt-free, invest carefully and never lose money. In *How to Master Your Time,* Tracy says, "The greatest time-saver of all is the word 'No.' Use it for anything that does not advance you toward your goals." He goes on to say, "Remember that everything you do counts. If you read a book on success, that is points in your favor. If you watch television in your spare time, that is wasting time — because either you are moving towards your goal or away from it."

Briefs

Greg Bear

Since he was a child, Greg Bear knew that he wanted to be a science fiction writer. He wrote his first story before his tenth birthday, and by fifteen his work had been published in a famous science fiction magazine. The San Diego State University graduate is now living his childhood dream as a successful and award-winning science fiction novelist.

Dr. Kenneth Blanchard

Blanchard originally came to San Diego in the mid-1970's on sabbatical from teaching. By the end of the decade, he and his wife established Blanchard Training and Development. The Escondido-based firm is still a leader in management consulting and training. In 1982, Blanchard co-authored *The One Minute Manager,* one of the most popular management books of all time. Since that success, he has written several other "One Minute" books, which have collectively sold several million copies.

Raymond Chandler

Considered one of the finest writers of detective fiction of all time, Chandler didn't pen his first novel until he was over forty. The late bloomer began studying pulp fiction after he was laid off from a job as an oil company executive during the Depression. He then created a new genre of detective fiction, featuring a tough, wise-cracking private eye named Philip Marlowe. Chandler's first novel, *The Big Sleep,* was published in the late 1930's, followed by *Farewell, My Lovely* and *The Lady in the Lake.* After moving to La Jolla, he wrote *The Long Goodbye.* He lived in the Bird Rock area until his death in 1959. He's buried in a nondescript grave in Southeast San Diego.

Cameron Crowe

This former San Diegan wrote, directed and co-produced the 1992 film *Singles,* starring Matt Dillon and Bridget Fonda. He also wrote and directed *Say Anything.* He is probably more famous for his portrayal of high school life in the 1981 best-selling book and later the film *Fast Times at Ridgemont High,* which is rumored to have been based on Clairemont High School. Crowe, who graduated from San Diego's University High School at age fifteen, skipped two primary school grades. He wrote for the school paper as well as an underground San Diego paper. Still in his teens, he wrote for *Rolling Stone* and hung out with Led Zeppelin and the Eagles. Signed to write a book about high school life, the wunderkind moved back home and into his old room. At twenty-one, he returned to high school incognito and relived his senior year as research before writing the book that made him famous.

Raymond Feist

This best-selling science-fiction writer was a graduate of UC San Diego in the late 1970's and worked as a social worker before cutbacks put him out of work. He moved back in with his mother in a Clairemont apartment and began writing. Out of money, Feist was about to apply for a job as a management trainee with a hamburger chain when a few of his friends offered to lend him some money so he could finish the book he was working on. That first effort, *Magician,* became the first of many successful books from this San Diego native.

Spencer Johnson

In 1982, this San Diegan co-authored *The One Minute Manager* with Ken Blanchard. Setting records for non-fiction sales, the book was on the *New York Times* best-seller list for more than three years; it has been translated into twenty languages. Johnson's knack for taking complicated problems and simplifying them so they can be readily understood has made his books immensely popular.

Anita Loos (1893-1981)

Loos began her writing career as a student at San Diego High School, then called Russ High School. She was best known for her book *Gentlemen Prefer Blondes,* published in 1925. It was later made into a successful play, a musical comedy and a film. It eventually went through forty-five editions, establishing Loos as a prolific writer and celebrity.

Dr. Carl Rogers (1902-1987)

Recognized as one of the nation's leading psychologists, Dr. Rogers was called "the father of humanistic psychology." He founded the Center for Studies of the Person, based in La Jolla. A highly-regarded author, two of his most popular books were *On Becoming a Person* (1961) and *A Way of Being* (1980). His final book was *Freedom to Learn for the '80's.* He called La Jolla home for the last twenty-four years of his life.

Victor Villaseñor

Throughout grade school, junior high and high school, teachers failed to recognize that Villaseñor was not, in fact, unintelligent. Today they would have realized that he suffered from dyslexia. He went on to become a successful author but, before his first book was published, he suffered rejection after rejection. He faced over two hundred rejections before *Macho!* was finally published in 1973. For more than a decade, he traced his family's Mexican roots while writing what was to become the nationally-heralded *Rain of Gold.* It was originally scheduled for publication by a large New York firm, but Villaseñor didn't want to compromise his work. He took a big risk and bought the manuscript back, publishing thirty thousand copies through a much smaller company. The epic has received extraordinary reviews, focusing national attention on its author. It provides Latinos with the hope that they can be anything they want to be.

Robert Wade

San Diego author Robert Wade is better known to readers around the world as Wade Miller or Whit Masterson. Under those pseudonyms, he turned out forty-six widely-acclaimed novels of mystery, suspense and intrigue. He met his long-time writing partner Bill Miller while the two attended Woodrow Wilson Junior High School in San Diego. After graduating from Hoover High School, Wade and Miller worked in tandem on campus publications and dramatic productions at San Diego State University. To help finance their productions, Wade worked as a truck driver, grocery clerk, shoe salesman, service station attendant and newspaper reporter. The two collaborated on over thirty novels until Miller died in 1961. Since then, Wade has published eleven more novels under the Whit Masterson name, as well as two which carry his own name. Over fifteen million copies of Wade's novels have been sold in the United States and around the world. Thirteen of his whodunits have been sold to Hollywood for films starring some of the biggest names in the business. In 1988, he was honored with the Private Eye Writers of America's Life Achievement Award for his contribution to the genre.

Dr. Denis Waitley

This San Diego native is not only a best-selling author but is also one of the most sought-after motivational speakers in the world. He launched his career as an international authority on high-performance motivation with the best-selling audio cassette program *The Psychology of Winning* after a career as a Naval aviator and years of studying human behavior. He followed that with several best-selling books. Denis Waitley's name is practically synonymous with success and motivation.

Sherley Day-Williams

The UC San Diego literature faculty member was unable to get her first novel published, so she turned to writing poetry. She was nominated for the National Book Award for *The Peacock Poems*, published in 1975. With this success to back her up, the Afro-American writer finally got her novel *Dessa Rose* published. She also founded an Afro-American fine arts museum.

Chapter 5: Baseball

Ray, Bob & Bret Boone

Jerry Coleman

Tim Flannery

Tony Gwynn

Kevin Mitchell

Alan Trammell

Ted Williams

Briefs

Eric Anthony · Bud Black · Earle Brucker
Chris Cannizzaro · Chris Chambliss
Clifford "Gavy" Cravath · John D'Aquisto
Bob Elliott · Terry Forster · Jack Graham
Mike Harkey · Doug Harvey · Deron Johnson
Randy Jones · Eric Karros · Mark Langston
Don Larsen · Randy Milligan
Dave Morehead · Graig Nettles · Matt Nokes
Phil Plantier · John Ritchey · Bob Skinner
Dave Smith · Dan Walters · John Wathan
David Wells · Earl Wilson · Whitey Wietelmann

Ray, Bob & Bret Boone
History-making Baseball Family

History was made on August 19, 1992 when Bret Boone started at second base for the Seattle Mariners against the Baltimore Orioles. That day the Boones became the first family ever to have three generations play major league baseball. Bret, twenty-three, is following in the footsteps of his grandfather, Ray Boone, a thirteen-year major league veteran (1948-1960) and two-time All Star – and his father, Bob Boone, the most durable catcher in the history of baseball, with a record 2,225 games (1970-1990). He won six Gold Gloves before retiring. Another thing these three San Diegans have in common is what the oldest Boone refers to as "heart." "Both Bob and Bret were mentally tough kids who had the desire to play baseball and weren't affected by temporary setbacks," Ray says proudly.

Ray Boone should know. He, too, had the drive and determination to be the best player he could be. He was born in San Diego's County Hospital on July 27, 1923. Growing up in Normal Heights, he began his baseball career playing in the hundred-pound league at John Adams playground. "San Diego was a small town at the time," Ray says, "and when I say small town, the city ended in El Cajon." There was no major league baseball team in San Diego at the time, so Ray and his buddies rode their bikes to Hoover High School every Friday to watch Ted Williams play ball. "Our idol was Ted Williams. He was simply awesome," Ray remembers. "Our team at the time was the Pacific Coast League Padres, and we knew every player in the PCL."

Hoover High was in the Coast League then, and in 1942 they became CIF champions. It was the first time Hoover had won a CIF title of that magnitude, and Ray was on the team. He got his first chance to play in the big leagues in 1948 after hitting .355 in the Texas League. That year, he got to play in the World Series as a rookie shortstop with the Cleveland Indians and eventually replaced future Hall of Famer Lou Boudreau as starting shortstop. "I was a regular for ten years, five at shortstop and five at third base and first base. I moved to first base to prolong my career a couple of years," Ray says. His bad knees prevented him from playing as much as he would have liked, and he was traded to the Tigers in an eight-player deal in 1953. He responded by hitting .296 with 26 homers and 114 runs batted in. In 1954, he made the All Star team. In 1955, he led the league in RBI's with 116. Ray retired after 1,373 games – 852 fewer than the record set by his son Bob.

Bob Boone was born in San Diego on November 19, 1947. While he grew up in the College area, his summers were spent with his father and teammates, playing baseball. Bob quickly moved up through the ranks, beginning in the Rolando Little League, playing on the Crawford High School team and then for Stanford University. He reached the major leagues as a catcher for the Philadelphia Phillies late in the 1972 season. He was traded to the Angels in 1981, where he continued an amazing career that included four All Star Games and six Gold Gloves. At age forty, he was released by the Angels after hitting a career high .295 in 1988. Still one of the best catchers in the game, he signed with the Royals and continued to be productive until 1990, when he was released by the Seattle Mariners before he had the chance to play on the same team with his son, Bret.

In 1992, Bret Boone hit .315 with thirteen homers and 73 RBI before being called up from Calgary (the Mariners' minor league team) to become part of baseball history. Bob Boone is currently the manager of Oakland's Class AAA affiliate in Tacoma, and Ray Boone has served as a scout for the Boston Red Sox since 1961.

Jerry Coleman
Broadcaster/Baseball Star/War Hero

You can "hang a star" and many medals on all of Jerry Coleman's careers. As a Marine pilot during World War II and the Korean conflict, he flew 120 missions, miraculously surviving two plane crashes (one when his plane literally flipped over), earning two Distinguished Flying Crosses, thirteen air medals and three Navy citations. Coleman played ball with the Yankees, achieving enormous success in his nine-year run with them. In 1949 he was the American League Rookie of the Year. In

1950, he was voted World Series MVP. His broadcasting career spans over thirty years. He has acted both as a network sportscaster and as the "voice of the Padres" for the last twenty-one years. He did play-by-play for the New York Yankees, also serving as their personnel director just after his playing career ended. He even tried his hand at managing the Padres in 1980, but returned to the broadcast booth the following season, where he continued to entertain listeners with more of his now-famous phrases. "Oh, doctor!" (to use a Colemanism) has this eternal optimist ever been successful!

Always a student of the game, Coleman's love for baseball developed while he was growing up in Northern California. He studied book after book, learning strategies and a real understanding of the sport. He was set to begin his own baseball career when World War II suddenly changed his priorities. In 1942, the eighteen-year-old joined the Naval Aviation V-5 program, willing and eager to go overseas and win the war. He was commissioned as a Marine second lieutenant in early 1944 and promptly became a war hero.

After the war, he polished his skills as an infielder in the minor leagues. Always known as a slick fielder, he led all American League second basemen in fielding his rookie year. Playing for the New York Yankees, he also hit .275, ending up American League Rookie of the Year in 1949. During his tenure with the Yankees, they dominated major league baseball, winning eight pennants and six world championships. One of the "Bronx Bombers," he played alongside Joe DiMaggio, Mickey Mantle, Yogi Berra, Whitey Ford, Johnny Mize and Phil Rizzuto. In 1950, he was named Most Valuable Player of the World Series as the Yankees swept the Philadephia Phillies. He was elected to the American League All Star team the same year.

Coleman retired from baseball in 1957 at the age of thirty-two and took a job in the Yankees front office as player personnel director. This new job involved too much travel, requiring him to spend as many as 200 days a year on the road, so he pursued two alternate lines of work. In 1959, he took a job with the Van Heusen shirt company, working his way up to Regional Manager and eventually National Sales Manager. About this time, he also began his broadcasting career with CBS radio. He still broadcasts for CBS on Sundays. He has covered the World Series and recently announced the All Star game from San Diego to an entire nation. Coleman jumped at the chance to work in San Diego with the Padres. He's currently teamed with Bob Chandler in the booth, handling both Padres radio and television.

Coleman, his wife Maggie and their seven-year-old daughter Chelsea reside in La Jolla.

Tim Flannery
Former San Diego Padres Infielder

Tim Flannery doesn't know how to do anything without giving 110 percent – or more. During his ten-year (1979-1989) career with the San Diego Padres, Flannery played the game full-bore. He became one of the best utility players in the league and a favorite of the fans. "I went on the field every night saying, 'If I die tonight, so be it,'" Flannery says. "I didn't care, and because of that I could go another notch up and I could play to my peak. It's a good feeling to look back on my baseball career and know I couldn't have played any harder."

A sixth-round draft pick by the Padres in 1978, Flannery showed he could play ball right from the start. His first year in the minors at Reno, he hit .350 with twenty steals in eighty-four games. In 1979 at Amarillo he hit .345 with six homers and seventy-one RBI's before being called up by the Padres at the end of the season. "I love baseball. It wasn't like I was motivating myself saying, 'Okay, if I can have a couple of good seasons I'm going to be in the big leagues,'" Flannery remembers. "I was playing for today and playing as hard as I could. And then all of a sudden the phone call came."

In his first major league at bat he stroked an RBI single off Ed Whitson (then with the Giants). In 1980, he lit up the minor leagues by hitting .346 in AAA before being called up and making a respectable showing with the Padres. In 1981, the Padres traded for Juan Bonilla, sending Flannery back down to the minors. Flannery was so frustrated he thought of quitting, but Doug Rader, his minor league manager at Hawaii, helped turn him around. "I had to adjust my sights," Flannery says. "I had a choice. I can sit on the bench and be miserable because I'm not playing every day, or I can say, 'Okay, if I can't play every day, then I'm going to be the best utility player I can be.' I didn't worry about the things I had no control over. I just gave it everything I had whenever I got a chance to play."

Flannery never won a batting title or a Gold Glove. He won't be remembered for the numbers he put up. But he played with a zeal that many of today's superstars lack. But before retiring on his thirty-second birthday, Flannery was considered one of the best utility players in the game. He could play second, third or shortstop. He was a valuable pinch hitter — the one who started the winning rally in the 1984 championship game against the Cubs. He played just as hard whether the Padres were going to the World Series (1984) or finishing near the bottom of the standings. And the fans responded. Flannery was their hero, and he became San Diego's own version of Pete Rose (aka "Charlie Hustle").

As a rookie, Flannery approached Rose and jokingly told him he was going to break Rose's streak of fifty-three consecutive games with a hit. Rose snapped back that Flannery would be lucky to start fifty-three consecutive games. One thing Flannery and Rose had in common was that they loved the game fiercely. Flannery played for passion, for the thrill of it and the desire to win. Maybe he didn't make the record books, but his numbers over the years aren't too shabby, either. In 972 games, Flannery hit .255 with nine home runs, 209 RBI's and twenty-two stolen bases in limited play. He only quit in 1989 because an ankle injury sustained in 1987 still bothered him and he wanted to make up for lost time with his family. But not before he stood in the opening-day line-up for the first time in his career. He went out as a Padre, just as he wanted, turning down an offer to play for good money in Italy. "I never played baseball for the money," he says. And he never played baseball for any team but the Padres. Being a Padre meant the world to him, and he loved playing his brand of head-first baseball for the San Diego fans.

Flannery's other passions include surfing and music. During his baseball career, he spent his off-seasons surfing twice a day, getting up at 5:30 a.m. to catch the glassy morning waves, then heading out again in the evening to watch the sun go down. Along with Cubs pitcher and good friend Dave Smith, he challenged twelve-foot waves at Tavarua, Fiji. He's caught the swells up and down the North County coast since 1970. "Surfing is a lot more than just riding waves to me," Flannery admits. "I have a real strong relationship with the ocean."

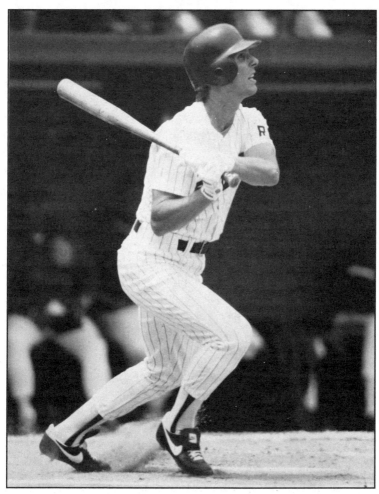

Tim Flannery   *Photo by Martin Mann*

Flannery also plays guitar and sings. In 1992, his band, Buffed Out, opened for Judy Collins. They've played their Jimmy Buffett-style music to capacity crowds throughout San Diego. "I've finally found people who have the same passion and the same love for the music I have. It started out innocently enough in the garage, just for therapy," he grins. But it wasn't enough just to play Jimmy Buffett's songs. Flannery became Buffett's friend, sharing the stage with the rock star in Chicago.

"I met Jimmy through Graig Nettles. He and Nettles were really close, and in 1981, during the fifty-day strike, I went and had a couple of beers with Jimmy. He loves baseball [Buffett is part-owner of a minor league team], so we've looked each other up when we were out on the road, and one thing led to another. My last year, he came in to Chicago and said, 'Hey, c'mon, we're going out tonight!' We went to this place called The Bridge. Everybody knew what was going to happen because his whole band showed up and in about two hours the whole place was jammed. He said, 'C'mon, you're goin' up with me,' and he pulled me up on stage and we played a couple of sets. It was a blast!"

Flannery always seems to be having a blast, as an exciting baseball player, serious surfer, motivational speaker, popular media personality — and, of course, when he's up on stage singing and playing his heart out to screaming "parrot heads"... which he had the opportunity to do recently.

A few days before Jimmy Buffett was to perform at the San Diego Convention Center, he called his buddy Flannery and said, "I've got some good news and I've got some bad news. The good news is you're opening for me. The bad news is you can't play any of my songs." That posed some unique problems for Buffed Out because, of the roughly seventy-six songs they know, seventy are covers of Buffett songs. But this was a once-in-a-lifetime opportunity for the band. On November 6, 1992, Jimmy Buffett himself introduced the band (Sharon Hancock, Mark Rutledge, Gary Seiler and, of course, Flannery) before a capacity crowd of 7,500, saying, "You knew him as an infielder. You knew him as a TV reporter. And now, finally, he has a REAL job!" On that note, Buffett left the band to fend for themselves, which they did admirably. On their sixth and final song, Buffett joined them again for a commanding performance of *Havana Daydreamin.'*

After his baseball career ended, he joined a new "club" at News Eight with teammates Hal Clement, Ted Leitner and Hank Bauer. A devoted family man, he relished being able to spend time with his wife Donna and children Daniel and Virginia. "I have a different philosophy about life than most people," he says. "I think our society is out of whack. I think too many times success is predicated on money made or positions held. The way I judge success is if you can walk away from whatever you do knowing that you've given it everything you had — then you're a successful person. Not everybody has the opportunity to play major league baseball or be a bank president or a corporation president, and not everybody has the opportunity to make big money. A lot of people spend their whole lives chasing these positions, thinking that's going to bring them happiness because that's what success is. People are being sold something that not everybody has the chance to attain. People have to realize there's more to life."

Flannery takes the time to enjoy the moment and realizes now more than ever what's important to him – his family and his children's future. "This is home. I love San Diego," he says proudly.

At thirty-five, he's already done more than the average San Diegan, but he doesn't take his good fortune for granted. He's always tried to take time out for his family, friends, surfing – the things that really matter. "Surfing is something I've always tried to keep pure," he says. "It's something I did all along, even when I played baseball. It balanced out the major league life and the crazy lifestyle, the pressures and the stress. Surfing has always been very important to me, because I knew when baseball was over surfing was always going to be there."

*NOTE: Lee Silber, a devoted follower and Jimmy Buffett fanatic, was finally able to meet his idol before the November 6 show. When he asked Buffett about Tim Flannery (for purposes of this book), Buffett jokingly replied, "Who the hell is Tim Flannery? Why not do a story about me?" Silber was so dumbfounded he agreed, saying, "Yeah, who the hell is Tim Flannery?"

Tony Gwynn
Baseball Superstar

Tony Gwynn may be the greatest player ever to wear a Padres uniform. He is certainly one of the best players in the game today, heading straight for the Hall of Fame. One of baseball's true superstars, he's been patrolling the outfield with his Gold Gloves and spraying line drives all over Jack Murphy Stadium with his Silver Bats for eleven years. (That's five Gold Gloves and four batting titles.) Yet Gwynn is unpretentious, truly a nice person. He freely gives his time to the fans – especially kids – and the media, as well as many worthy causes in San Diego.

Born May 9, 1960 in Los Angeles, Gwynn grew up thinking he'd like to be a professional basketball player. A graduate of Long Beach Poly High, he went on to San Diego State University, where he made himself the finest point guard in the Western Athletic Conference. Although he didn't play baseball his freshman year at SDSU, he also had an outstanding college baseball career. Picked by the Padres in the third round of the 1981 free-agent draft, he was claimed by the San Diego Clippers on the same day. Gwynn chose to focus on baseball, and began to earn his reputation as a left-handed hitting machine in the minor leagues. In forty-two games at Walla Walla, he hit .331 with twelve homers. He hit .462 in twenty-three games at Amarillo. Nobody doubted he could hit, but many scouts felt he was lacking in defensive skills. "There were always coaches who said I had ability but that I couldn't do something. I couldn't throw, I couldn't hit with power, I couldn't run, I couldn't field my position — whatever," Gwynn says. "I think that's one of the reasons I've been successful. They can measure everything you do on the field, but they can't measure what's inside of you and what drives you. In Little League, high school, college, the minor leagues and the big leagues, there's always been something people said I couldn't do."

When he made Triple-A ball, he showed his critics he was ready for the next step, hitting .328 at Hawaii in 1982. Only twenty-two, he got the call to join the Padres. He flew to San Diego on the red-eye and began his major league career on July 19, 982 against the giants. He went two-for-five with one RBI. Since then, he's been one of the most consistent hitters in baseball history. After hitting .289 his first year, his average has never been below .309 and has reached as high as .370 (in 1987). He rarely strikes out. A four-time batting champion (1984, 1987, 1988 and 1989), he was a contender in three other years. "I try to stay within myself and what I'm capable of doing, and not what other people think I should be doing," Gwynn says seriously. "My forte is to put the bat on the ball and put it in play." His proudest individual accomplishment is his five Gold Gloves. "Everybody said I had a quick bat and I'd be able to hit major league pitching, but nobody — and I mean absolutely nobody — would have said I'd win a Gold Glove. So I worked harder on my defense than anything."

Gwynn holds virtually every offensive record for the Padres. He's an eight-time Padre representative to the All Stars, dazzling hometown

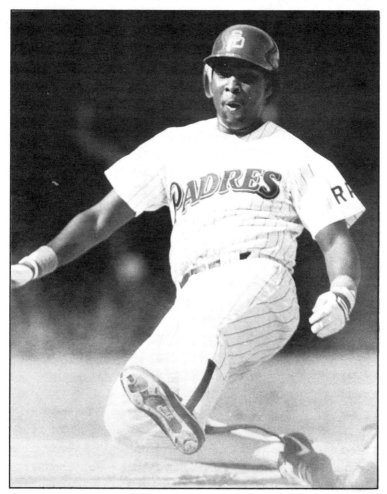

Tony Gwynn   *Photo by Martin Mann*

fans as he tied a record for assists by an outfielder in the 1992 All Star game. A team player, Gwynn knows he's got a job to do as the number two hitter in the Padres' lineup. "To me, that's what this game is all about," he says. "It's about going in there and fulfilling your role and watching everybody come together and fit into these roles. If everybody does what's asked of them, everybody will benefit and the team will have success. My role in the lineup is to get on base and get in position for McGriff and Sheffield to knock me in. This year it's been a blast, because they can hit two homers in a game or two doubles, and they usually drive in runners in scoring position!" Although the Padres have seen their share of ups and downs, Tony Gwynn has been a model of consistency. Still, playing for what is often considered an "also-ran" team has kept him from getting the national recognition he deserves. He's never received the National League MVP award. On top of that, at five-foot-eleven and 219 pounds, he doesn't *look* like a ballplayer. But he's the first to arrive at the ballpark and the last to leave. He records other National League pitchers, evaluating and categorizing them, then reviewing them on game day. He also videotapes himself, constantly reviewing and analyzing his swing. He takes extra batting practice as a matter of course, working through the off-season on both his batting and fielding skills.

Gwynn has always had the ability to overcome. "As a shy, skinny kid, I wasn't outgoing at all," he says. "I didn't want to say anything because I didn't want to be rejected. I wasn't sure of myself when I was younger, but once I got a grasp of who I am, I started to open up. Now I run my mouth with the best of them!"

In 1987, Gwynn and his wife were forced to file bankruptcy when his former agent failed to make good on loans Gwynn had co-signed. At twenty-seven, he found himself over a million dollars in debt. "The financial stuff was tough for me, because it involved my family. There's nothing like being on the front page of the newspaper, *Gwynn and His Wife File for Bankruptcy.*" He looked at it as a chance to start over, to learn from and to never let anything like that happen again. "Interestingly enough," Gwynn says, "I had my best year that year, because once I hit the baseball field I was able to get away from all the other stuff." Then Jack Clark accused Gwynn of being a selfish player. Nothing could be farther from the truth, and the whole thing blew over after a couple of months of turmoil..

Gwynn's most recent challenge came right before the 1991 season started. Diagnosed with what was thought to be a polyp behind his ear, he checked into Scripps Memorial Hospital for a simple operation to have it removed before spring training. "The doctor got in there and it was a tumor and it was growing," Gwynn remembers. "The doctor told me it was five and a half hours of the most delicate surgery you've got to perform. He had to go into my lymph nodes and down into my neck and into my head a little bit. I went to sleep with a mustache and woke up without one, and I had this gigantic rope-like incision going down the side of my neck." The doctor explained how lucky Gwynn was, giving him a new perspective on his life and his career. "My basic premise for playing baseball is if you work hard, good things will happen. And for the last ten and a half years I've worked very hard and things have happened for me that I didn't believe could happen," Gwynn says. "Only you know if you're working hard enough, because it's easy to cheat yourself and do just enough to get by. But that's what everybody can do — just enough to get by. Those who want to be successful and maintain that level of success have got to push a little bit harder and do a little bit more."

Kevin Mitchell
MVP Outfielder

After brief stints with the New York Mets and the San Diego Padres, Kevin Mitchell lived up to and even surpassed his baseball potential with the San Francisco Giants in his fifth year in the major leagues. 1989 saw Mitchell batting clean-up behind Will Clark as the strong, stocky (five-foot-eleven, 210 pounds) right-hander led the league in home runs (forty-seven), RBI's (125) and slugging percentage (.635). That year, Mitchell played in the All Star game and was voted the National League's MVP. He was already MVP for San Diego youths. During the off-season, he returns to his Southeast San Diego neighborhood to sponsor Little League teams, pass out baseball equipment and play football in the streets with the kids who look up to him. Traded to the Seattle Mariners after the 1991 season and to the Cincinnati Reds just before the start of the 1993 season, he still calls San Diego home.

Born January 13, 1962, the San Diego native was raised by his grandmother. Mitchell used baseball as his ticket to escape Southeast San Diego street gangs, but not before having to dodge bullets on a couple of occasions. After showing his stuff in a San Diego camp for free agents, he was signed in 1980 by Joe McIlvaine, then scouting director for the New York Mets. He played seven games for the Mets at the end of the 1984 season, before he became a jack-of-all-trades for the world champion Mets in 1986. Mitchell hit .277 with twelve homers while playing six positions in 108 games, finishing third in the National League Rookie of the Year balloting. He was traded to the Padres as part of a seven-player deal before the start of the 1987 season, and got a chance to play in front of his friends and family. He was the Padres' starting third baseman for three months and sixty-two games before being traded to the Giants. In his Giants debut, he hit a pair of home runs and hasn't stopped hitting them since. Mitchell finished 1987 with twenty-two home runs, helping the Giants win the National League West divisional crown. After an off-year, he began wearing contact lenses and spending time working with Giants hitting instructor Dusty Baker. The results were phenomenal. The now-full-time outfielder set the league on fire, hitting thirty-one home runs by the All Star break. He was on pace to tie the major league all-time home run record. With sixty-two home runs over two seasons with the Giants (1990-91), he was traded to the Seattle Mariners and then to the Cincinnati Reds.

Kevin Mitchell serves as an example that there is a productive alternative — a way out for those willing to take a chance on themselves. And he definitely made his way out. He's now one of the game's highest-paid players.

Alan Trammell
All Star Shortstop

1992 was Alan Trammell's fifteenth season in the major leagues, all of them with the Detroit Tigers. Only twelve other players have been with their present team more then ten years. His longevity has helped Trammell become Detroit's all-time leader in a number of offensive categories. After an MVP year in the minors, he made his major league debut at the age of nineteen in 1977. Trammell at shortstop and Lou Whitaker at second base formed the most productive double-play combination of the late 1970's and 1980's.

Trammell is one of the game's best all-around players. An outstanding fielder, he was a consistent Gold Glove winner. He hit .300 or better six times during his career, with 160 career home runs. He was a team leader who did whatever it took to win as the Tigers reeled off eleven straight winning seasons with him at shortstop. In 1987, he just

missed winning the MVP award. His personal accomplishments include frequent trips to the All Star game and career numbers which
include over 2,000 hits, over 1,000 runs scored and nearly 900 RBI's.
All this while having to overcome nagging injuries to his shoulder, arm,
back, knee and ankle.

Born February 21, 1958, Trammell grew up in San Diego rooting
for the home team and his favorite Padre, Nate Colbert. He and his
friends would arrive at the ballpark early to sneak in before the gates
were closed. Once in, they tried to get into the box seats, carrying old
General Admission ticket stubs in their pockets. Later, he started selling Cokes as a stadium vendor. A graduate of Kearny High School,
Trammell was taken in the second round of the June 1976 draft by the
Detroit Tigers. After a short season with the Tigers in 1977, he went on
to have four solid years before he suffered an off-season injury in 1982.
He came back strong, winning the American League's Comeback Player
of the Year award in 1983 at the age of twenty-five.

Trammell the 1984 World Series MVP when the Tigers defeated
the Padres in five games. A year earlier, an elbow injury had threatened
to cut his career short. Slightly built, Trammell took up weight training
in the off season as part of his rehabilitation under the supervision of
then-Padre trainer Dick Dent. After hitting just .258 with thirteen
homers in 1985, the once-lean right-hander returned in 1986 bulked up
and able to hit twenty-one home runs while remaining quick enough to
steal twenty-five bases. He followed that with a .343 average, twenty-
eight homers, 105 RBI's, 205 hits and 109 runs in 1987.

Early in the 1992 season, Trammell was hurt again and forced to
miss most of the season. No doubt the resilient San Diegan will be back
to wind down what looks to be a Hall of Fame career.

Ted Williams
Hall of Fame Baseball Player

Ted Williams is one of baseball's all-time greatest hitters, and by far
the best ballplayer San Diego has ever produced. Route 56 was recently
renamed Ted Williams Parkway in his honor. The Hall of Famer started
his phenomenal career in San Diego, first at Hoover High School and

then as a local hero playing for the Padres of the Pacific Coast League. After a brief stint in the minors, Williams spent two decades dominating professional baseball with the Boston Red Sox (1939-1960). His career was interrupted twice when he served as a Marine fighter pilot in World War II and again in Korea, losing nearly five years of playing time. He finished his distinguished baseball career with an incredible lifetime batting average of .344 while powering 521 home runs and driving in 1,839 runs. Williams finished the 1941 season with a batting average of .406, becoming the last player ever to hit over .400. The secret to Ted Williams' success is practice, practice, practice. Many said he was the best natural hitter baseball has ever seen, but he still spent countless hours perfecting his swing.

Born August 18, 1918 in San Diego, he grew up on Utah Street in North Park. He spent his days at the University Heights playground, where he practiced more than any other kid in the neighborhood. He later said he was fortunate to have grown up in San Diego because it allowed him to play his beloved baseball twelve months out of the year. He threw himself into the game out of both love and desperation. His mother, a devoted Salvation Army worker, spent much of her time helping other people, sometimes neglecting her own family. Williams' father had a political appointment as an inspector of prisons and spent a great deal of time traveling. There were nights when Williams and his brother Danny would have to wait until well after dark for someone to come home and let them into the house.

A student at Horace Mann Junior High and then Hoover High School just after it opened, Williams remembers San Diego as a small town of roughly 100,000 people. He always tried to be the first one at school in the morning, waiting for the janitor to arrive so he could grab a bat and be the first in line to hit before school started. He practiced hitting during lunch and after school, keeping his grades just high enough to maintain his eligibility to play. In high school, "The Kid" was also a pretty good pitcher, although he wasn't known as much of an outfielder. When he wasn't playing baseball, he liked fishing in Coronado and off Crystal Pier and hunting in San Diego's back country, which at that time wasn't too far from his home.

After becoming Hoover High's Athlete of the Year in 1936, Williams joined the PCL Padres. In forty-two games, he managed to hit

.271. In 1937, at six-foot-two and 145 pounds, the "Splendid Splinter" improved his average to .291 in 138 games, while playing beside guys like Vince DiMaggio and Bobby Doerr, both much older. The Padres sold him to the Red Sox for $25,000 and five players when he was only seventeen. He spent 1938 hitting up a storm for Minneapolis, leading the American Association in homers (forty-three) and RBI's (142) while hitting an impressive .366. He broke into the majors in a big way in 1939 and was awarded Rookie of the Year honors after winning the RBI title with 145 runs batted in while batting .327 with 31 homers.

Over the course of his major league career, Williams won six batting titles. He led the league in home runs and RBI's four times each, was American League MVP in 1946 and 1949 and a six-time All Star. In 1941, with a week left in the season and a batting average over .400, the coach asked if he'd like to sit out the remaining games, guaranteeing that he'd end the year with his incredible average intact. Not only did he refuse, he played both games of a double-header on the final day of the season. He needed four hits in two games to finish the season over .400. He went four-for-five in the first game and two-for-three in the nightcap. The same year, he hit a dramatic home run to win the All Star game in the bottom of the ninth. Williams only hit below .300 once in a long career. In 1959 he hit a slump, but bounced back to lead the league in hitting in 1960 at the age of forty-two. He went out hitting his 521st home run in his final major league at bat in 1960. He was named the 1950's Player of the Decade.

Williams spent untold hours studying opposing pitchers and talking with the game's greatest hitters. He wasn't afraid to ask questions, because his quest for knowledge was insatiable. After retiring from baseball, he spent time fishing in Florida, but returned to the game as the Washington Senators' manager in 1969. He passed his knowledge of the game on to his players and improved the team's record by twenty-one games, raising the team batting average by twenty-seven points. He was named American League Manager of the Year in 1969.

Now in his seventies, Williams spends his time in the Florida Keys catching fish instead of baseballs. He wrote an autobiography fittingly entitled *My Turn At Bat,* and recently returned to his hometown to throw out the first pitch at the sixty-third All Star Game in 1992. That year July twelfth was declared Ted Williams Day in San Diego.

Briefs

Eric Anthony

This twenty-five-year-old San Diego native and Houston Astro out-fielder proved that he could hit with power in 1992 when he slugged nineteen round-trippers and drove in eighty runs in 440 at bats.

Bud Black

A teammate of Tony Gwynn at San Diego State University, Black has accumulated over 100 wins in his eleven major league seasons with the Royals, Indians, Blue Jays and Giants. His best year was 1984, when he won seventeen games for the Royals, helping his team win the American League West divisional title.

Earle Brucker

Brucker was the catcher for San Diego High School's national championship team in 1921. He didn't appear in his first major league game until 1937, when he became a thirty-six-year-old rookie with the Philadelphia Athletics. In four seasons, he played 241 games, retiring with a lifetime batting average of .290. He went on to become a coach and minor league manager.

Chris Cannizzaro

This former Padre catcher holds two very unique Padre firsts. He was in the opening lineup for the 1969 San Diego Padre major league expansion team, where he batted eighth, just ahead of pitcher Dick Selma. The same year, he was chosen to represent the Padres in the All Star game, another first. In thirteen major league seasons, he played in 758 games.

Chris Chambliss

This Oceanside High School graduate entered the major leagues with a bang, winning Rookie of the Year honors in 1971. During his lengthy career with the Indians, Yankees, Blue Jays and Braves, he was known for his consistency and winning ways. The Gold Glove first baseman appeared in thirteen World Series games in a career that saw him hit 185 homers and drive in 972 runs in 2,173 games. A successful minor league manager, Chambliss was recently named the hitting instructor for the St. Louis Cardinals.

Clifford "Gavy" Cravath

He was the home run king of baseball during what was known as the "dead ball" era. A gruff and tough player, Cravath was nicknamed "Cactus" for his prickly personality. Born in 1881, he was the sensation of the Pacific Coast League before breaking into the big leagues with the Boston Red Sox in 1908. He was the first San Diegan to make it to the majors. His 119 career home runs was a major league record until Babe Ruth came along. After his baseball career ended, Cravath became a judge.

John D'Aquisto

The hard-throwing right-hander pitched for eight teams during his major league career, including three seasons with the Padres. A San Diego native, he was All-CIF in baseball and football at St. Augustine High School. A first-round draft pick by the San Francisco Giants, D'Aquisto made the Major League All Star Rookie Team.

Bob Elliott

In 1947, this Braves third baseman hit .317 with twenty-two home runs and 113 RBI's, good enough to earn him National League MVP honors. Elliott also appeared in five All Star games. He later played for the Pacific Coast League Padres and managed the team from 1955 to 1957.

Terry Forster

An All-CIF pitcher from Santana High School in 1970, Forster was immediately drafted by the Chicago White Sox. They tested his ninety-plus mph fastball in all of ten A-ball games before calling him up. In 1972, the left-hander set a club record with twenty-nine saves. Over his sixteen-year major league career, the reliever pitched for the White Sox, Dodgers, Braves and Angels, notching 127 career saves.

Jack Graham

He was the home run king for the Padres in the late 1940's, consistently driving balls out of Lane Field along with teammate Max West.

Mike Harkey

This San Diego native was the Chicago Cubs' number one draft pick in 1987. The six-foot-five-inch right-hander made his major league debut in 1988. In 1992, Harkey led the Cubs ERA with an impressive 1.89 while winning four games.

Doug Harvey

One of the most respected umpires of his time, Harvey was a native San Diegan. He retired in 1992 after thirty-one years as a National League umpire.

Deron Johnson (1938-1992)

Born July 17, 1938 in San Diego, Deron was one of the greatest high school athletes in San Diego history. He starred in both football and baseball at San Diego High School. In his senior year (1955), the Cavers dominated prep football, with Johnson playing an important role as end, linebacker, punter and kicker. He earned first-team All American honors. Instead of choosing a college football career, however, the muscular slugger chose baseball. In 1956, while playing in only sixty-three games in the Nebraska State League, Johnson hit .329 with twenty-four homers and seventy-eight RBI's. In 1963, he led the Pacific Coast League with thirty-three home runs, playing for the Padres. The following year he hit twenty-one home runs for the Reds and in 1965 he put it all together, driving in a league-leading 130 runs while hitting .287 with thirty-two home runs. He finished his sixteen-year major league career with 245 home runs after hitting 162 in the minors. The popular Johnson also spent twelve years as a coach. He died in 1992 of lung cancer at the age of fifty-three.

Randy Jones

Jones is listed among Padre leaders in almost every pitching category — except strikeouts. He used his incredible control and an effective sinker ball to get many of the best hitters to ground out. He tied the National League record by going sixty-eight consecutive innings without a walk. The Padre lefthander also led the league with twenty-two wins in 1976, took the ERA title (2.24) in 1975, earned the Cy Young Award in 1976 and was National League Comeback Player of the Year in 1975. That year he became the first Padres pitcher to be invited to an All Star game. In 1976, he appeared again as an All Star.

Eric Karros

Following the 1992 season in which he hit twenty homers and drove in eighty-eight runs as the Dodgers' starting first baseman, Eric Karros was chosen National League Rookie of the Year. He grew up in the Del Cerro area of San Diego and attended Patrick Henry High School. As a kid, Karros idolized Pete Rose and, like Rose, became a hard worker who gets the most out of his abilities. In his minor league career, Karros consistently hit over .300 and, in 1991, the six-foot-four-inch first baseman was chosen Dodgers minor league player of the year, hitting .316 with twenty-two home runs and 101 RBI's. In fourteen at bats with the Dodgers in 1991, he had only one hit, a double. He came to spring training in 1992 and hit .370, earning a spot on the roster and eventually a starting job.

Mark Langston

One of the most overpowering left-handed pitchers in baseball, Langston is regularly among the league leaders in strike-outs. In 1984, the San Diego native was voted *Sporting News* American League Rookie Pitcher of the Year, winning seventeen games and using his blazing fastball to take league honors for most strike-outs while pitching for the Seattle Mariners. Today the Gold Glover is a starting pitcher for the California Angels, with nineteen wins in 1991 and thirteen in 1992.

Don Larsen

On October 8, 1956, Don Larsen made baseball history by becoming the only man to pitch a perfect World Series game. Before then, the native San Diegan was just another pitcher. In fact, pitching for the Orioles in 1954, his record was a dismal three and twenty-one. He was then traded to the Yankees. By the end of his career, Larsen had pitched for several teams and earned a career record of eighty-one wins and ninety-one losses. At Point Loma High he was considered a better basketball player than baseball player and, in January 1947, was chosen San Diego's Star of the Month for his hoopsterism.

Randy Milligan

This native San Diegan was a first-round pick by the Mets in 1981. His best years have come while playing for the Baltimore Orioles, where he's hit fifty-six of his fifty-nine career home runs. The powerful first baseman, who stands just over six feet tall and weighs 235 pounds, finished the 1992 season with eleven home runs, fifty-three RBI's and a team-leading 106 walks. Three of his Oriole teammates were also from San Diego. All Star outfielder Brady Anderson attended Carlsbad High School, while Sam Horn and Mark McLemore both went to Morse High. Milligan signed with the Reds in 1993.

Dave Morehead

Dave Morehead was All-CIF at Hoover High School and went on to pitch for the Boston Red Sox in the 1960's. He became the fourth San Diegan to hurl a no-hitter.

Graig Nettles

Nettles' father came to San Diego in 1934, attended Grossmont High School and, along with his twin brother, became a football star at San Diego State University. Graig Nettles graduated from San Diego High School in 1962 and attended San Diego State University on a basketball scholarship. He began his baseball career with the Minnesota Twins as an outfielder, but made his mark as a slick-fielding, power-hitting third baseman with the Cleveland Indians, Yankees and later the Padres. He led the league in homers in 1976 with thirty-two, but had his best year in 1977, when he won the Gold Glove, crushed thirty-seven homers and drove in a career-high 107 runs. Nettles was traded to San Diego in 1984 and helped the Padres win their first pennant, providing timely hitting and experience. The three-time All Star finished his illustrious career with 390 home runs and 1,314 RBI's. Graig's brother Jim also got his start as an outfielder with the Twins. On September 14, 1974, the brothers both homered in the same game while playing for opposing teams. In a July 1984 interview in *Tuned In* magazine, Graig commented on what it takes to be a champion: "Determination, concentration and confidence. Attitude is everything. You must have a winning attitude if you want to be a champion."

Matt Nokes

A San Diego native, Nokes was drafted in the twentieth round by the Giants in 1981. He appeared briefly in 1985 and 1986, but in 1987 the catcher exploded for thirty-two home runs to help spark the Tigers to win the American League East division title. That year, he also appeared in the All Star game. Over the next few years, Nokes' production dropped off, but in 1991 he bounced back with the Yankees, hitting twenty-four homers with seventy-seven RBI's in 135 games. He finished the 1992 season with twenty-two home runs and 59 RBI's.

Phil Plantier

The former Poway High star was drafted by the Boston Red Sox in 1987. During his first four minor league seasons, he hit a total of sixty-six homers and drove in 225 runs. His first call-up came in 1990. The left-handed outfielder played in fifty-three games for the Red Sox in 1991, hitting eleven home runs and batting an impressive .331. After a disappointing 1992 season, he was traded to the San Diego Padres in exchange for Jose Melendez. Now the former member of the Junior Padres Club will have a chance to play for the team he rooted for as a kid.

John Ritchey

In 1948, this catcher became the first black to play triple-A minor league baseball. Known as the Jackie Robinson of the Pacific Coast League, he played in 103 games for the Padres. He hit .323 that year in 217 at bats. Ritchey was a graduate of San Diego High School and San Diego State University.

Bob Skinner

A three-time .300 hitter with the Pittsburgh Pirates, the La Jolla native batted a career-high .321 and was the National League's All Star left fielder in 1958. He played on two world champion teams — the

Pirates in 1960 and the Cardinals in 1964. In six World Series games, he batted .375. In 1967, he was named minor league manager of the year as he guided the Padres to the Pacific Coast League championship. As interim manager of the major league Padres in 1977, he compiled a perfect record: one win, no losses. Skinner's son Joel was a thirty-sixth round draft pick for the Pirates in 1979 and has played ten years in the majors as a reliable back-up catcher known for his defense and a rifle arm.

Dave Smith

This long-time San Diego resident notched over 200 saves in his thirteen-year career with the Astros and Cubs. He's the Houston Astros' all-time leader in saves and games pitched. "Smitty" and pal Tim Flannery are both avid surfers.

Dan Walters

A Santana High School graduate, Walters grew up in Santee dreaming of someday playing for the Padres. After several seasons in the minors, his dream became a reality in 1992. He was called up after hitting .390 with Class AAA Las Vegas, finishing the year with the Padres with a respectable .251 batting average in 179 at bats. He's likely to be the Padres' regular catcher in 1993.

John Wathan

The versatile Wathan played catcher, first base and outfield during his ten-year major league career, all with the Royals, a team he would later manage. He set a major league record for catchers with thirty-six steals in 1982. The former St. Augustine High School and University of San Diego standout was nicknamed "Duke" for his John Wayne imitations. In 1992, he coached third base for the Angels until he took over as manager for Buck Rogers, who was injured when the team bus crashed in New Jersey.

David Wells

Wells is a 1982 graduate of Point Loma High School, where he was named Conference Player of the Year. The lefty made his major league debut with the Blue Jays in 1987 and compiled forty-seven wins against thirty-seven losses in six years with the club. His best year was 1991, when he won fifteen games against ten losses. He pitched four-and-a-third shutout innings in the 1992 World Series, helping the Blue Jays win over the Atlanta Braves.

Earl Wilson

While pitching for MCRD in 1957 and 1958, Wilson won forty-two games, losing only two. He tossed a no-hitter for the Boston Red Sox in 1962 and won twenty-two games for the Detroit Tigers in 1967.

Whitey Wietelmann

During this infielder's nine-year major league career (1939-1947), he played for the Boston Braves and Pittsburgh Pirates. He joined the PCL Padres in 1949 and has been a San Diego baseball fixture ever since. "Mr. Indispensable" has been in professional baseball for over fifty years.

Chapter 6: Football

Marcus Allen

Hank Bauer

Rolf Benirschke

Jim Laslavic

Junior Seau

Irvine "Cotton" Warburton

Ed White

Briefs

Eric Allen · Lance Alworth

Willie Buchanon · John Butler

Shawn Collins · Don Coryell · Keith DeLong

Tom Dempsey · Dan Fouts

Gary Garrison · Sid Gillman · Ed Goddard

Charlie Joiner · Mark Malone

Bill McColl · Harold "Brick" Muller · Art Powell

Bert Ritchey · Dan Saleaumua · Brian Sipe

Webster Slaughter · Tommy Vardell

Marcus Allen
Heisman Award-winning Running Back

Marcus Allen began his brilliant career as a defensive back at Lincoln High School in San Diego. After switching to quarterback, he led Lincoln to a twelve-zero-one record and a thirty-four to six win over Kearny High in the 1977 City Championship during his senior year. That year he also compiled some very impressive numbers on the offensive side of the football: 1,900 yards passing for eighteen touchdowns and 1,198 yards rushing for twelve touchdowns. On defense, he intercepted eleven passes for four touchdowns while leading the team in tackles. He used all of his talent on December 9, 1977, carrying the football nine times for 197 yards, scoring four touchdowns rushing and another on an interception return of sixty yards for the city championship. Lincoln retired Allen's jersey, #9.

Because of his success in high school, Allen was avidly recruited as a defensive back. He chose the University of Southern California, where he majored in public administration. After his fourth day of practice as a defensive back, however, the six-foot-two, 210-pounder was shifted to tailback. In his freshman year, he rushed for 171 yards and one touchdown. In 1979 as a sophomore, Allen was switched again, this time to fullback, where his job was to block for eventual Heisman Trophy winner Charles White. On his first day of practice at fullback, he broke his nose. "I looked down and saw blood all over my jersey and I said, 'Hey! Did I hurt somebody?'" Allen remembers. He became an effective blocker while still managing to rush for 649 yards. In 1980, he returned to tailback, where he finished second in the nation in rushing with 1,563 yards. He was starting to realize his potential as a runner. He made the bold prediction that in 1981 he'd win the Heisman and rush for 2,000 yards, something nobody had ever done before. Allen made good on his promise, setting fifteen new NCAA records, including most yards gained rushing in a single season (2,342). His statistics also included twenty-two rushing touchdowns and thirty-four receptions for 256 yards. He was named UPI Player of the Year, won the Heisman and evoked favorable comparisons to O.J. Simpson.

Still, many pro scouts felt Allen was too slow to make an impact in the NFL. The Raiders decided otherwise, and made him the tenth player chosen in the first round of the 1982 draft. Allen silenced his critics during his first year, leading the NFL in touchdowns (fourteen), playing in the Pro Bowl and being voted AFC Rookie of the Year. 1983 saw Allen rush for over 1,000 yards, taking his team to the Super Bowl, where he earned MVP honors, setting a Super Bowl record with 191 rushing yards as the Raiders defeated the Redskins. Allen had another Pro Bowl year in 1984, when he rushed for 1,168 yards and scored fifteen touchdowns. In 1985 he set another NFL mark, this time for combined yards running and receiving (2,314) while winning both NFL MVP and NFL Player of the Year honors. That year he became the first Raider to lead the NFL in rushing, with 1,759 yards. Allen's not only a fine runner, but he's a dangerous receiver out of the backfield, with 418 career catches.

A solid, all-around player, Allen regularly sacrifices his body as a lead blocker opening holes for other runners who have tried to take his job. First it was Bo Jackson, then Roger Craig and, in 1992, Eric Dickerson. Allen is a team player and, although he's the Raiders' all-time leading rusher and the third leading active NFL rusher with 8,244 yards, he isn't above doing the dirty work. Early in the 1992 season, he filled in on special teams for an injured player, serving as a blocker on the kickoff return team. He's deservedly known as a class act.

One of six children, Allen was born in March, 1960 and grew up in Southeast San Diego. He managed to stay out of trouble and keep his focus on sports. His proud parents, Gwen and Harold Allen, often drive up from San Diego to watch their future Hall of Fame son play.

Hank Bauer
Pro Football Player/Media Personality

During his days with the San Diego Chargers, Hank Bauer was a specialist who did whatever it took to help the team. He was the team's designated scorer, using his five-foot-eleven-inch, 204-pound frame for short yardage bursts into the end zone as a running back for Air Coryell, scoring twenty-one touchdowns in his seven seasons on the team. Three of those touchdowns were in one game against the Saints in 1979. As a so-called designated hitter, he set an NFL record with fifty-two special teams tackles in 1982.

Bauer played the game with abandon and disregard for his body, earning the distinction of being named Most Inspirational Player in 1978. "I'm proud of the fact that I'm thirty-eight years old," he said, "because I honestly never thought I'd live this long. I've always been pretty reckless in the way I played the game."

Bauer was forced to retire due to a broken neck in 1983, just as his career was starting to take off. "I was forced to make the decision to retire," he says. "I had no choice. My neck was broken. But that didn't make it any easier. Here I was at the top of my career, the first year I started making any kind of money, top of my game, Special Teams Player of the Year in the NFL, team captain, we were winning... Everything was just going great, and then it was all taken from me." He became one of the youngest coaches in the NFL, taking over as Chargers coach for special teams and running backs. In 1987 he left the team for a career in broadcasting, and he is now a member of the News Eight team.

Bauer was born July 15, 1954. He played both football and baseball in high school and was named to the Orange County Hall of Fame. He set twelve offensive football records for California Lutheran University while getting a Bachelor's degree cum laude in physical education. He signed as a rookie free agent with Dallas in 1976, but was released before ever playing a game with the Cowboys. He taught school in Oxnard, California before signing as a free agent with the Chargers in 1977. "People said I couldn't make it in the NFL," Bauer remembers. "I was too small, too slow, came from a small school. But I did! Not only did I make it, but I lasted and I excelled. People would say, 'Look at this guy, he's an overachiever. How can this guy do the things he's doing?' There's no secret. I did it with hard work. I did have some talent — not a lot — but I did have some ability. I think the thing I'm most proud of is not so much what I've accomplished, but what I've overcome."

As a reporter, Bauer has taken his viewers on a bull ride, off a waterski jump and parachuting out of a plane at 3,000 feet. "It's part of my job. I choose to do it because I don't want to just do my job like every other reporter," he says. Still, he believes that he's just your average, quiet, sensitive, private, sane person. "People think I'm this totally whacked-out, reckless, carefree, hell-bent type of individual. And I am, but I'm not like that all the time. There's a side to me that's very sensitive, very family, very private and quiet."

Bauer certainly isn't afraid to take chances, and he isn't afraid of hard work. "Everybody has a certain talent, and the people who really excel are those who take that gift and work overtime. There's no shortcut to success. Nothing but hard work, period," he says. "The guys I've been around who have excelled and have lasted in any arena are those guys who've put in the extra work. I look at Charlie Joiner. Charlie was the first guy on the practice field and the last guy off the practice field. And that's what made him a [soon-to-be] Hall of Famer."

Although Bauer isn't heading for the NFL Hall of Fame, he's proud of his career as a football player, and his hard work has paid off in his broadcasting career. He received an Emmy Award for Best Sports Feature for a story he did on golf. That makes him happy – to be recognized for excellence in a field where he was told he couldn't make it. But then, he's used to that.

Rolf Benirschke *(Ben-ER-shKA)*
Pro Football Player

In 1979, at the age of twenty-four, Rolf Benirschke was dying from an intestinal disorder known as ulcerative colitis. Before his illness, he was successfully kicking field goals for the San Diego Chargers, but after two emergency abdominal operations in which he almost died, he went from a healthy six-foot-one-inch, 180-pound football player to a frail, 125-pound young man just trying to survive. He battled back and amazingly returned to action the following year, going on to become one of the most accurate place kickers in NFL history.

Benirschke provided Charger fans with some of the most memorable moments in the team's twenty-seven-year history. He's the team's all-time leading scorer with 766 points. He played in the 1982 Pro Bowl and in 1983 was voted NFL Man of the Year. He also used his place kicking skills to benefit endangered species. Contributing fifty dollars for each field goal he made and encouraging others to pledge money as well, Benirschke launched "Kicks for Critters." The program raised $1.3 million for the San Diego Zoo's Center for Reproduction of Endangered Species (CRES), founded and directed by his father, Dr. Kurt Benirschke.

After retiring from football in 1987, Benirschke has been extremely busy. "I had never planned to play professional football," he says. "This was something I kind of fell into. There were other things I wanted to do, and I began to understand that my purpose for being here, my mission, was not just to kick a football, but was to impact peoples' lives." He spent several years as a motivational speaker, sharing his inspirational story. Eight years ago, he founded "Great Comebacks," a program that finds role models for over two million people with the same illness he has. He's also a partner in a financial firm that works with a select group of individuals. "We work with people who are farmers, not miners. People who reap but then replant instead of just stripping the land." He took an interesting detour in his life with a spin as host of *Wheel of Fortune,* when Merv Griffin tapped him to replace Pat Sajak, who left to host his own late-night talk show.

Having come so close to dying, Benirschke is thankful for every day he's alive. "In my desire to get a lot out of life and impact a lot of different people," he says, "there are some trade-offs. One is I am very busy — but I still try to live each day to the fullest." He now shares his life with his wife, the former Mary Michaletz, a speech pathologist. The couple also shares a commitment to their Christian faith.

Benirschke was born in Boston and grew up in New Hampshire before his family moved to the San Diego area in 1970. He became interested in soccer when he was five, but had to stop playing when he entered La Jolla High School because they didn't have a team. He tried his hand at wrestling and tennis until a soccer team was started in his junior year. When his friends saw how far he could kick a soccer ball, they convinced him to try out for the football team his senior year. He not only made the team, he discovered he had a knack for kicking field goals.

In 1973, Benirschke enrolled at the University of California at Davis as a zoology major. While there, he combined academics and athletics, graduating with honors and kicking the ball well enough to

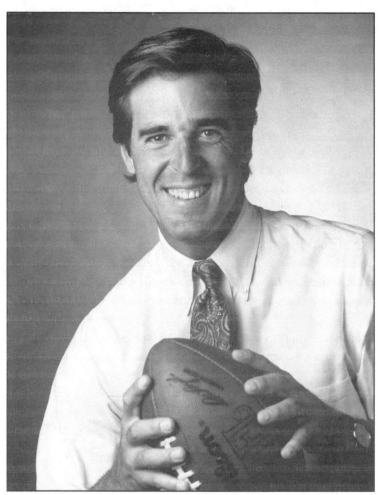

Rolf Benirschke   *Photo by Martin Mann*

be drafted in the twelfth round by the Oakland Raiders in 1977. He recalls his first and only training camp with the Raiders before being picked up by the Chargers on waivers. "I'll never forget meeting Kenny Stabler," he says. "UC Davis was an hour and a half from Oakland, so I was a Raider fan, and he was The Man. I had seen him pull out so many games in the last two minutes... He was a great player. When I walked into the locker room, the lockers were in numerical order. I was #6, Ray Guy was #9 and Stabler was #12. Stabler was sitting at his locker and I remember being really nervous. So I walked in with my head down, put my bag in my locker and began to change. And then Kenny Stabler turned to me and said, 'Hey, Rolf, nice to meet ya!' I was so surprised that he even knew my name. I said, 'Hi, Mr. Stabler, it's nice to meet you.' I shook his hand and he kind of laughed and said, 'Hey, call me Ken, and I'm really happy you're here. I've read about your great college career. Congratulations!'" This taught the young Benirschke a valuable lesson. "The people we admire in our lives are ordinary people who have been able to accomplish some extraordinary things. The things that make them extraordinary are things we all possess."

In his first two seasons with the Chargers, Benirschke was successful on thirty-five of forty-five field goal attempts. During the 1978 season, he began feeling dizzy and weak. He played through the season, despite the constant pain and dizziness, and the discovery of his incurable illness. He started the 1979 season with a club record of four field goals in a row against the Seattle Seahawks, but he'd been losing weight fast – as much as six pounds a week – and literally staggered over to the bench after each kick. Flying back from a game in New England, he toppled over in the aisle of the plane with a temperature of 105 degrees. He was admitted to the hospital the following day to face a life-and-death struggle. Six days after his first surgery, his condition worsened and doctors had to operate again. He came very close to dying. He told his father he didn't want to be kept alive by a machine if it came to that, but it never did. He began the long, hard road to recovery forty-three pounds lighter than he'd been just a year before. He had trouble walking. He took it step by step, however, and with the help of Chargers trainer Phil Tyne and a lot of courage, he built himself back up, running and training with weights.

In less than a year, Benirschke was ready to resume his football career – only this time he was wearing an ileostomy bag taped to his side. On kickoffs, he had to run what the coaches called "Rolf's L pattern." He'd kick the ball, then run a direct route to the sidelines and safety. "My illness was a terrible thing to go through for a twenty-four-year-old," he admits. "It was the beginning of my career, it didn't look like I'd survive. Then I did survive and I had to wear an ileostomy bag. How am I ever going to play again, or date or get married? It turns out that the illness became the biggest blessing of my life. The reality is at the time I would have done almost anything to get rid of the illness. As people deal with major struggles, I'm convinced that most people would do anything just to get over them, whether it be a financial struggle, the break-up of a relationship, divorce or illness – whatever it is. But after major struggles like that, we come out of them changed people. When going through tough times, instead of trying to control them, I began to understand that maybe I'm supposed to be learning something here."

Benirschke was a changed person after his brush with death. He had a new perspective on his life and career. He didn't get as upset about his mistakes. "There were times when I was fearful and I wished they could score a touchdown, but most of the time I was excited because I have a chance to contribute now," he remembers. "Sometimes the fear of failure is so great that we forget that what we're doing is really neat. I think we have to fail sometimes. The great ones have all failed at one time or another." Since retiring from football in 1987, Benirshke's life has taken many interesting turns, and he's taken the time to enjoy the ride. "Life is a journey and not a destination," he says firmly.

"A few years ago, my secretary buzzed me and said, 'The Vice President is on the phone.' I buzzed her back and said, 'The vice president of what?' She answered, 'He just said the Vice President.' I picked up the phone and he said, 'George Bush calling.'" He was calling from the recovery room of the hospital where his son Marvin had just gone through ileostomy surgery and was wondering what to do now. Benirschke offered encouragement and eventually visited the future President and his family. All part of the journey.

Benirschke has immense respect for both of his parents. Although he and his father, a highly respected doctor, have taken very different paths to success and have different outlooks on life, they have a mutual admiration. "My dad was one of those people who always seemed to know what he was doing," Benirschke says ruefully. "I like to explore."

Jim Laslavic

Pro Football Player/Sports Director

No one would question that Jim Laslavic, sports director at KNSD

Channel 39, has paid his dues. He began his football career playing quarterback, fullback and tight end on a twenty-two man squad at Etna High School in Pennsylvania. At Penn State he became a star linebacker for the Nittany Lions before being drafted by the Detroit Lions in 1973. "Laz" spent the bulk of his professional career with the Lions and San Diego Chargers before retiring in 1983. A decade later, many viewers forget that this polished and professional on-air personality even played in the NFL. That comes as a compliment to Laslavic as he builds his reputation as a credible and successful television sports anchor and color analyst.

Laslavic is fortunate in being able to live out two of his childhood dreams — playing professional football and becoming a sports broadcaster. His role model while growing up in Pennsylvania was his older brother, a star football player in high school and captain of his college team. Laslavic credits his brother (now a counselor and coach in Pittsburgh) for his growth as a football player and as a person.

In high school, Laslavic took an interest in sports writing and served as editor of the school paper, showing a talent that has been helpful in his second career. At Penn State University, he became one of the team's best defensive players, starting in two major bowl games and recording 105 tackles in his senior year. After becoming the first Penn State player chosen in the 1973 draft, he was voted to the All Star rookie team. He went on to become the Detroit Lions' leading tackler in 1974 and 1975. "I had the attitude when I was playing football that it was going to be a temporary thing," Laslavic remembers. "I hoped to play five years. That was my goal." During the third quarter of the last game of the season against the Rams in 1976, his knee was seriously injured. Having his knee reconstructed and not knowing if he'd ever play pro football again proved to be the most trying time in Laslavic's career. He overcame both the injury and the fear of getting back on the field with determination and hard work, his trademark in both careers.

After being traded to the Chargers in 1978 for fifth and sixth round draft choices, Laslavic missed the entire 1979 season with an injured left knee. He used this off time to begin paying his dues in broadcasting. He began covering high school sports for the *Los Angeles Times San Diego Edition.* He paid attention to reporters' techniques when he was being interviewed. He started taking adult education courses to learn as much as he could about broadcast journalism. He worked for WOMC-FM radio in Detroit and interned at Channel 10 in San Diego during his off seasons. When his playing career came to an end with the Green Bay Packers in 1983, he was ready to begin his new trade in the sports department at Channel 8. He spent six years at Channel 8 as Ted Leitner's understudy, but it was Hal Clement who took the time to show him the ropes. "I enjoyed watching the way Hal did the sports when he did them," remembers Laslavic. "I thought he was comprehensive, had a good sense of humor and was an excellent writer."

Laslavic came into his own when he took over as KNSD's sports director in July, 1989. He brought credibility, respect and higher ratings to the News San Diego team since becoming their sports anchor. He's turned down offers from competing stations and remains loyal to KNSD because he respects the people he works with, feels that they put out a quality product and enjoys the working atmosphere. In addition to his duties at KNSD, Laslavic serves as analyst for Chargers radio broadcasts on XTRA Radio.

Laslavic enjoys spending his free time with his wife, Susan, and their two young children. Occasionally, he sneaks off for a round or two of golf. He's quick to point out that he works very hard at his job and at being a good husband and father. "I'm just a normal guy who works hard at his job," he insists. Today, he enjoys the fruits of his labor and his success as one of San Diego's most popular media celebrities.

Junior Seau

Pro Bowl Linebacker

Junior Seau is one of the most talented and dominating players in the NFL, and he happens to be a homegrown talent playing for the local team. In his first three seasons with the Chargers, Seau has been selected to the AFC Pro Bowl team every year. He's earned the respect of his peers, his coaches and, especially, Charger fans. "I'm a performer, and I perform for the people who come to watch the game," he says. "I approach the field as a stage, so if I'm doing my job, you should have a good time. If not, then I did something wrong, and I feel like I cheated the people who came to watch." He certainly hasn't cheated local fans who come to see him do his thing at San Diego's Jack Murphy Stadium.

Seau's road to success hasn't been easy, and he worked hard for what he's accomplished. "If you're going to sit down and cry, you're never going to get anywhere in life," he says earnestly. "You can be the greatest athlete, but it doesn't necessarily mean you're going to make it. It takes being able to get off your butt when you're down and not taking no for an answer." He's also a firm believer in setting goals. "Goals are always a priority for anyone to succeed, because they help you focus on what you want," Seau says. His goal was to dominate in the NFL, and he has done just that.

Just twenty-three, Junior Seau remembers clearly what it was like sharing a two-bedroom home with his parents and five brothers and sisters in Oceanside. "We didn't have the luxuries that a lot of people did, but it's warming to see that we made it after what we had gone through," he says. "I see growing up in Oceanside as being a positive aspect in my life. Oceanside was a tough town even then, but I think my mom and dad really sheltered us away from the drugs and violence." Born January 19, 1969 in American Samoa, Seau has immense respect for his father, who is a deacon in their church and gave his son a focus in life. "My dad was a role model," Seau explains, "raising six kids and not knowing the English language or the English ways. You've got to respect someone like that."

Seau grew up constantly competing with his older brothers. "I wanted to be better than my brothers," he admits. "I didn't want to settle for second, and my biggest fear was failure. For me to fail is a hard thing to take, but it's a learning experience. So I'll take it, and then I make sure it never happens again."

In high school, Seau's focus was on getting a scholarship so he could further his education, and he saw football as a way to accomplish that goal. "I knew we didn't have the funds to pay for an education, so I had to take advantage of what I did have — and that was talent," he says. "And luckily I had that." He chose to continue his career and education at University of Southern California after becoming one of the best football players ever to take the field at Oceanside High School, where they recently retired his number. He put all of his energy into becoming the best football player he could be, while taking full advantage of the opportunity to learn. Early in his college career, Seau's grade point average was many points below his time in the forty-yard dash (4.61). He went on to become an honor student, but there was never any doubt about his athletic ability. He was rated one of the best linebackers in the nation, the fifth player taken in the first round of the 1990 draft. The Chargers were lucky to get the six-foot-three-inch, 250-pound linebacker.

Seau immediately established himself as an impact player at inside linebacker and was selected a second alternate to the Pro Bowl. Despite missing much of his first training camp negotiating a contract, he finished second on the team with eighty-five tackles. While waiting for the chance to show the hometown folks his style of football, Seau kept himself in shape by working out at Gold's Gym in Pacific Beach (he bench-presses 440 pounds) and bodysurfing. Growing up, it was exercise he took to naturally – the ocean was always there and bodysurfing was free. After signing with the Chargers, he's got the money to play expensive sports like golf and tennis, but he sees his good fortune more as a way to show his parents a better way of life.

In 1991, only his second year in the NFL, Seau was voted a starter to the AFC Pro Bowl squad after leading the Chargers with 129 tackles (111 solo). He became an effective pass rusher, recording seven sacks. In 1992, the Chargers moved Seau to outside linebacker, turning him loose on opposing quarterbacks and taking full advantage of his drive and versatility. Known as the team cheerleader, he frequently turns to the crowd, hands up, calling for the support the team deserves. The fans love #55, and respond with a roar to fill the heart of their hometown hero.

Irvine "Cotton" Warburton
Football Player/Oscar-Winning Editor

Irvine "Cotton" Warburton is a perfect example that might, not height, is the true measure of a man. At just over five-feet-six-inches tall and weighing in at 148 pounds, he was one of the smallest, yet most effective men ever named an All American football player. Nicknamed "Cotton" because of his curly white hair, the speedy quarterback led

USC to twenty victories in two years (1932-1933), including a thirty-five-to-nothing rout over the Pittsburgh Panthers in the 1933 Rose Bowl, when he scored two touchdowns.

A brilliant all-around athlete at San Diego High School, Warburton starred in basketball, baseball and track as well as football. In 1931 he was the California State High School Quarter-Mile champion in track with a run of :49.1. As a shortstop for San Diego High, he could hit, field and run the bases with the best. As a football player, he was an undersized but elusive runner who knew how to use his blockers, which made him a tough competitor. In a sport filled with big men, Warburton's talent and determination to excel helped him overcome the handicap of size. The rugged quarterback led USC's Trojan football team from 1932 through 1934 in Howard Jones' single-wing attack.

After his football career ended, Warburton went on to become an Oscar-winning film editor at Walt Disney Studios. His Oscar came in 1964 for editing the classic and much-loved film, *Mary Poppins*. He died in 1981 at the age of 70.

Ed White
Future Hall of Fame Lineman/Sculptor

In his seventeen years in the National Football League, Ed White established himself as one of the best offensive linemen in the game. He rarely missed a game, absent only six times in his entire career, playing an amazing 241 games before retiring in 1986. White played in four Pro Bowls and was an alternate in three others. He also had the good fortune to play for winning teams, appearing in twenty-four playoff games with the Vikings and Chargers. Only three other players can claim they played in more.

Ever since he was a kid growing up in La Mesa, White knew exactly what he wanted to do. "I've always had a great desire to play in the NFL," he admits. His dream not only became a reality, but he's now a candidate for the exclusive NFL Hall of Fame.

Off the field, White has had success as well. He put his degree in Landscape Architecture to work and, with a partner, built a business in North County. It grew so big — with over eighty employees — it began to interfere with his football career. That's when he sold his interest in the company. Football came first.

"Big Ed" was the league's arm-wrestling champion and a promoter of that sport, also. After his playing career ended, he became a member of the Chargers coaching staff, spending his free time developing into an accomplished sculptor. He provided the trophies for John Madden's "All Madden Team." He's proudest of his achievements as a professional football player, but admits he paid a price for success. During his playing days, he spent a great deal of time away from his wife of twenty-four years and his three children. After seventeen NFL seasons, he owns up to being a little more beat up than your average forty-five-year-old. "I did what I had to do to earn a living and provide for my family," White says. "Football was the area I chose to work in. I was driven in that sport to be successful, and I gave it my best shot. Achieving it has been really satisfying. I'd do it again."

Both White and his father are native San Diegans. His grandmother was born in the Fallbrook area. His Southern California roots go back even further – his great-aunt and uncle were among the earliest settlers of Murietta Hot Springs. Born June 4, 1947, White fondly recalls his early days growing up in San Diego. "It was all country back then. In La Mesa, where I grew up, it was all hills with a few scattered houses. Where I spent a good many years at the stadium in the valley, there was nothing but an old farm. Going up to the fair seemed like it took an entire day." His younger brother knew every player in major and minor league baseball, but White was more concerned with what it took to be a professional athlete, both physically and mentally. "I can remember the hours I spent visualizing myself carrying a football, running through people to where I had a very clear image of what I was doing," he says. "In my high school album, I put I was going to be a pro football player. I spent all of my focus and concentration doing that."

In college, his hard work started to pay off. He was a Consensus All American guard at the University of California before the Minnesota Vikings drafted him in the second round (thirty-ninth overall) in 1969. After years of successfully protecting Fran Tarkenton in Minnesota, he came to San Diego in a trade in 1978. With the Chargers, he provided protection for another great quarterback, Dan Fouts. He and Fouts have remained best friends since their glory days as part of Air Coryell and the winning Chargers of the early eighties. "In the end, that's all it is," he says, "the friendships that you've made."

After retiring from football as a player and a coach, White tried to take it a little easier. "I don't feel like I'm driven like I was driven to be successful in sports," he says. He now lives in Julian and enjoys the relaxed pace of country living. "I've always felt I needed to be in the country. I consider myself a country person," White admits. As Julian's resident celebrity, he donates much of his spare time helping the community he's grown so fond of. "I've spent most of my free time in Julian trying to help the high school," he says. "Education is a high priority to me, and I'm going to direct a lot of what I'm doing to help the school financially." He's planned a celebrity golf tournament to raise funds to help with the school's budgetary problems.

White's oldest son is twenty-two and wants to coach football. He'll be working with San Diego State University's football program this year. White's other son, Randy, recently graduated from the Culinary Institute of America and is heading to Europe to become a chef. "My daughter, Amy [still in high school], is probably the best athlete," he says proudly.

So the next time you're in Julian and see a six-foot-two-and-a-half-inch, 270-pound man walking your way, give him a friendly country smile and say hello to "Big Ed" White, future Hall of Famer.

Briefs

Eric Allen

As a senior at Point Loma High School, Eric Allen rushed for over 900 yards and caught 26 passes. Yet it was his skill as a defensive back that led the Philadelphia Eagles to draft him in the second round out of Arizona State University. With the Eagles, the two-time Pro Bowl cornerback has established himself as one of the game's best defensive backs. When he was growing up in Southeast San Diego, he used to watch and admire another Allen playing local football. Now the two go face-to-face in the NFL.

Lance Alworth

Alworth became the first player from the old American Football League to be inducted into the Pro Football Hall of Fame. Nicknamed "Bambi," Alworth was one of the most fluid and graceful wide receivers of all time. The Chargers retired his number (#19) after he starred for the AFL team from 1962 through 1970. He finished his illustrious career with over 500 receptions, 84 touchdowns and 10,000 receiving yards.

Willie Buchanon

This native of Oceanside was a two-sport star at Oceanside High School — football and track. In 1969, he added baseball to his list of credentials at MiraCosta College and became a second-round draft pick by the San Diego Padres the same year. At San Diego State University, Buchanon became an All-American defensive back, voted MVP in the 1971 East-West Shrine game after intercepting three passes. A number one pick of the Green Bay Packers, he was the NFL Defensive Rookie of the Year. The Pro Bowl cornerback also played for the Chargers.

John Butler

This San Diego native and football star at St. Augustine High School earned All-Conference honors three seasons in a row in the 1930's.

Despite his lack of stature, he had continued success as guard and linebacker at San Diego State University. During World War II, Butler was a Naval aviator. Following the war, he became a practicing attorney, then Deputy District Attorney and finally Mayor of San Diego from 1951 through 1955.

Shawn Collins

The Atlanta Falcons used their two number one draft picks wisely in 1989. They chose Deion Sanders and then took a large wide receiver named Shawn Collins out of Northern Arizona University. The San Diego native caught fifty-eight passes for 862 yards his rookie season, becoming a Consensus All-Rookie selection in 1989. He remains an effective receiver in the NFL.

Don Coryell

Coryell is the first coach ever to win 100 games at both the college and pro level. As the San Diego State University Aztecs' head coach from 1961 to 1972, he amassed 104 wins against a mere nineteen losses. Known for his wide-open offense, he guided the St. Louis Cardinals to three divisional championships. He also led the Chargers' explosive Air Coryell teams of the late 1970's and early 1980's to three divisional championships. He was named NFC Coach of the Year in 1974 and NFL Coach of the Year in 1979.

Keith DeLong

This San Diego native was the San Francisco Forty-Niners' number one draft pick in 1989. The rugged linebacker is used primarily to defend the run. His father, Steve DeLong, was a defensive lineman for the Chargers and Bears in the late 1960's and early 1970's.

Tom Dempsey

Born with a malformed hand and foot, Dempsey's outstanding NFL career proved that physical obstacles do not limit a person with talent, determination and a desire for excellence. Growing up, he participated in a number of sports. At San Dieguito High School, he played defensive end and was a shot putter for the track squad. He excelled as a six-foot-one-inch, 250-pound defensive lineman at Palomar Junior College.

In 1967, he played semi-pro football before joining the San Diego Chargers as a place kicker in 1968. He signed as a free agent with the Saints the following year and was selected to the Pro Bowl as one of the NFL's premier kickers. On November 8, 1970, Dempsey kicked a record sixty-three-yard field goal against the Detroit Lions. He finished his outstanding career with 718 points, making 158 of 252 field goal attempts for a .622 average.

Dan Fouts

Dan Fouts is considered the finest quarterback in the history of the Chargers and one of the all-time greats in the NFL. From 1973 through 1987 he led one of the most potent passing attacks in NFL history. He was tough, competitive, accurate – and above all, he was a winner. The six-time Pro Bowl quarterback finished his career with over 43,000 passing yards, second only to Fran Tarkenton. Fouts completed 3,297 of 5,604 passes, including 254 touchdown tosses. In 1979, he was NFL Player of the Year although, statistically, it was not his best year. In 1981, he completed 360 of 609 passes for 4,802 yards and thirty-three touchdown passes with only seventeen interceptions. He guided the Chargers to three division championships and two AFC Championship games. In 1992 he was inducted into the Pro Football Hall of Fame and the Chargers Hall of Fame.

Gary Garrison

The speedy wide receiver was voted the SDSU Aztecs MVP in 1964, when he caught seventy-eight passes for 1,272 yards and fifteen touchdowns. He was a number one draft pick by the Chargers and caught over forty passes a year in his first seven years in the pros, twice for over 1,000 yards. In 1970, he was voted Chargers MVP. He went to the Pro Bowl in 1971, 1972 and 1973 before retiring in 1977.

Sid Gillman

Elected to the Pro Football Hall of Fame for his accomplishments as a coach, Sid Gillman was an offensive genius. He coached for twenty years in the college ranks with tremendous success, later becoming an AFL and NFL coach. During his winning years with the Chargers, he won five divisional titles and an AFL championship in 1963.

Ed Goddard

Goddard lettered in four sports at Escondido High. An All-American quarterback at Washington State during the mid-1930's, he also played defense and served as the team's punter.

Charlie Joiner

Voted the Chargers' most inspirational player seven years in a row, Joiner was inducted into the Chargers Hall of Fame in 1992. He was usually the first to arrive at practice and the last to leave. It was this work ethic, along with his ability to focus and concentrate on catching the ball after running precise patterns, that made him one of the NFL's all-time best wide receivers. The durable Joiner played in 239 games, catching an amazing 750 passes for 12,146 yards.

Bill McColl

At Hoover High School during the mid-1940's, McColl proved that he could block, run, tackle and catch passes. He went on to become an All-American end at Stanford, occasionally playing defensive tackle as well. He starred for the Chicago Bears from 1952 to 1959 while attending the University of Chicago. He later became known as Bill McColl, MD. His sons Milt and Duncan also played in the NFL.

Mark Malone

An El Cajon native, Malone was one of the nation's top-rated quarterbacks while a senior at El Cajon Valley High School in the late 1970's. An outstanding athlete, he also played basketball and excelled in track and field. A number one draft choice out of Arizona State by the Pittsburgh Steelers, he was a starter at quarterback, leading the team to an AFC championship in 1984. He also played for the Chargers.

Harold "Brick" Muller

The West Coast's first All-American, Muller was named to *Sports Illustrated's* all-time college football team in 1969. At San Diego High School, the big, rugged superstar was a local football hero. He played end on Cal's Wonder Teams of the 1920's and went on to play professionally for a brief time. He earned a medical degree and became an orthopedic surgeon.

Art Powell

An All Star wide receiver for a number of pro teams, Powell amassed 478 receptions and eighty-one touchdowns in eight AFL seasons. With the New York Titans in 1960, he caught sixty-nine passes and led the league with fourteen touchdown catches. In 1963, undcı first-year coach Al Davis, the Oakland Raiders won nine more games than the year before, thanks in part to Powell's 1,304 yards receiving and sixteen touchdowns. The San Diego native attended San Diego High School, starring in both football and basketball. As a senior, he was named the City Player of the Year. At San Diego City College, Powell was again a two-sport star. At San Jose State, he led the nation with forty receptions in 1956.

Bert Ritchey

A former San Diego police officer, this star athlete graduated from Cal Western Law School and began a practice in Southeast San Diego. A San Diego native, Ritchey starred in both football and track at San Diego High School and later for the USC Trojans.

Dan Saleaumua

The six-foot, 295-pound Kansas City Chiefs nose tackle was born in San Diego on November 25, 1964. After beginning his career with the Detroit Lions, Saleaumua joined the Kansas City Chiefs. He led the Chiefs' linemen in tackles in past seasons, registering thirteen fumble recoveries in three years.

Brian Sipe

During his fourteen-year professional career, twelve with the Cleveland Browns and two in the USFL, Sipe was regarded as one of the best quarterbacks of his day (1972-1985). A graduate of Grossmont High School, he attended San Diego State University, where he set numerous passing records. Sipe played on the El Cajon-La Mesa Little League team that won the world title in 1961.

Webster Slaughter

This former San Diego State University star is considered one of the NFL's top receivers. In 1991, he led the Browns with sixty-four catches for 906 yards and three touchdowns. The veteran wide receiver signed with the Houston Oilers in 1992.

Tommy Vardell

"Touchdown Tommy" of El Cajon was a nine-letter athlete and an honor student at Granite Hills High School. At six-foot-one and 238 pounds, he rushed for 1,084 yards and scored twenty touchdowns in his senior year at Stanford in 1991. He was selected to the All-Pac 10 Conference first team after setting six Stanford records. Vardell is now a fullback with the Cleveland Browns after being selected in the first round of the 1992 draft.

Chapter 7: Other Sports

Florence Chadwick

Maureen "Little Mo" Connolly

Kevin Crow

Brad Gerlach

Greg Louganis

Scott Simpson

Ivan "Ironman" Stewart

Scott Tinley

Jesse Valdez

Bill Walton

Briefs

Mark Allen · Willie Banks · Jud Buechler
Malin Burnham · Billy Casper · Florence Chambers
Michael Chang · Chris Chelios · Tiffany Chin
Dennis Conner · Gail Devers · Gerry Driscoll
Chris Dudley · Phil Edwards · Charles Fletcher
Dave Freeman · Broc Glover · Karen Hantze Susman
Tony Hawk · "Bud" Held · Jeff Jacobs · Rick Johnson
Tommy Johnson · Cliff Levingston · Gene Littler
Phil Mickelson · Bill Miller · Billy Mills · Archie Moore
Bill Muncey · Jean "Cheesy" Neil · Terry Norris
Lowell North · Margo Oberg · Larry Penacho
Milton "Milky" Phelps · Clarence Pinkston · Lee Ramage
Mark Reynolds · Arnie Robinson · Paul Runyan
Craig Stadler · Mike Stamm · Willie Steele
Mary "Mickey" Wright

Florence Chadwick
Record-Setting Channel Swimmer/Stockbroker

Florence Chadwick has always pushed herself to do better. No matter what she does — swimming the English Channel in record time or creating money-making portfolios for her clients as a top-producing stockbroker — she doesn't go halfway. Long-distance swimming taught her that discipline and hard work do pay off. On her first attempt at swimming the English Channel, she broke the record set by Gertrude Ederle. One of the most consistent and famous Channel swimmers in the world, Chadwick was also the first woman to complete the more difficult England-to-France trip. Of her four successful crossings, she started in England three times. She's the holder of sixteen world records in long-distance swimming and won over 100 trophies for swimming. In her early forties, she studied to become a stockbroker, and became a champion in that field also. Thirty years later, Chadwick is still making money for her clients in San Diego.

Chadwick was born in San Diego in 1918. Her father was a policeman and her mother owned and operated two restaurants bearing the family name. At Loma Portal Elementary School, Chadwick swam in her first race at the Mission Beach Plunge. She boasted to her family that she'd easily win the event, but she came in last. Chadwick learned a valuable lesson that day: Don't talk about it — just go out and do it. At ten, she won the San Diego Bay Channel Swim. At eleven, she won her first cup — a two-and-a-half-mile night swim in Hermosa Beach. She finished fourth among the seniors and first junior swimmer.

Growing up, Chadwick swam her heart out and trained just as hard. Her father built a gym in their home, and Chadwick worked to develop her shoulders so she could swim stronger and better. She was constantly training, constantly improving. Swimming was her passion, and she sacrificed plenty for her sport before graduating from Point Loma High School in 1936. She didn't attend the prom, Ditch Day or the baccalaureate sermon because of her training schedule. But it paid off. She became the champion of San Diego County, the Pacific Coast and finally the Far West. She won the La Jolla Rough Water Swim seven times.

After working in her mother's restaurants as hostess, manager and bookkeeper (all at the same time), Chadwick went to Hollywood to appear in *Bathing Beauty* opposite swimming great Esther Williams in 1945. Then she made a bold move and took a job with the Arabian American Oil Company in Saudi Arabia. While there, she rigorously trained in the shark-infested waters of the Persian Gulf, preparing for an attempt on the English Channel. She saved $5,000 to finance it, and her father cashed in his savings and flew east to join her. Awaiting his arrival in Wissant, Chadwick heard that the *London Daily Mail* was sponsoring a Channel swim. She sent in an application, only to be rejected. They wrote to say she didn't have a chance and shouldn't be wasting her time. It was a shattering letter but, when she thought about it, she got angry. The angrier she got, the more determined she became. On August 8, 1950, two days before the *Daily Mail's* contest, she entered the chilly water at 2:30 a.m. and emerged in Dover thirteen hours and twenty minutes later with a new world record.

When Chadwick returned to San Diego's Lindbergh Field, she was surprised to be whisked off by seaplane to a ticker tape parade in her honor up Broadway, where she was given a brand-new Chevrolet. With barely a dime left of her savings, she wondered how she'd pay for gas. A year later, she was back in Europe, this time to make the first of three England-to-France trips, breaking more records along the way. She moved to New York, where she taught swimming at her two swimming schools when not touring the United States making radio and television appearances. She got up at 4:00 a.m. to get in four to seven hours of training in preparation for upcoming challenges.

Chadwick swam the difficult Catalina Channel in 1952 and made her last long-distance swim in 1969 at the age of forty-two. In that final swim, she attempted to become the first woman to cross the twenty-two mile North Channel of the Irish Sea. The fifty-two degree water proved too much for her; she became incoherent from hypothermia toward the end of the swim and had to be pulled into the boat. Always a fighter, she refused to quit. The crew was trying to save her life, but she didn't want to give up, no matter what the cost.

After keeping an apartment in New York for eighteen years,

Chadwick returned to San Diego to care for her ailing mother. She opened a swimming school in Mission Valley, but quickly tired of spending fourteen hours a day in the pool. She was ready for a new challenge. Driven to achieve, she longed for the sense of accomplishment she felt after a long-distance swim. She found that challenge and that satisfaction in stockbrokering, a field few women had entered in the early 1970's. In typical fashion, she used discipline, hard work and passion to become a success. Now in her mid-seventies, Chadwick is known to work eleven to fourteen hours a day, six days a week in the La Jolla office of First Wall Street Corp., and shows little signs of slowing down.

Maureen "Little Mo" Connolly
Tennis Legend (1934-1969)

Although her playing career ended abruptly at age twenty-one, Maureen Connolly was considered by many experts to be the best women's tennis player in the world. Stocky and intense, she played a powerful game even as a youngster. She was only twelve when *San Diego Union* sportswriter Nelson Fisher dubbed her "Little Mo" after the battleship *Missouri* (or "Big Mo"), likening her rapid-fire style to the big guns of war. Her meteoric rise to success began before her sixteenth birthday, when she became the youngest winner of the U.S. Open at Forest Hills. She went on to win a total of three U.S. Open titles. In 1953 she became the first woman to win a Grand Slam — taking all four of tennis's major championships in a single year. She won the women's Wimbledon crown for three consecutive years, 1952-1954, and was ranked the world's best. Named female athlete of the year three times by the Associated Press, Connolly was everybody's favorite before she was twenty. Overall, she won twelve major international tournaments while still in her teens. Her success focused national attention on San Diego, making it a tennis mecca and Little Mo a hometown hero.

Connolly's career was cut short on July 20, 1954, when she was struck by a cement truck while riding her horse, Colonel Merryboy, down Friars Road. Her right leg was severely injured and, despite extensive rehabilitation, she was never able to regain the form that won her so many titles. She retired seven months later on February 22, 1955. Ironically, the golden palomino Tennessee Walker she was riding that fateful day was a gift from San Diego well-wishers after her triumphant tour of Europe in 1952.

Born September 17, 1934 in San Diego, Connolly grew up on Idaho Street, just around the corner from the University Heights playground (now the North Park Recreation Center). At age nine, she watched two of San Diego's best play tennis there, and decided she wanted to learn. She asked tennis legend Wilbur Folsom, who ran a local tennis shop and gave lessons, if he'd teach her how to play. In exchange for the lessons, young Connolly shagged balls for Folsom. He taught her the fundamentals of the game and helped prepare her for her first competition, which she lost in the final match. Showing a real aptitude for the game, she won the San Diego Junior Tennis Championship soon afterward and was awarded a complimentary membership in the Balboa Tennis Club, where she practiced with the boys. At twelve, she began taking lessons from coach Eleanor Tennant and started on her incredible winning streak. Harry Hopman took her to her highest level of play, however. Tennant taught her to truly hate her opponents; Hopman believed in concentration and conditioning. In addition to endless hours on the court, she ran and jumped rope, went to bed early and watched what she ate. She was so focused on her game, it was said not even an earthquake could break her concentration during a match.

Off the court, Connolly was full of smiles, friendly to just about everyone. She enjoyed going to the movies, dancing and having a good time. She met Norman Brinker, then a world-class polo player and equestrian, at a Mission Valley stable where they both kept their horses. They were married on June 11, 1955. She worked part-time as a sports columnist for the *San Diego Union,* contributing to various magazines and serving as a television commentator. She also taught tennis at the Town and Country Club and the Balboa Tennis Club, where she had more students than she could handle. She and her husband, an extremely successful businessman and multimillionaire, moved from San Diego to Texas some years after their marriage. Connolly died of stomach cancer in 1969 when she was only in her mid-thirties. She died with strength, dignity and happiness, knowing she'd lived a full life. Her extraordinary story was told in the 1978 television movie, *Little Mo.*

Kevin Crow
Soccer Star

A graduate of San Diego State University in 1983, Kevin Crow has done it all in the sport of soccer – indoors and out. In four years with the SDSU soccer team, he helped put the building blocks in place for a soccer program that still enjoys national prestige. He earned All-American honors twice, and his professional career was about to bring him success and honors that few individuals receive in their sports.

In 1983, as a rookie with the Sockers playing outdoors in the prestigious North American Soccer League, Crow was named runner-up in the Rookie of the Year balloting. The following year, he became the only player in the Sockers' outdoor history to earn All-NASL first team honors. The summer of 1984 saw Crow wearing the red, white and blue of the United States National Soccer Team in the Los Angeles Summer Olympics. He represented the U.S. one more time in the Seoul Olympics in 1988. In 1984-85, it all came together for Kevin Crow as a star indoor soccer athlete. With an indoor championship already under his belt, he earned his first of eight consecutive MISL All Star selections in just nine years of play. He's the only player to win the MISL's Defender of the Year award more than twice (he won it five times), and he received six All-MISL first team selections. Needless to say, these are all league record marks.

Off the field, Crow has been honored for his work with San Diegans. In 1987, he received the inaugural Met Life Community Service Award and in 1989 he was inducted into SDSU's Hall of Fame. A favorite among Sockers fans, he missed only two games in his career. "I always kept in shape during the off-season," he says, "mostly because I just couldn't stand to have to get fit again during the preseason training camp."

In all, Crow has won eight championships in nine years of play. "We always felt we had the capability to win any game when we stepped on the field," he says, "but we still had to play hard. I think people took for granted how hard the team really worked. We weren't always the most talented team in the league. A lot of our success was a result of our work ethic and commitment to winning." Crow has carried that winning aura into the private sector, where he made the difficult transition into the business world. He made the most of his degree in Finance from SDSU, joining former Sockers owner Ron Fowler as a sales and financial analyst for Mesa Distributing Co., Inc.

Crow was born September 17, 1961, with a true sports pedigree. His father played for the NFL Oakland Raiders (1959-1961) and the Buffalo Bills (1961-1963) as a running back and punter. After trying a number of sports, Crow decided to make soccer his main focus when he was fourteen. "I was able to make the soccer team in high school and then in college," he remembers. "It wasn't until the summer between my sophomore and junior years at SDSU that I decided to make an all-out effort to get to the pros. For three years, that was my goal, and I was lucky enough to get drafted by the Sockers. I went on to reach all the goals I wanted to reach. The greatest success of my soccer career was representing the United States in the Olympics twice. Essentially, success means setting goals and achieving your goals. You have to set realistic goals, but you also have to set goals that are going to stretch you."

Crow and his family – Brenda, his wife of seven years and four-year-old Kendalle – are proud to call San Diego home. "I think San Diego has a lot to offer," Crow says. "I've been fortunate to have done a lot of traveling, and I think, as large cities go, it's by far the best. It's true... this is America's finest city."

Brad Gerlach
Professional Surfer

In 1991, Brad Gerlach finished runner-up to world champion Damien Hardman on the Association of Surfing Professionals (ASP) World Tour. A consistent top-sixteen ASP performer, he moved up twelve places from the previous year, earning over $200,000 in the process (including $127,400 in endorsements). In 1992, Gerlach finished sixth in the *Surfer Magazine* annual reader's poll.

At twenty-six, "The Gerr" was ready to start a new phase in his surfing career, taking time away from competitive surfing in 1992 to explore a more creative approach, experimenting with different boards, trying new maneuvers and traveling to places that had never been surfed before. "I just want to take the same focus and drive towards creativity, experimentation and adventure," he says. "I think by doing that I'll be able to make more of a contribution to surfing than if I won contests. I want to show people that you don't always have to go down a beaten path, but that you can go your own way. I hope this will open up alternate routes for surfers to make a viable living in surfing." He says his sponsors, Life's a Beach, Oakley and Xanadu Surfboards are a hundred percent behind his new approach. He's going to spend his winters in Hawaii, competing at selected events. But he won't really have a shot at being the second Californian to win the world title.

Born in Miami in 1966, Gerlach has called Encinitas home for most of his life. His parents split up when he was seven, and he lived with his mother until he was fifteen. "I had a really happy childhood. We weren't really well off — we had food in the house, and that's about it," he remembers.

Gerlach's father, Joe (better known as "Jumpin' Joe Gerlach), defected from the 1956 Hungarian Olympic diving team and made his living jumping out of hot air balloons and off tall buildings as a high-diving showman. His mother was a professional water skier. Gerlach's parents gave him the freedom to make his own decisions, and generally he made the right choices. "I was the kind of kid that there was no way you were going to tell me not to do something, and you couldn't guard me twenty-four hours a day. Nor would you want to!" he grins.

He learned to surf at the age of ten, when he found a surfboard that had been thrown off the cliff in Leucadia. After surfing for three months, he almost gave it up completely when his board hit him in the head. He had to undergo plastic surgery to hide the scars made by the 150 stitches needed to close the wound. But he kept learning about surfing, up and down the North County coast at places like Beacons, Stone Steps, Swami's, Pipes and Cardiff Reef before he moved to Huntington Beach for his senior year of high school. At sixteen, he almost gave up surfing again, but his dad intervened and became his coach — a major turning point in Gerlach's career. "I came home when

I was sixteen-and-a-half and said to my dad, 'I'm not going to make it. I'm just not going to do it.' And he said, 'All right, I'll come down there and have a look at what you're doing.' It started right there." After his father coached him for a week, Gerlach took second place in a pro-am contest. His dad has been a major part of his career ever since.

Gerlach has a powerful style of surfing, with an amazing ability to pull off maneuvers in critical parts of the wave. The first time he made the ASP top sixteen, he was constantly pitted against Tom Curren, who was on his way to a second world championship. "I decided to take a look at my surfing and change it – not change my style, but change my technique," Gerlach says. "It took three years, and during that time I was barely scraping into the top sixteen, which was extremely frustrating for me." After he figured it all out, he was still unable to get past tenth place. Then in 1991 he began to use visualization. "I just totally visualized myself getting past that thing [tenth place]," he remembers. "I had set a goal and I wanted to be in the top three." He finished second that year and, much like with an earlier goal he made in high school to make the top sixteen, he went beyond the limits of what he thought was possible.

Since becoming a pro surfer, Gerlach is always challenging the dangerous waves of the North Shore of Hawaii. "The main reason I spend my winters in Hawaii is because I'm constantly dealing with big waves. I don't want to just ride these waves. I want to attack them. One of the reasons the Hawaiians are so good in big waves is that they're constantly dealing with fear. The only way to overcome fear is to keep pitting yourself against it all the time until you get used to dealing with fear," he emphasizes. "The only way to not get hurt surfing in Hawaii is to not hesitate, and just go for it." Despite his changing aspirations and his yen to explore the many sides of surfing, Gerlach's "go for it" style – of surfing and living – isn't likely to change.

Greg Louganis
Olympic Gold Medalist/Diving Champion

San Diego native Greg Louganis is possibly the greatest Olympic diver who ever lived. During his remarkable career, he won forty-seven national titles, five world titles and five Olympic medals. He retired after competing in his third Olympics, the 1988 Summer Games in Seoul, Korea, going out in dramatic fashion. After hitting his head on the springboard in the first round of the competition, he had the courage to go on, winning two gold medals. In 1984, Louganis received the Sullivan Award as the nation's most outstanding amateur athlete. He was also inducted into the Olympic Hall of Fame. Yet, on his way to greatness, he had to overcome quite a few hurdles, both as an athlete and an individual.

Born January 29, 1960, Louganis was adopted at nine months by Frances and Peter Louganis. By the time he was eight, he was an exceptional gymnast. About then, his father signed him up for diving lessons, after watching him perform acrobatic leaps into the family pool. Unfortunately, his school days were unhappy. He was subjected to racial slurs because of his dark Samoan skin, and he suffered further harassment because of a stutter and a reading disorder known as dyslexia. Called a "dummy" by his classmates, Louganis withdrew and became shy, a loner. By the time he was eleven, he was a proficient diver, attracting the attention of coaches all around the country. At fifteen, he began training under the guidance of Dr. Sammy Lee, a gold medalist in both the 1948 and 1952 Olympics. After a year with Dr. Lee, Louganis qualified for the 1976 Summer Olympics in Montreal, where he took home the silver medal in platform diving. In 1980, the United States and other free countries boycotted the games, so he had no choice but to set his sights on the 1984 Games in Los Angeles. It was there that he won gold in both the springboard and platform events. On his final dive, he scored a perfect 10.0 to win the gold medal by sixty-seven points, setting a new world record for points scored.

After that, many speculated that Louganis would retire from competition to pursue other interests, including acting. Instead, he prepared for the 1988 Olympics. At twenty-eight, he was considered ancient by diving standards, competing against divers only half his age. The odds were already stacked against him, but then he developed a fever and sore throat and injured his wrist. During one of the dives in his springboard competition, he miscalculated and hit his head on the board, giving him a three-inch gash in his forehead. Undaunted, Louganis returned to finish the competition, capturing the gold medal and the hearts of all those watching. For his courage, he was honored with the Olympic Spirit Award.

Louganis not only overcame his injuries, he also conquered bouts of alcohol abuse and smoking on his way to becoming a sports legend. With the physique of a Greek god (five-feet-nine, 150 pounds and only seven percent bodyfat), it's hard to believe he ever did anything to abuse his body, but he did. Now he uses his influence and experience to educate kids about the positive alternatives to alcohol when dealing with their problems.

A graduate of the University of California at Irvine with a degree in theater and dance, Louganis has worked as a model, actor and dancer since retiring from competitive diving.

Scott Simpson
Pro Golfer/Winner of the 1987 U.S. Open

"My goal was to be as good as I could be and to become one of the best," Simpson says. When he beat Tom Watson to win the U.S. Open in 1987, the San Diego native reached his goal to be included among the finest golfers on the PGA Tour. That win stands as his greatest accomplishment in a career that began over two decades ago, when young Scott Simpson learned to play golf at the Stardust Golf Club in Mission Valley.

His father, Joe Simpson, was an accomplished amateur golfer. He split a set of golf clubs between Scott and his younger brother David when the two were just kids, to see if they'd stick with the sport long enough to make buying them their own set of clubs worthwhile. Golf was practically all Scott Simpson thought about while growing up. "I played a lot of golf," he admits. "I never really did much else. From the start I just loved the sport, and I played every chance I got because I wanted to get good at it."

Eventually equipped with his own set of clubs, he began competing in and winning junior tournaments in San Diego. "I played Tecolote [a golf course in the Clairemont area] a couple of times, but mainly I played at the Stardust [in Mission Valley] because we had a family membership there," Simpson remembers. As a member of the San

Diego Junior Golf Association, he won the California State Juniors at age fifteen.

Simpson continued his rise in amateur golf while attending USC, winning two consecutive NCAA golf titles (1976 and 1977). He set his sights on turning pro, but getting a proper education came first. "School was always pretty important, and I always did well in school," he says. "I realized there was a good chance I wouldn't be playing professional golf. There were a lot of good juniors and a lot of good college players and very few made it to the pros." Some of golf's all-time greatest players have come from San Diego, however, and that fact stood in his favor. Native San Diegan Gene Littler was one of Simpson's heroes, while his good friend and USC alum Craig Stadler also went on to become a successful pro.

Simpson experienced his first PGA win at the Western Open in 1980. A steady professional player in 1985, he felt he needed to add distance to his tee shots in order to win more. He began experimenting with his swing, but had less than positive results. He added length off the tee, but couldn't hit the ball straight. He dropped in the standings and eventually dropped out of the tour for eleven weeks late in 1986. He returned in 1987, realizing that if he wanted to win, he'd better go with his strengths and return to "his" game. It worked. 1987 was a dream year for Simpson. He won the U.S. Open, and his winnings for the year topped $600,000. Only three other PGA players won more money that year, and only two won more PGA events. When he beat Tom Watson by a shot in the Open, Simpson – with birdies on three of the last five holes – became a star.

But that win brought with it high expectations for 1988. "Every golfer has a tough time, because golf is a frustrating game," explains Simpson. "But my toughest time was in 1988. 1987 was my best year ever, and then I followed it up with my worst year ever." At the 1988 and 1989 U.S. Opens, he tied for sixth, tied for fourteenth in 1990 and then bounced back with a second place finish in 1991. Still, to Simpson, success isn't necessarily tournament wins. Being happy, enjoying life and spending time with his wife and two kids are what's really important to him.

Simpson and his wife, Cheryl, whom he met while the two attended Madison High School in Clairemont, now call the Big Island of

Hawaii home. "I love San Diego, and I have many fond memories of growing up and living there," Simpson says. "Hawaii is the only place I'd ever move to from San Diego." His parents, both teachers, still live in San Diego and, when Simpson is in town, he and his father usually play a few rounds together. "I love to play golf. I enjoy the social aspect of being out and playing with friends, and I have a great time playing with my dad down at the Stardust," he says. Especially since his dad gave in and got him that full set of clubs.

Ivan "Ironman" Stewart
Off-Road Racing Legend

Ivan "Ironman" Stewart began competing in off-road racing in 1971, when the sport was still in its infancy. Twenty-one years later, Stewart has won over sixty-five trophies and has been instrumental in taking off-road racing out of the backyard and into the realm of professional sport. "To be a leader and able to help set the standards for off-road racing and to watch it grow so more and more people can make a living at it is real special to me," Stewart says. Since clinching his first race in 1973, Stewart has been an unstoppable force in the desert, winning numerous Baja 500 and 1000 races. In stadium events, he's equally dominating, with three driver's championships and a record thirteen main-event triumphs. "I'm still the only person to win stadium and desert championships in the same year," he says proudly, "and that was 1990."

Stewart, now forty-seven years old (born June 4, 1945), shows no signs of slowing down. He drove his V6 Toyota truck to his fourteenth overall victory in a desert race in 1992 — another record. Even when he's not racing, Stewart is consumed by off-road racing. His arcade game, *Ivan Stewart's Off-Road,* was the most popular arcade game in 1989, and now he has a Nintendo game. You can see him in commercials promoting his primary sponsor, Toyota. A recent spot shows Stewart searching his home for a place to put his newest trophy, but even the refrigerator is full with old ones.

Stewart and his wife, Linda, live in a unique custom ranch house on eight acres near Alpine. "I couldn't be happier," he says. "I'm doing

Ivan "Ironman" Stewart

exactly what I want to do. What a great lifestyle! How could it get any better? When you go out and work hard for something and you make it happen, you really appreciate it."

His passion for off-road racing has rubbed off on the whole family. Linda follows in a helicopter when he races in the desert. Stewart's son Brian, 27, competes against his dad in both desert and stadium races, which causes the occasional awkward moment. "Obviously, I want him to do very well," Stewart says. "He wants to make a career of off-road racing. Yet I'm committed to driving Toyota trucks, and I've obligated myself to do the very best I can, so part of my job is to beat him." Trying to pass his son in a stadium race in Los Angeles, Stewart forced his son's truck into a wall. "It was nothing to do with him being my son," he says. "It was just another competitor out there, and he happened to be the one in the way."

Stewart's other two sons, Gary and Craig, aren't competing directly against their dad yet. When they're ready to challenge their famous father, maybe they should listen to his advice about achieving success. "It just started off with a flicker, an idea... then it became a goal. Then you set up a game plan and work toward that goal. Years ago, it started as a flicker and I made a dream come true. But not without a lot of hard work and a lot of dedication."

Scott Tinley
Triathlete/Entrepreneur

Scott Tinley is considered one of the true pioneers of the sport of triathlon. In the sixteen years he's been competing, he's helped the sport grow from a day-long exercise for a few crazies to the ultimate challenge for endurance athletes around the world. A top competitor since 1976, Tinley is grateful for what the sport has given him. "I've been able to carve out a lifestyle for myself that allows a lot of my passions to be my career," he says. His longevity in the sport, his consistency, durability and ability to win races is legendary.

Tinley was born in Santa Monica in 1956 and moved to San Diego when he was twenty to attend San Diego State University. He's lived in the area ever since. Independent, he has been on his own since leaving home at eighteen. He began competing in triathlons in 1976, when the sport was very new. In 1982, Tinley won the Bud Light Ironman World Championship in Hawaii, setting a new world record, and he took the Ironman title again in 1985. That year he was voted Triathlete of the Year, and he's finished in the top five of the world-wide poll every year since. He's competed in over 300 triathlons, winning nearly a hundred of them. He's unfailingly near the top in almost every event he enters but is known for the steadiness of his disposition as much as for his consistency in racing.

In 1984, he helped launch Tinley Performance Wear, designed with the triathlete in mind. He and many of his top-caliber triathlete friends "wear tested" the clothing, offering valuable feedback to the designers. The company was immediately successful in the triathlon market and grew rapidly, leaving Tinley less and less time to devote to training. "Some of my competitors are able to put 100 percent of their effort into training and racing – in the afternoon they can go home and take a nap and get ready for the next workout. I often spend that time on company business," he says. He serves as the company's vice president of advertising and promotions. The company is based in San Diego and manufactures roughly ninety-eight percent of its line locally. Tinley's business interests also include a retail sport shop near his home in Del Mar. He's also the author of three books on triathlons and writes a monthly column for a number of publications.

Tinley originally got involved with the apparel business just in case something happened to him physically, making him unable to earn a living on the racing circuit. He has since found that the business allows him to keep a sense of balance in his life. "Compared to my athlete peers, I have carved out a niche for myself on the business side, and it may affect me competitively because I'm distracted with other things," Tinley admits, "but I think I have a more well-balanced life." He credits much of his success to his partners, Jim Riley and Jeffrey Essakow, and an excellent staff.

When not training, competing or working with the business, Tinley spends time with his wife, Virginia, and their two children. He's looking forward to slowing down a little in the future. "Because I've been somewhat obsessive and driven in the past to accomplish these things, success really would be, in the end, being able to back off a little bit and start to enjoy the fruits of my labor instead of continually trying to stack up more and more points," he says.

Still, Tinley believes more people would compete in triathlons if they understood what is involved. "If you were to believe only what you see on television about triathlons," he points out, "nobody would ever compete in them. They'd think they were too hard and just for the criminally insane or masochistic types who are into this high pain threshold thing. But they really are a lot more achievable than people realize."

Scott's training takes him into the backroads of San Diego, where he's seen a big change in the amount of open space left. "I'm out on the roads training all the time," he says. "I'm in the environment so much that I see it more than most other people. It's an unhealthy environment to train in compared to what it used to be. I'm almost forced, if I'm going to maintain my stature in this sport, to go to other places to find fresh air, to get clean water to swim in and get less-crowded roads to train on. It's unfortunate that a place I've been in for almost twenty years has been let go to the point where people want to move away."

Tinley does offer some encouragement for those quintessential San Diegans who choose to stay and fight to protect the San Diego lifestyle: "The thing about hard-core San Diegans is they're going to stick it out and they're going to give it their best shot. They're a resilient bunch, and I think most of them are in it for the long run. I just hope that the power brokers in this area will listen to what these people have to say and do what's right."

Jesse Valdez
Olympic Boxer/Award-Winning Cameraman/ Entrepreneur

Although boxer Jesse Valdez never turned pro, his amateur record includes an estimated 600 bouts. He was the Texas State Champion four times and national AAU Golden Gloves Champion five times. At sixteen, he qualified as the first alternate for the 1964 U.S. Olympic Team. Three years later, he qualified as a member of the Pan American Team, winning a bronze medal in the welterweight division. The following year, he again qualified as a first alternate for the 1968 Olympic Games. For four years afterwards, Valdez won awards as the All Air Force Champion and All Inter-Service Champion, ultimately becoming the World Military Champ. The highlight of his boxing career was when he won the welterweight bronze medal at the 1972 Olympics in Munich. "It's not gold, but I guess third place in the world isn't too bad," he says.

Valdez brought his expertise to the 1975 American boxing team at the Pan American Games, serving as an assistant coach for a team that included Sugar Ray Leonard, Michael and Leon Spinks and Howard Davis, all of whom have since gone on to become world champions in professional boxing. He also has a successful career as an award-winning, seventeen-year cameraman for Channel 10. He recently opened the San Diego Boxing Academy in downtown San Diego, where a person can learn the skills of boxing without ever having to take a punch. Boxercise is a unique way to get in shape and relieve stress by working out like a champ, hitting the heavy bag, jumping rope and shadow-boxing with Jesse Valdez.

Valdez was born July 12, 1947 and raised in a tough part of Houston, Texas. One of seven children, his parents worked long hours trying to put food on the table, leaving the kids to fend for themselves. "We were low income, barely making it, and we ate a lot of rice and beans," Valdez remembers. While his father worked as a waiter and his mother cleaned offices for a living, Valdez got mixed up with the wrong crowd. "I hung around with a group of guys. Back then we didn't call them gangs, we just hung around in groups. If it hadn't been for the Boys Club, I don't know what I would have become," he admits.

Valdez got his first taste of boxing at the Boys Club when he was twelve. Through boxing, he gained discipline and self-esteem and learned about real determination. "I would never quit," he says. "I was always the last one to take the gloves off, and that was only because I wanted to, not because I wanted to quit." He was also winning, often against guys much bigger than he was. He began to see boxing as a stepping-stone to a better life and an education. "My goal and focus was to win the local tournament and then the state tournament," he remembers. After he accomplished that, he set his sights on the Olympics.

"People were telling me that the Olympics would open doors for me, and eventually it did," he says. Valdez received a scholarship to a college so small that he was the only member of the boxing team. Later he made it to a larger university on a scholarship as a physical education major while working part time as a television reporter in his home town of Houston.

"I almost went pro," Valdez says. "I'd gotten a lot of offers to turn pro." One offer came from Bill Daniels, who owns the Denver Nuggets basketball team and cable companies in the Denver area. "I'd been called by Mr. Daniels to come down and check out the gyms. I went down there with my friend and was made an offer that I couldn't refuse. But I did."

At twenty-five, he turned down sixty thousand dollars and a chance to become a professional boxer. After thirteen years in the ring, he was burned out. He had other options – he could stay in the service and become the Air Force coach or he could take a job as a television reporter in Houston. "I was a reporter for six weeks," he says, "and I realized that was not what I wanted to do. But I did want to stay in the business, so I ended up becoming a photographer." Valdez sent resumés all over the western states in an attempt to get out of Houston. "Once you leave Houston, you realize there's a better world," he says with a grin. Ron Mires of Channel 10 flew Valdez to San Diego and offered him a job as a cameraman in 1975, and he's been there ever since.

His toughest bout wasn't against another boxer but with alcohol. "I did have a rocky road, and it's something I don't normally share with the public," Valdez admits, "but I was an alcoholic. It started with a beer here and a beer there, and then it started to get real bad. I drank and drank, even though I knew what I was doing was wrong, and I knew what it could do to me." His father died from alcoholism and, as a kid, Valdez remembers saying he'd never let it happen to him. Yet, it nearly did. "I can remember as a little kid, taking a sip of his booze while he lay there on the floor passed out. At the time, it tasted terrible – and even when I was an adult it tasted terrible." With the support of his wife, Jackie, and his two sons, Jimmy and Jeremy, Valdez made the decision to quit eight years ago. He hasn't had a drink since. "When I quit drinking, it was the hardest thing I'd ever done in my life," he says. Jesse Valdez has shown his true colors – champion colors – both in boxing and in life.

Bill Walton
Basketball Star/Broadcaster

Bill Walton is considered one of the greatest centers to ever play professional basketball, despite being plagued by injury. After dominating the local basketball scene at Helix High School, he went to UCLA, where he became a three-time collegiate Player of the Year. He led UCLA to the NCAA championships in 1972 and 1973 and was rewarded with two tournament MVP's. In 1973, Walton received the James E. Sullivan Award for top U.S. amateur athlete. As the Portland Trail Blazers' top draft pick in 1974, the six-foot-eleven-inch center began a professional career that also saw him play for the San Diego Clippers and Boston Celtics before injuries forced him to retire after the 1987 season. Constantly hobbled by injuries over the course of his career, Walton still scored over 6,000 points with almost 5,000 rebounds and well over 1,000 blocked shots. He was voted the NBA's MVP for 1976-77 and was a two-time NBA All Star. In early 1993, Walton was elected to the Basketball Hall of Fame.

Walton was one of the most feared centers of his generation because of his intensity, which allowed him to play hard in spite of constant pain. He was a team leader who, although an outstanding individual talent, played a team-oriented game. He used his great instincts, mastery of the fundamentals and height while participating on a number of winning teams. In 1986, as a member of the Boston Celtics, he performed on aching feet to help bring the Celtics their sixteenth NBA championship. He won the Sixth Man Award for his outstanding contributions off the bench.

Today, Walton lives in San Diego, raising four sons, serving as a television and radio sportscaster and teaching basketball. Recently, he released a spoken-word album, *Men are Made in the Paint,* where he shares his vast knowledge of basketball.

Briefs

Mark Allen (Triathlete)

This Cardiff resident has won every Nice (France) Triathlon ever run (nine at last count). In 1992, he set a new record, winning his fourth consecutive Hawaii Ironman Triathlon in 8:09:09, besting his 1989 record time by six seconds. Paula Newby-Fraser of Encinitas set a record in the same triathlon, taking her fifth women's title at the same time.

Willie Banks (Track & Field)

This Oceanside track and field star won the Jesse Owens award in 1985 and became the U.S. Olympic Committee's Sportsman of the Year after setting a world record in the triple jump. He is the first American to hold the record since 1912.

Jud Buechler (Basketball)

A San Diego native, Buechler led the Warren Junior High School basketball team of Del Mar to fifty wins in two years. He then helped Poway High School win three San Diego Section basketball titles from 1984 to1986. The six-foot-six-inch forward led Arizona State in scoring and rebounds as a senior and was named to the All Pac10 team. After scoring over 1,100 points in his college career, Buechler was taken in the second round of the NBA draft in 1990.

Malin Burnham (Sailing)

In 1945, at seventeen, this Point Loma High School graduate became the youngest sailor to win the coveted World Star Class Championships. Burnham later earned respect as an ocean racing skipper. In the mid-1980's, he headed the Sail America syndicate that successfully recaptured the America's Cup.

Billy Casper (Golf)

At Chula Vista High School, this San Diego native had to choose between his two passions — golf and baseball. Casper chose golf, turning professional in his early twenties while still enlisted in the U.S. Navy. Since then, he has won 51 tour tournaments. He was the PGA Player of the Year in 1966 and 1970. In 1982, he became a member of the prestigious PGA Hall of Fame and is considered one of golfing's all-time greats. He has been on the senior PGA tour since 1981. Casper told *City Magazine,* "There are a lot of men and women blessed with ability and talent. But it's what's inside that ultimately separates the professionals from the amateurs. It's concentration and control that really decide the games."

Florence Chambers (Swimming)

One of San Diego's first champion swimmers, Chambers competed in the 1924 Olympic Games in Paris at the age of sixteen. She went on to win more than 300 medals and over 130 trophies. As a coach, one of her prize pupils was Florence Chadwick.

Michael Chang (Tennis)

Seven-year-old Chang won his first tennis tournament at San Diego's Morley Field. The La Costa resident won many national junior titles and became a dominant junior boys tennis player. While only in the eighth grade, he competed for San Dieguito High School, winning a CIF section championship in 1986. The following year, he became the youngest male to win a U.S. open match (at fifteen). In 1988, Chang turned professional. At five-feet-eight and 145 pounds, he doesn't possess the physical assets to be a big serve-and-volleyer. Instead, he uses his quickness to defeat opponents much larger than he is.

Chris Chelios (Hockey)

An All Star National Hockey League defenseman, Chelios attended Mira Mesa High School. He occasionally played pick-up games at a local skating rink. After graduation, he tried out for USIU's hockey team, but was cut. Determined to play in the NHL, he played in Canada, in college and for the 1984 U.S. Olympic Team.

Tiffany Chin (Ice Skating)

Local talent Chin was not only the World Junior Champion, but in

1985 she became the national ladies figureskating champion as well. She was the first Asian-American ever to qualify for the USFSA world team, and she did it at age fifteen.

Dennis Conner (Sailing)

Conner wrote *The Art of Winning, No Excuse to Lose* and *Comeback* over the course of a sailing career that includes four America's Cup victories and one defeat. He began sailing at eleven, when he joined the San Diego Yacht Club. He took a bronze medal in the 1976 Olympics, skippered America's Cup winners *Freedom (1980)* and *Stars and Stripes (1987)* and was selected Yachtsman of the Year three times. He also skippered the luckless *Liberty,* which lost the Cup to the Australians in 1983. San Diegans were nearly hysterical with joy when he brought the cup back in 1987. Almost singlehandedly, he broadened the base of interest in his sport, involving even Sunday sailors and landlubbers in the excitement of the race.

Gail Devers (Track & Field)

A little over a year before the 1992 Olympic Summer Games, San Diegan Gail Devers couldn't even walk. She was bedridden, suffering from Graves disease, a thyroid disorder. Her condition was so severe that she nearly had to have her feet amputated. In one of the greatest comebacks in Olympic history, she won the gold in the 100-meter dash. For her courage, she was honored with the Olympic Spirit Award.

Gerry Driscoll (Sailing)

Following an extraordinary sailing career spanning four decades, Driscoll earned international acclaim as a builder of fine yachts in San Diego. In 1968, he organized the first West Coast challenge for the America's Cup and skippered *Columbia* in trial competition. Driscoll was selected as San Diego's Yachtsman of the Year in 1966 and 1974. As skipper of *Intrepid* in 1974, he barely missed winning the right to defend the America's Cup; an equipment casualty cost him the final trials race.

Chris Dudley (Basketball)

Now a six-foot-eleven-inch, 240 pound center for the New Jersey

Nets, the Torrey Pines High School graduate was a longshot to make it to the NBA. Dudley didn't even make the varsity roster at Torrey Pines until he was a senior – at six-feet-seven and 185 pounds. He developed outstanding shot-blocking and rebounding abilities while attending Yale, not exactly known as a basketball school. Dudley was a fourth-round draft pick by the Cleveland Cavaliers in 1987 and has established himself as a solid NBA player.

Phil Edwards (Surfing)

Edwards is best known as the designer of the Hobie Cat, a sailboat made popular by Hobie Alter. A graduate of Oceanside High School, he graced the cover of *Sports Illustrated* in 1966, the same year he was voted the world's best surfer in a *Surfer Magazine* poll. Edwards was inducted into the International Surfing Hall of Fame.

Charles Fletcher (Aquatics)

A member of the pioneering Fletcher family, he was a world-class swimmer and water polo player. A founder of HomeFed Savings Bank in 1934, he served in the Navy during World War II and was elected to Congress in 1946.

Dave Freeman (Badminton)

The world's best badminton player of all time retired from competition in 1954 to devote his full attention to his second career as a neurosurgeon in San Diego.

Broc Glover (Racing)

Glover was the childhood friend of another Supercross champion from El Cajon, Rick Johnson. Since 1977, Glover, a Valhalla High School graduate, became the first rider in history to win three Super Bowls of Motocross and five national championships.

Karen Hantze Susman (Tennis)

Before she became the world tennis champion in 1962, Susman dominated junior girls tennis, winning the first of numerous titles while still in her early teens. In addition to her many national championships in women's singles, she was also a highly successful doubles player.

Tony Hawk (Skateboarding)

This Torrey Pines High School graduate began riding skateboards in the late 1970's. In 1982, while still in his teens, he turned pro. He's been a top-ranked professional ever since.

"Bud" Held (Track & Field)

Held became the first American to hold the world javelin record when he threw the spear 268 feet, two-and-a-half inches in 1955. In 1956 he topped that mark with a toss of 270 feet. After graduating from Grossmont High School, he went on to win three NCAA titles and six AAU titles at Stanford University.

Jeff Jacobs (Racing)

Jeff Jacobs of El Cajon has won five national Jet Ski racing championships and more than 100 races since turning professional in 1987 at the age of fifteen.

Rick Johnson (Racing)

Johnson has far surpassed his motocross mentor, Broc Glover. Johnson, who recently retired, holds the record for most Supercross event wins with twenty-eight. Not only that, he's a seven-time American motocross champion. Before a hand injury ended Johnson's career, he was only two wins shy of eclipsing Bob Hannah's career total of sixty-four wins. The El Cajon native now races on four wheels, taking on the Mickey Thompson Off-Road Grand Prix tour with the same drive and skill that made him a champion at motocross.

Tommy Johnson (Golf)

At Hoover High, the five-foot, 100-pound Johnson excelled not only at golf, but at baseball and basketball as well, sometimes competing against guys well over a foot taller than he was. He eventually grew to five-foot-five-inches, weighing in at around 120 pounds. But despite his lack of size, he dominated amateur golf in San Diego during the late 1940's and early 1950's, winning championship after championship. Although he did turn pro briefly, Johnson made his mark teaching others the game and later working to keep scholastically troubled youngsters in school at Hoover High.

Cliff Levingston (Basketball)

Since being drafted by the Detroit Pistons in 1982, the Morse High School alumnus has played for Atlanta and Chicago. The forward was fortunate to be part of the Chicago Bulls' machine the past two seasons, helping them win their second straight title. He is currently playing in Europe.

Gene Littler (Golf)

This San Diego native began his professional golfing career in 1954 after winning the San Diego Open as an amateur. A Hall of Famer, he was a tour regular from 1954 to 1977, winning twenty-nine titles before switching to the senior tour. In the early 1970's, Littler was diagnosed with cancer and most people thought his golfing career was over. But he battled back after surgery to surprise the golfing world, winning four tournaments in three years following his recovery.

Phil Mickelson (Golf)

As a senior at the University of San Diego High School, Mickelson was considered one of the best junior golfers in the country. While at Arizona State, he joined Ben Crenshaw as the only golfer to win three NCAA championships. His collegiate awards include College Player of the Year, Heisman Trophy of College Golf and selection to the golf coaches' All American Team. In 1991, Mickelson became the first player born in the 1970's (and only the fourth amateur ever) to win a PGA Tour event when he shot a sixteen-under-par 271 to win the Northern Telecom Open in Tucson.

Bill Miller (Track & Field)

In 1932, pole vaulter Bill Miller won an Olympic gold medal and set a world record in the process. The San Diego High School graduate won two national intercollegiate vaulting titles in college.

Billy Mills (Track & Field)

Part Sioux Indian, this USMC record-setting runner (based at Camp Pendleton) was an Olympic gold medal winner in the 10,000-meter run at Tokyo in 1964. His incredible victory inspired the movie *Running Brave*. Nobody believed he could win, except himself.

Archie Moore (Boxing)

Voted Mr. San Diego in 1968, Archie Moore is one of San Diego's most respected citizens, "Not only because of his amazing accomplishments in the boxing ring, but also for what he has done outside it." Moore began fighting out of San Diego in 1936, and over a thirty-year period fought over 200 bouts, winning nearly ninety percent of them. He still holds the world record for most knockouts. He took the world light-heavyweight title from Joey Maxim in 1952 and held it for ten years, during which time he was called the greatest light-heavyweight of all time. In 1955, "The Mongoose" challenged the great Rocky Marciano for the heavyweight title, but lost. He also lost a bout to another legendary fighter, Floyd Patterson. The durable boxer finally hung 'em up in 1965 at the age of forty-eight. In 1960, Moore made his motion picture debut as Joe in *The Adventures of Huckleberry Finn*. At his training facility in Ramona, he worked with many great fighters, including Muhammed Ali. Archie Moore, who grew up in central San Diego, devoted his life to working with youngsters in an effort to keep them off drugs and away from violence.

Bill Muncey (Racing)

Muncey, a resident of La Mesa, was the most successful driver in the history of unlimited hydroplane racing, winning over sixty races, seven national championships and eight Gold Cup titles during a twenty-five year career. He was killed on October 18, 1981, when his Atlas Van Lines boat went into a backward loop and crashed in Acapulco. Muncey was fifty-two years old.

Jean "Cheesy" Neil (All-Around Athlete)

Neil was one of the Marine Corps' greatest athletes, winning awards in six different sports and earning twenty-one sports letters at MCRD during the early 1930's. As a coach and administrator for MCRD and later at San Diego State University, he was also immensely successful. A thirty-year veteran of the Marines, he retired as a captain in 1959. During World War II, he saw action with the Fourth Marine Division.

Terry Norris (Boxing)

Terry Norris won the World Boxing Council super welterweight title from John Mugabi with a first-round knockout in 1990. Less than a year later, he scored an impressive victory over Sugar Ray Leonard in Madison Square Gardens. The East County resident was a unanimous choice as WBC Boxer of the Year. The five-foot-ten boxer, still only in his mid-twenties, has amassed over thirty wins, many by knockout.

Lowell North (Sailing)

Today, North is considered the world's foremost sailmaker, yet he's also remembered as one of the all-time best Star Class sailors. He won the world Star Class championship title in 1957, 1959, 1960 and 1973. A medal winner in the 1964 Olympics, he captured the Gold in 1968. His company is based in San Diego and located near the San Diego Yacht Club.

Margo Oberg (Surfing)

This former women's world champion surfed regularly at La Jolla Shores at one time. She now gives surfing instruction in Kauai.

Larry Penacho (Water Skiing)

San Diegan Larry Penacho was a world waterski champion in 1961, 1963 and 1965.

Milton "Milky" Phelps (Basketball)

This Hoover High School and San Diego State University star (1938-1941) was considered the Aztecs' greatest basketball player for many years. During an era when fewer points were scored per game, "Milky" compiled a career total of 1,043 points for a 10.7 per game average and was twice named Little All American. Phelps was killed in an aviation training accident during World War II.

Clarence Pinkston (Aquatics)

In 1920, Pinkston became the first San Diegan to win an Olympic gold medal. The high-dive and springboard champion also won silver and bronze medals during his career.

Lee Ramage (Boxing)

During the 1930's, Lee Ramage was a ranking heavyweight who

compiled a record of over seventy wins against twelve losses. Two of those losses were to Joe Louis, who knocked Ramage out in the eighth round in 1934 and in the second round in 1935 while he was challenging for the heavyweight title.

Mark Reynolds (Sailing)

Reynolds, who has been involved with sailing for over twenty-five years, won his first Olympic gold medal in 1992 after narrowly missing it in the 1988 Olympics, settling for the silver in the premier Star class. He and crewman Hal Haenel were the first Star team to appear in two consecutive Olympics. The Point Loma High School graduate went on to become an All American at San Diego State University. In the early 1970's, he taught sailing to juniors for the San Diego Yacht Club. Two of his students also won medals in the 1992 Olympics: Brian Ledbetter won a silver in the Finn class and J.J. Isler took a bronze in the women's 470 class.

Arnie Robinson (Track & Field)

A native San Diegan, Robinson was one of the best long jumpers in American track & field history, with six National AAU titles and two Olympic medals. In 1970, he captured the NCAA title, won a bronze medal in 1972 and then captured a gold medal in the 1976 Olympics. The Morse High School graduate attended Mesa College before graduating from San Diego State University.

Paul Runyan (Golf)

Nicknamed "Little Poison" because he was so small, Runyan's golfing career spanned many decades. The Hall of Famer won over twenty-five tournaments, two national PGA championships and two world senior titles.

Craig Stadler (Golf)

This five-foot-ten-inch, 200-pound La Jolla native is one of the world's outstanding professional golfers. A top competitor in the San Diego Juniors program, he also excelled in college competition at USC before joining the PGA tour. Stadler won the 1982 Masters Tournament, among many others.

Mike Stamm (Swimming)

Stamm was one of the best swimmers to come from San Diego. At Crawford High School, he was a three-time prep All American from 1968 to 1970. At Indiana University, he helped the Hoosiers win three NCAA titles while becoming a four-time All American. In the 1972 Olympics, he won a gold and two silver medals.

Willie Steele (Track & Field)

Steele won an Olympic gold medal for the broad jump in the 1948 Olympics. A member of San Diego State University's Hall of Fame, he was also a basketball and football star. As a track star, he helped SDSU win two NCAA titles (1947 and 1948), as well as three National AAU championships (1946-1948). Steele was drafted into the Army during World War II and became a decorated war hero, awarded five battle stars.

Mary "Mickey" Wright (Golf)

Wright dominated the women's golf tour from 1956 to 1973, winning an incredible eighty-two tournaments, four U.S. Opens and four LPGA Championships. In 1963 and 1964, the San Diego native was the AP Woman Athlete of the Year.

Media

Chapter 8: Television

Mike Ambrose

Hal Clement

Larry Himmel

Carol LeBeau

Ted Leitner

Marty Levin

Gloria Penner

Briefs

Johnny Downs · Charlie Jones

Susan Peters · Sarah Purcell · Laurie Singer

Bree Walker

Mike Ambrose
Weatherman

Mike Ambrose is the cool and confident Channel 10 weatherman whose career spans over thirty-five years. He still videotapes every one of his performances and critiques it. He is, and always has been, hard on himself, perhaps because of his struggle to overcome the stage fright and panic attacks that plagued him early in his career. Blessed with a deep and distinctive voice, Ambrose has been successful in both radio and television.

Born in 1939 in Handley, a small town in Texas, Ambrose dreamed of coming to California. His parents, just teenagers at his birth, led a modest life. His father was a glass cutter who earned fifteen dollars a week. His mother, an only child born into a very wealthy family, had rebelled by marrying the poorest guy she could find. Ambrose idolized his well-to-do grandmother, and he loved escaping into her world of lavish luxury and elegance. A lonely child, Ambrose spent many nights with a radio under his pillow, listening to the on-air legends in the early years of radio's Top 40 format. Wanting to be liked, he fantasized about being on radio someday, thinking, "If there was ever a way to be popular, this is it!" He was never athletic – always the last to be picked for team sports – and was often relegated to the outfield in baseball. At sixteen, he was hired by a radio station just outside Ft. Worth for a dollar-fifty an hour. He was on his way.

By the time he was twenty, he moved to the number one rock station in Texas. Two years later, Ambrose was a twenty-two year-old kid living out his childhood dream, spinning records for KFWB in Los Angeles, the largest rock station in the nation at the time. When he was twenty-five, he came to work for KOGO radio in San Diego. The television studio was just across the hall, and he became fascinated with the lights, camera, action! of this new media. He spent his free time hanging around the studio until they finally gave him a job as fill-in weekend weatherman. For three years, Ambrose hyperventilated his way through the weathercasts. He managed to control his stage fright so well, however, that he was moved to the coveted weeknight slot. But Ambrose still had his worries. "I was always concerned with what the engineers were thinking," he remembers. "'Gee, what an idiot! How did this guy ever get on the air?'" Many of his concerns were real. "As a news anchor, you have a desk for a security blanket. As a weatherman, you're on a stage with a blue wall behind you, and there's nothing else there," Ambrose explains. To cope with the stress, he lay down before each newscast and visualized himself successfully doing the weather, using positive affirmations to reinforce this image.

Today, Ambrose is a picture of success, a fixture on the award-winning Channel 10 newscast team and a true San Diego celebrity. He is very well paid for his efforts, and had the honor of being been chosen to appear on Good Morning America as a guest weatherman for a week. He loves what he's doing so much that the highlights of his week are the twelve-hour days he puts in at the station. Time off the air is spent at his spectacular home in the La Jolla hills. His recipe for success is a happy mixture: "A small amount of ability, overwhelming desire, meaningful goals – and you can accomplish anything."

Hal Clement
Award-Winning News Anchor

Hal Clement's television career in San Diego began at KGTV Channel 10 (then KOGO) in 1970, while he was still a student at San Diego State University. He started as an intern, earning a mere two dollars an hour. His job included everything from paste-up to shooting and editing film to writing and filing. He did it all – whatever was asked – without question. Now, over twenty years later, Clement is an Emmy Award-winning reporter and writer who co-anchors the 5:00 p.m. and 6:30 p.m. weekday editions of News Eight. He also writes and produces the *Words and Pictures* segments seen weekdays.

Clement started his career in San Diego and, although he's not a native San Diegan, he feels that he has a unique understanding of the city and its people. "I've lived here long enough and seen enough go on here that I really do have a tremendous affection for the city. I care about what happens here," he says.

Born in New York City, Clement grew up in Connecticut. His father died when he was two and, when his mother remarried, the new family moved to Los Angeles. There, his mother worked as a writer for television and radio. "I had a terrific childhood," Clement says. "I remember my parents always being there for me, and I've tried to make that same commitment to my children." He prefers not working nights, so he can spend more time with his wife, Patty, and their two daughters, Stacey (fourteen) and Brooke (eleven). He loves his work, and is gratified by his success in television, but he enjoys life away from the station as well. "I'm not a workaholic," Clement admits. "I put in my eight to ten hours, and when I'm at work I try to give it all I've got. When I go home, I try to leave the office at the office. Success to me is to enjoy what I do and to be happy in the overall picture of my life."

After graduating from SDSU in 1971 with a degree in journalism, Clement became a sportscaster on the highly rated Channel 10 News. He was promoted to sports director in 1974, but became restless, feeling he was just doing the same thing over and over again. He made a surprising move to News Eight, becoming the number two sports commentator behind Ted Leitner. Surprising because he willingly took a pay cut just to stay in San Diego. People in the news business frequently change markets for new jobs offering more money. This gutsy move put his career on a new and challenging course away from sports. In 1983, under the guidance of Channel 8's news director, Jim Holtzman, Clement moved to feature reporting. In June 1984, he began anchoring the 4:30 p.m. news, and in March 1989 he began to co-anchor the 6:30 p.m. news also.

What does the future hold for Hal Clement? "My daughter Stacey said that she would like to co-anchor with me someday, and after reading a story she would turn to me and, instead of saying 'Hal', she would say 'Daddy,'" Clement chuckles

Larry Himmel
Media Celebrity

Since Larry Himmel moved to the then-sleepy resort town of San Diego in 1972, the wisecracking disc jockey from Chicago has grown up along with the city. Now Himmel is forty-five, and has done and seen more in his twenty years as a San Diego celebrity than most will accomplish in a lifetime. He's been "The Cruiser" on KGB-FM, "Swami Sweatsocks," an off-the-wall sportscaster, and a stand-up comic and emcee at the Comedy Store. He was an Emmy Award-winning hippie commentator in the late 1970's and early 1980's. "Himmel At Large" on TV Channel 8 grew into the unprecedented "San Diego At Large" and later into a live show on Channel 39. He even tended bar at the Sunshine Company in Ocean Beach for a short time. Today, he's back at Channel 8 as their weekday weatherman, and he continues to spin jazz records once a week at KIFM radio. About his long career in San Diego, Himmel says, "At least life has been exciting. I don't think any of my career moves have been forward. They've just been kind of lateral moves, but I'm a survivor and that's all I try to do."

As a kid, Himmel knew that he wanted to go into radio because "Disc jockeys were the wise-ass guys who seemed to be bucking the system." Himmel himself had a problem with authority. "I've been kicked out of high school for it and lost a few jobs when people tried to tell me what not to say and what not to do," he says ruefully. "I always thought it was easier to apologize than ask permission." After earning his Master's in broadcasting from Bradley University in Peoria, he has worked at and been fired from radio stations in three states and two countries. In his defense, Himmel points out that getting fired in radio and television is very often the only way you move ahead in your career.

Himmel's career in radio was slow to get off the ground, but the worst part was when he went to apply for jobs. Basically, and frequently, he was told he just wasn't any good. As he puts it, "They would call me into their office and say, 'I want to be really honest with you. You don't have what it takes and you're not going to make it.' I just arched my back and said, 'I'm going to show you!'" He left Chicago for a radio job in Canada, where he hit the lowest point of his career.

After emigrating to Canada, Himmel's money and what few possessions he had were tied up at the border. He had to go on air and perform every day, keeping himself "up" and funny when he had no money for food and he had to sleep on the floor of his empty apartment with a single blanket to keep out the cold. After his shift, he just went home and cried. But radio was what he'd always wanted to do, and he knew things would get better.

Himmel came to San Diego to work at KPRI-FM, but lasted only a few months there before moving on to KGB-FM for a six-year run. In 1978, he moved to San Francisco, following a girlfriend's career. When he couldn't find regular radio work there, he started doing stand-up comedy. He met Robin Williams, who told him that if he ever wanted to make it in comedy, he should go to the Comedy Store in Los Angeles. Himmel took his advice, and began flying to Los Angeles on Monday afternoon, taking a taxi to the Comedy Store for amateur night, waiting in line, doing his five minutes and flying back to San Francisco the same night. His dedication caught the attention of the Comedy Store's owner, who hired Himmel to emcee at his new club in La Jolla. From that perspective, he studied the surge of great comics passing through town. Michael Keaton, Robin Williams, Gallagher, David Letterman – they all left an indelible impression on Himmel.

Channel 8 Executive News Director Jim Holtzman saw Himmel's act and hired him to do "at large" commentary, poking fun at San Diegans. Later, Holtzman was instrumental in getting Himmel his own show. *San Diego At Large* ran for three-and-a-half years, cranking out well over 800 shows. Himmel put his personal life on hold to take advantage of this once-in-a-lifetime chance. He worked six days a week, fifteen hours a day, writing most of the material and performing on the commercial half-hour comedy program.

Today, Himmel still keeps his hand in radio with a Sunday morning show on KIFM. He uses his skills as a stand-up comic to spice up the weekday weather on Channel 8. He says, "I never thought I'd like doing the weather. I always thought it was the dufus job, and one bad career move away from hosting the Home Shopping Channel. But I'm not a weatherman. I just play one on television. I want to be the next Bob Dale. I'm even ready to put on the bow tie and do weather for the next thirty years."

Himmel and his wife of ten years just had their first child, Miles Daniel Himmel, named after jazz great Miles Davis. "It's funny," he says, "my son is already showing some of the signs of his namesake. He was born with his back to the doctor. He will not do requests, and he's really distressed that his parents are white." Asked why they waited so long to have children, Himmel cracks that this way, by the time the kid is old enough to hate him, he'll be senile.

When Himmel talks about success, he gets very serious. "Be so focused on what you want that when you go through all the BS you have to go through to get there, you're so focused that you say, 'I'm going through this now, but I'm going to get there.' Don't ever stop, and don't ever let anyone tell you that you can't achieve your goal. Just keep going. Success really has to be a personal issue, because we so often judge our own success against other people's achievements. You have to realize that, given whatever limited resources and whatever the odds were, that you did the best you possibly could. That's what success is."

Carol LeBeau
Award-Winning Newscaster

All of her life, Carol LeBeau has felt pressure to succeed, and succeed she has. As an anchorperson on Channel 10 News, she is an integral part of San Diego's top-rated nightly news. Teamed with Kimberly Hunt on 10 News Nightcast, she forms part of the country's top two-women news team. She earned the prestigious Golden Mike Award for her popular *Staying Healthy* segment, which she also co-produces. Not one to rest on her laurels, LeBeau says, "Success — once you've achieved it, it's gone and you have to set the next goal. What they say in Hollywood is that you're only as good as your last film. In sports you're only as good as your last touchdown. In my business, it's the same way." Under constant pressure to do her best, LeBeau knows how many women are after her job. Their tapes arrive every day.

LeBeau is totally into fitness and loves working off the stress of her job through exercise. Competing as a runner and rough water swimmer are relaxing for her. "I've always been a compulsive exercise-a-holic," she admits. Another stabilizing force in her life is her husband, Tom Hamilton, a successful businessman and ex-Navy pilot she met on a blind date. "He understands what it's like to be married to a high-visibility individual, and he handles it beautifully," she says. The two also share a Christian faith that helps put their lives into perspective.

LeBeau grew up in Davenport, Iowa, the oldest of three children. She was raised in a high-performance family and felt pressure to do well right from the start. She discovered that bringing home "A's" and excelling at sports got her lots of attention. "I equated success with love, and it took me a long time to figure out that somebody could love me just because I exist," she says. LeBeau painfully recalls being called "Carol the barrel" in junior high school because of her weight. She joined the Davenport YMCA and learned to swim competitively, shedding the weight and nickname. "While it was painful," she points out, "it helped me find other areas in my life that I could excel at, so that I could still be somebody even if I wasn't the prettiest one or the fittest one." Described as shy and reserved in high school, she made a brave move when she got involved in drama, taking on the lead role in the school play. "It was always the fear of failure," LeBeau says. "If I did not get up and make that speech in my speech class, then I would really be a failure. At least if I got up there and made the effort, there was a chance that I could succeed."

LeBeau graduated from the University of Northern Iowa at Cedar Falls. She switched from being a theater major to radio and television after two years, realizing that she didn't want to be an actress. From 1976 to 1978, she worked as a reporter, writer and talk show host at WOC-TV in Davenport. In June of 1978, she joined WMBD-TV in Peoria, Illinois. Looking to move into a larger market, she sent out resumes and audition tapes all over the Midwest, only to have them returned with a "Don't call us, we'll call you" response. She was considering a move to Lexington, Kentucky, when Ron Mires in San Diego called. "I think they must have been looking for a wholesome brunette from the Midwest who had a standard American dialect. They already had all the glamorous blondes and beautiful people," LeBeau says ironically. In March of 1981, she joined 10 News as a weekend anchor and weekday reporter. Since then, she's become a fixture at the station. "I'm proud of the fact that we're a number one team here," she says, "and I think it has a lot to do with people working together."

At one time, LeBeau wanted to move up to the network level. Today, she's unwilling to pay the price. She's happy staying in San Diego doing the local news. "I got sucked into that whole superwoman thing in the 1980's where you think you have to have it all," she admits.

"Thank goodness we're in the nineties, because the eighties were a travesty. Women were exhausted. They were lonely. They had anxiety disorders, relationships that were in shambles and kids who were on drugs. I heard Connie Chung say once that sure, she makes a lot of money, but she doesn't even have the time to spend it. What kind of life is that?"

Ted Leitner
Sportscaster/Announcer/Media Celebrity

Nobody would ever accuse Ted Leitner of being boring. His unique brand of unscripted and unrehearsed sportscasting airs weekdays at 5:00 p.m. and 6:30 p.m. on News Eight – and audiences eat it up. When Leitner came to San Diego in January, 1978, he was hired as sports director and sportscaster for News Eight. Fifteen years later, he's still at it, but he's added many other jobs to his portfolio. You can hear him mornings on KFMB radio, joking with Hudson and Bauer as the morning sports anchor. Afternoons when the Padres are in town, he fields callers' questions about "his Padres" as the host of *Padre Talk,* also on KFMB. For the past thirteen years, Leitner has served as a play-by-play announcer for Padres radio and cable television broadcasts, blending his personal opinions with the facts, always in an entertaining way. Over the years, he has done play-by-play for San Diego State University football and basketball games, Charger football and Clipper basketball. He wrote *Leitner Strikes* and, in 1990, branched out to do social commentaries for News Eight. He says he's trying to cut back, but he's also the first to admit that when offered paying work he has a hard time saying no.

Much has been made of Leitner's three divorces and subsequent alimony payments, his six-figure salary and his controversial style, mixing politics with sports. He's one of San Diego's most talked-about and successful television personalities. In a 1987 national survey, Leitner was voted the country's best sportscaster. He's won his share of Golden Mike Awards for sports commentary, too. "I never gave success that much thought," he says. "I never considered myself successful, but now that I'm older, I appreciate it more and I think about it more." He appears to have it all. Still, while he's certainly famous, the price of fame can be high. Ask almost any San Diegan who Ted Leitner is and they'll know. They're also likely to tell you they either love him or hate him. "I'm very sensitive," he admits. "I've always been that way, very sensitive. I like to be liked, but I can't make people like me." As for his fortune, he admits he's a prisoner of his luxury lifestyle, even though he rarely has the time to stop and enjoy it.

Born July 9, 1947 in New York City near Yankee Stadium, Leitner's family moved to Yonkers, a lower-middle-class neighborhood, when he was four. They didn't have much more than a roof over their heads and food on the table. His father was a wine salesman and his mother a bookkeeper. They slept on a pull-out couch in the living room while Ted and his brother shared a room in their tiny apartment. It was not a happy childhood. He remembers his parents constantly fighting with each other. When his father wasn't shouting at his mother, he was calling young Ted a moron, an idiot and a jerk. His father's verbal abuse made Leitner withdrawn, shy and lacking in confidence.

The skinny, introverted youngster turned to sports and to his kind and affectionate mother. His happiest childhood memories are of summers spent at the Jersey shore, where he was able just to be a kid, playing baseball and swimming all day. At eleven, he took a job folding towels in a laundry, earning five dollars a week, because his father wouldn't give him an allowance. The next summer, he filled cigarette machines. Leitner's dad never took his son to Yankee Stadium, but he and his brother, Lew, rode the subway to see his first ballgame in the summer of 1961, gorging themselves on hotdogs as they sat in the upper deck.

Leitner got his regular sports fix by listening to broadcast greats Marty Glickman, Red Barber and Mel Allen. In junior high school, he decided to become a sportscaster, but his parents mocked his dream. Although he matured into a 190-pound dynamic defensive end, earning all-city honors at Roosevelt High School, Leitner was still terribly shy and insecure. It took a lot of guts for him to pick up the microphone and become the public address announcer for his high school basketball team, but he did it.

Leitner left New York to attend Oklahoma State University for a number of reasons. His brother was there, he couldn't afford tuition at

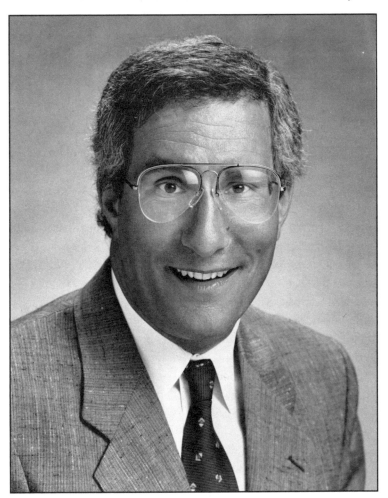

Ted Leitner

a school in New York State, Oklahoma had a good football program and he wanted to put some distance between his father and himself. He majored in radio/TV/film, intending to go into sports broadcasting. When a counselor suggested he might want to do play-by-play for the campus radio station, he took the job and hung up his football helmet for good. He gained valuable experience during his five years behind the mike at Oklahoma State. Add to that a part-time job with a commercial radio station, summers doing baseball play-by-play and a degree — and Leitner was on his way. Still afflicted with shyness (I know it's hard to believe), he earned his Master's in speech communications from the University of Oklahoma. While there, he also handled basketball and radio broadcasts. In 1974, he was named Oklahoma Sportscaster of the Year by the National Sportscasters and Sports Writing Association.

His first big-time job came at twenty-six, when Leitner was paid $30,000 a year by WFSB-TV in Hartford, Connecticut, a lot of money for someone with his upbringing. At Hartford, he developed his ad-lib style of going on the air unscripted (although he did use an outline) to help fill the five minutes he was allotted for sports. After two years, he moved to WCAU-TV in Philadelphia to become sports director in the fourth largest market in the country. Unfortunately, his abrasive style of sports reporting didn't go over well with the fanatical Philadelphia sports fans, and he was fired. While he was in Philadelphia, however, he met Michael Tuck, who moved on to Channel 8 in San Diego. Channel 8 News Director Jim Holtzman brought Leitner to San Diego, where he and Michael Tuck had a long run as the undisputed ratings kings of San Diego television news. Described as opinionated, controversial, entertaining and outrageous, Leitner has endured and prospered here. His "sports is just a game" attitude has amused some and angered others − but nobody seems to be indifferent to him. He continues to attract viewers and listeners, doing the work of four or five men on radio and television. "Co-workers say I hardly work at all, yet I'm always hearing from listeners and viewers that I work too hard. I work frequently. I don't work hard − I work often," he says.

The Leitner you see on-air is a ranting and raving lunatic who isn't afraid to let his opinions be known. Off the air, he's a very private person. He spends as much time as possible being the kind of father he never had. Married for the fourth time on April 16, 1990, he and his wife, Debrah, are the proud parents of twins. His son Mark, from his first marriage, also lives with him. His two other sons, Matthew and Jordan, live with his second wife.

Leitner, who once weighed as much as 250 pounds, lost fifty pounds thirteen years ago by jogging, working out and taking karate lessons. Both of his parents died in their sixties from heart disease, so he tries to keep his weight and Type A personality in check. He doesn't smoke and rarely drinks. Although he's on the road more than seventy-five days a year, sometimes working nineteen-hour days, he denies that he's a workaholic, because he loves what he does. Sometimes he gets so busy, however, that he finds it hard to enjoy his favorite pastimes — seeing a good motown concert or spending time on the ocean. He sold his thirty-three-foot Bertram yacht because he only used it once or twice a year.

Despite the confidence he exudes on-air, deep down Leitner fears it will all be taken away someday. His brother, a psychotherapist, told him once that he lives his life as a warning to others.

Marty Levin
Award-Winning Anchorman

Marty Levin is the highly-respected and award-winning Channel 39 news anchor, writer, editor and producer. His advice to anyone who wants to get into the news business is to "be a jack-of-all-trades, somebody who knows a little about everything and hopefully a lot about a couple of things." A broadcast veteran of more than twenty-five years and a successful anchor at all three San Diego stations, he knows what he's talking about. Levin's peers call him an outstanding newsman, a dedicated professional whose work is honored as the best, time and time again. To viewers who see him anchoring the news at 5:00 p.m., 6:00 p.m. and 11:00 p.m. or hosting his award-winning ninety-minute monthly show, *Third Thursday,* he is always a friendly and familiar face.

Levin was born in Maine and grew up in Los Angeles. He enrolled at Oregon State University as a pre-law major. While still in college, he got his first taste of broadcasting at a local PBS station. He worked as a news reporter for a local radio station from midnight to 8:00 a.m. and still made it to class every morning. He graduated with a degree in communications in 1969. Levin became a radio news director, then a public affairs officer with the police department in Eugene, Oregon while he completed his training at the police academy. His career in television news took him to stations in San Jose and Seattle before he came to work at San Diego's Channel 10 in 1977. In 1980, he left San Diego to become a highly-paid, Emmy-winning news anchor at NBC-owned WRC-4 in Washington D.C. During his tenure there, the news

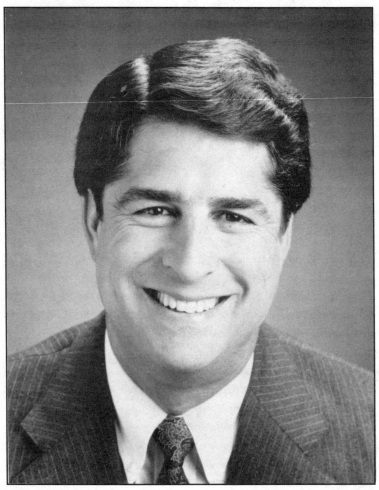

Marty Levin   *Photo courtesy KNSD-TV Channel 39*

program rose from its usual position at the bottom of the ratings to compete for the top spot.

In 1982, Levin returned to San Diego as an anchor at KFMB-TV Channel 8 for a fraction of his former salary, because he didn't feel the hassles and stress of Washington were worth it. "I got there and almost immediately wanted to come back to San Diego," he remembers. In August of 1987, he took his talents to KNSD-TV Channel 39 and, along with Denise Yamada, has been there ever since. During his career, he has won the coveted Golden Mike award, seven Emmys, accolades from the New York International Film and TV Festival and has been a co-anchor on two different number-one rated local news stations.

What's the secret to his success? "Learn as much as you can and work as hard as you can. I have been lazy at times in my life, but I don't think anyone will tell you I don't work hard. In fact, I work harder now than I ever did before. I've had a lot easier jobs than this," Levin says.

Levin spends his mornings getting his eight-year-old son ready for school, making his breakfast and packing his lunch. He uses up the rest of the morning doing his own homework, reading the *Los Angeles Times* and *San Diego Union-Tribune,* watching CNN and checking Compu-Serve on his computer for any late-breaking stories. His day at the office begins at 2:00 p.m. and lasts until he's off the air at 11:30 p.m. During the summer, he takes a long dinner between broadcasts and sneaks in a little fishing, his favorite pastime.

Asked if his son is aware of how much of a San Diego celebrity his father is, Levin answeres, "My son's more of a sports fan and gets a big kick out of Laz [Jim Laslavic, KNSD sports director] and Jerry Coleman. He's a baseball fanatic."

His son might not know it yet, but his colleagues and many viewers give Marty Levin all the respect he deserves.

Gloria Penner
Director of KPBS-TV

Gloria Penner has interviewed everyone who's anyone in San Diego during her twenty-three years at KPBS. She's won many awards doing it, including several local Emmys. But it's the issues facing San Diego that she most loves discussing. "My interest is always public affairs and politics," she says.

As the director of program production, she decided to change formats from her respected half-hour interview show to one that delved into the kinds of things that directly impact San Diego. In 1989, it was clear to her that San Diego was heading for tough times with an impending economic downturn, disenchantment with local politicians and deficiencies within the infrastructure of the city. She felt it was important to do a weekly show that dealt with these issues, and put together *San Diego Week.* The show, like its producer, tackles the issues head-on.

Because KPBS-TV is short on staff, she serves in a multitude of roles. She is producer, executive producer, director of program production and one-third program manager as well as on-air personality. She's responsible for an annual budget of over a million dollars, and oversees all production work at KPBS.

At sixty-one, Penner shows no signs of slowing down. "I expect to be the oldest living woman on television ever," she says. Her mother, now eighty-seven, retired from her job in a Manhattan department store when she was eighty-five, and then only because the store's new owners no longer catered to her regular clientele. "As I've matured, I've come to recognize that a lot of me is modeled after my mother, a very independent woman who raised me all by herself," Penner explains. "I think a lot of what I do is done to satisfy my need to demonstrate that women can make it and make it independently. I love the fact that my mother not only appreciates but encourages me to do what I'm doing."

Penner grew up in New York City, crowded into a two-bedroom, one-bath apartment along with her mother, grandmother, two aunts, cousins and an uncle. Her family was blue-collar, salespeople and factory workers. In fact, she was the first in her large family to complete college and graduate work and use her education in a profession that benefited from her studies. "College was my bridge to what I'm now doing," she says. "The fact that I was able to pull myself out of a poor family and achieve some success in both teaching and broadcasting is my greatest accomplishment." Always a superachiever, writing was Penner's passion. "I started writing as soon as I could handle a writing instrument, and I started winning awards in elementary school," she says. "I wrote poetry, anything I could." She decided to be a journalist, and became the first female editor of her high school newspaper.

After graduating from Syracuse University with a Masters in English, she worked as a researcher for NBC's *Today* show in the early 1960's. She then moved to Hawaii with her husband, a physician and major in the Army. In Hawaii she had a stint working mornings on-air with KULA radio. Given her background, she had a difficult time pronouncing some of the Hawaiian words. Later, while working as chief speech writer on a candidate's campaign for the Senate, she met Margita White. The two became lifelong friends as White worked her way up through the Republican party, serving in the Goldwater, Nixon and Ford administrations, eventually becoming assistant press secretary and the first-ever female Federal Communications Commissioner.

Penner took time off when her husband was transferred back to the mainland to raise their two adopted children. In 1969, when Penner and her husband moved to San Diego, she was ready to go back to work. She heard that a new station was staffing, so she came to KPBS. "They only had one job available," she remembers. "It was a half-time job as a community relations director, which meant that, since the station was just a year-and-a-half old, they were going to start a membership campaign. They wanted a magazine begun, public relations in the community – all the tough stuff. That was my job, and that's how I started."

Her secret to success? "I'm very persistent," Penner smiles. "I will not be squelched. You can just imagine what it must have been like for a woman broadcaster in the later 1960's and early 1970's to move into a position of management. I'm a New Yorker, and as a New Yorker I think you see the world as a big contest, and I think I have a real need to win." After interviewing literally hundreds of successful people, she noticed that the most prevalent trait is that they believe in themselves. "You don't hear too many self-doubts from these people. They know what they're doing, they're organized, they knew what they wanted and they went after it in the same way I did."

Things have turned out well for Penner. She has the respect and admiration of both her peers and her viewers and enjoys renown in San Diego. She is now married for a second time, to Bill Snyder, a man she met while he was vacationing here. "I'm married again to a wonderful man. He's a typical Southerner except that his eyes have been opened up, and he doesn't attempt to control me," she says. Her husband now lives in San Diego and runs his Tennessee company via phone, fax and modem from his home.

Penner is in fantastic shape and keeps fit by doing aerobic walking on a treadmill five times a week. She also has a trainer who takes her and her husband through a weightlifting program that includes flexibility stretching three times a week. She plans to start open water swimming this summer. "I'm an absolute exercise nut," she says. "I get up early in the morning, at 6:00 a.m., and at the latest I am on that treadmill by 6:30 a.m. I work out for forty-five minutes to an hour."

With her fitness regimen and her past success with KPBS, Penner should have no problem reaching her goal of being the oldest living woman on television ever. She's already one of the most interesting.

Briefs

Johnny Downs

This long-time Coronado resident got his start in show business back in the 1920's. After roles in silent movies, he became a member of Hal Roach's Our Gang comedies. He returned to San Diego in the 1950's and became the popular host of his own children's show, *The Johnny Downs Show,* seen weekday afternoons on KOGO-TV Channel 10 through 1971.

Charlie Jones

A long-time resident of La Jolla and a popular sportscaster, Charlie Jones has been with NBC Sports for over twenty-seven years. He's had two Olympic assignments (including 1992 at Barcelona), has done NFL play-by-play for years and was fortunate enough to cover the sport that also happens to be his passion – golf.

Susan Peters

A San Diegan since the age of ten, Peters' family moved here from the Midwest when her father became general manager of KFMB-AM/FM radio. Peters graduated from Grossmont High School in 1974 and attended San Diego State University. She returned to the Midwest to begin her broadcasting career before coming back to San Diego to join the News Eight team as a co-anchor and reporter in 1991.

Sarah Purcell

The former KFMB-TV weather reporter and co-host of *SunUp San Diego* was raised in San Diego and graduated from UCSD before leaving her hometown for fame and fortune in Los Angeles. After hosting a Los Angeles morning talk show, she became internationally famous as part of the successful network program, *Real People.* She can currently be seen with Gary Collins weekday mornings on *The Home Show.* She told *Tuned-In Magazine* (July 17-23, 1982) that there was a time in her career when she had "just enough money for one meal of spaghetti."

But she adds that what's important is not how much money you have but "how much you believe in yourself that counts. What matters, in the final run, is that you believe you can do it. The fact is, we can do anything – absolutely anything – we believe we can do."

Laurie Singer

This San Diego native and Hoover High School graduate made television news history in the early 1970's by becoming the first woman sportscaster in the Western United States. She broke the all-male barrier in the locker room a couple of years later, when she entered the San Diego Mariners hockey team's locker room to conduct interviews. A sports fan since she was a kid, Singer would sneak in sports stories she wrote for her high school newspaper by signing them with a male pen name. She heard of a job opening for a production assistant at KFMB-TV, got the job and worked there in a number of capacities from 1969 to 1976. She has since gone on to become a successful on-air sports reporter and television news producer.

Bree Walker

Like many young girls, Bree Walker dreamed of becoming a glamorous television star when she grew up. But the odds were stacked against her, because people with physical deformities are rarely, if ever in the spotlight. Walker was born with a rare hereditary deformity of the feet and hands called syndactylism. It became painfully obvious to her at an early age that she was different. She was called names like "gimp" and "lobster claws" in school. But she refused to let anything get in the way of her dreams. Discovering writing and journalism in high school, she worked to become the editor of the school newspaper and yearbook. After studying journalism in college, she tried to get a job as a reporter but she found it difficult to make it without typing skills. She turned to radio and began to see some real success as a DJ in New York. Walker came to San Diego in the late 1970's and continued her broadcasting career at KPRI-FM. Still determined to make it in television, she went back to school at San Diego City College. Armed with her new knowledge, she made an audition tape and began introducing herself to local news directors, asking for a chance to show what she could do. Ron Mires of KGTV Channel 10 gave her that chance in 1980, and Walker began doing the local newscast during *Good Morning America.* She went on to become an award-winning local anchorwoman and popular television personality before leaving San Diego for New York and then Los Angeles. Bree Walker is a big believer in two little words: "You can!"

Media

Chapter 9: Radio

Sam Bass

Sue Delany

Art Good

Roger Hedgecock

Jeff & Jer

"Shotgun Tom" Kelly

Ken Kramer

Ernie Myers

Russ T. Nailz

Briefs

Bill Ballance · Don Howard
Hudson & Bauer
Harry "Happy Hare" Martin
J.D. Steyers · Nick Upton

Sam Bass
Radio Personality

Sam Bass found success when he stopped trying to emulate other on-air personalities he admired and started acting more like himself. He has consistently remained number one in the afternoon slot (10 a.m. to 3 p.m.) on KYXY since switching from mornings in 1986. He's like an old friend to his baby-boomer audience, spinning soft hits for over fifteen years. Being on-air comes very easily to Bass, who at times during his career didn't take his job seriously. Now, under the guidance of his program director, he is more focused. He tapes a condensed version of his show and listens to it on his way home every day, always looking for ways to improve.

Growing up in the 1950's in upstate New York, Bass had a fascination with tape recorders. He liked hearing his own voice and had a thing for microphones. His father, an engineer at an NBC affiliate and on the cutting edge of television at the time, discouraged him from pursuing a career in the often flaky entertainment business. His parents suggested he go to college and learn a "legit" profession such as law or medicine. Bass followed his parents' advice and attended Boston University in the late 1960's as a pre-med major, only to drop out and join the merchant marines in Vietnam. When he returned to college in the 1970's, his studies took a new direction. He decided to study film and broadcasting. Suddenly his grades improved, his attitude changed and he started making the Dean's List. Bass decided to become a film major because he'd been around film all his life, it was something he enjoyed working with – and he thought it would be a good way to meet girls. He noticed that the guys who got the girls either played guitar or carried 16mm cameras. While he still didn't get many girls, he did get a degree.

Getting into radio was an accident. After college, Bass found himself unemployed and living in a tiny town near the Canadian border. One day he scanned the job possibilities posted on the bulletin board at the laundromat and saw that the local radio station was looking for an announcer. "I called the guy up and he heard my voice. I was born with a broadcasting voice," Bass says, "and he hired me right over the telephone, even though I didn't know a darn thing about radio. He found that out in a hurry when he put me on the air." After botching his first fifteen minutes, Bass was pulled off the air and his brief radio career was over. "I had so much fun during those fifteen minutes," he remembers, "even though I was screwing up, I decided I'm going to give this a try." He had a brief stint in Pomona but, although he tried to be flexible, he was fired. "When they changed their format to Spanish, and I didn't speak Spanish, they said, 'Adios,'" he laughs. After working up and down the East Coast, he landed in 1977 at KYXY as the morning DJ broadcasting from the El Cortez Hotel. He's been at KYXY ever since.

Success to Sam Bass means doing well enough in radio so that he can provide for his family. He and his wife have three children. "We live in a nice part of town," he says. "My wife doesn't have to work, and I'm able to provide for my family." He has great admiration for Mike Ambrose, who is an ex-radio personality. "I have a lot of respect for Mike because he is so natural and fun to watch. He's been in San Diego a long time and has always done positive things for the community."

Although this ex-hippie has hit some lows in his career, he's now riding a wave of success that has him taking his career very seriously. He feels fortunate to be working for a station and a station owner who have stuck with him through the years.

Sue Delany
On-Air Personality

There's no mistaking that distinctive, super-sexy voice on San Diego radio — it's Sue Delany. A veteran of many years in local radio, ten with KGB, Delany's incredibly popular afternoon drive-time show has made her one of the most successful disc jockeys on-air anywhere. Although she's proud of her "lady rocker" image, there's much more to this complex woman than meets the eye. She's just as busy off the air as she is on, providing listeners with a warm, friendly voice to ease the drive home. She spends a great deal of her spare time backing causes

Sue Delany   *Photo by Martin Mann*

that she really believes in. Delany is an animal rights activist who supports the Humane Society and the Helen Woodward Animal Center.

Born in Dallas, Texas, Delany grew up in the Los Angeles area. Her mother, Pat Delany, is an actress; her father is a financial consultant. She was an excellent student and a cheerleader at Grant High School in the San Fernando Valley. She knew she wanted to become an entertainer, but she didn't want to follow in her mother's footsteps.

After attending Grossmont College for a year, Delany sent tapes to radio stations all over the country. She got her first break in radio with

KKXX in Bakersfield at the tender age of eighteen. In 1981, she came to 91X in San Diego but switched to KGB after two years. "KGB has always allowed me to be me," Delany says. "I love what I do. I have so much fun doing it, it doesn't even seem like a job."

Delany has never been one to hold back. When asked about her feelings on success, she offered the following advice: "If there is something you want to do, don't sit on your butt – go do it! Be confident and persistent and always be yourself. Don't be afraid to be human." Her advice to women interested in a career in radio: "Don't hesitate. There's plenty of room out there. Just keep your pride and don't sleep around to get it. I'm gonna die with my boots on!"

Although she's most taken with the rock stars whose music she plays during her show (especially Robert Plant and Led Zeppelin), Delany is also a big fan of Mel Gibson because "he's true to his wife and kids" and is, of course, one of Hollywood's sexiest leading men.

Art Good
Entrepreneur/On-Air Personality

To know who Art Good is, you first have to know what he does – and that's not easy. Art Good is not only a veteran radio personality and newsman with KIFM radio, he's also a concert promoter (Catalina Jazz Trax Festival), syndicated radio show host *(Jazz Trax)* and entrepreneur. "So much of what I do is connected to what I do," he says. "I go to concerts. That's work. I buy records. That's work. I go to a Padre game and, because I report on sports in the news, that's work, too."

Good has achieved success in all the fore-mentioned endeavors, but it hasn't been easy for the man originally from Marion, Indiana. He grew up listening to the sounds of Montovani, Lawrence Welk and the Top 30 Countdown on Fort Wayne's WOWO radio. His start came while attending college in Los Angeles in 1975. During the 1980's, he became a cult figure on San Diego's KIFM radio, always on the cutting edge of new, contemporary jazz. He was responsible for making jazz into something more than just bedtime music in the city. But gaining respect as a radio personality isn't a simple thing to do. Friends and family would ask him, "Haven't you had enough fun playing around in radio? Isn't it about time you got a real job?" Well, Good does have a real job. Several, in fact. And he's earned respect from the people who count most — his listeners.

When Good created his syndicated radio show, *Jazz Trax,* in 1985, he struggled in smaller markets, not really knowing what he was doing. "When starting out, you're so ignorant and so eager, filled with such lofty dreams..." Good muses, "you just know it's going to work, and so you keep driving forth." *Jazz Trax* showcases contemporary jazz artists with new music, old classics and insightful interviews with today's jazz stars. The show is now heard weekly on almost three dozen stations across the country, marked by pins on the map hanging in Good's personal studio. The state-of-the-art studio has a commanding view of a lake below. The show is just turning the corner, making money at last, and Good is planning to enter larger markets such as Chicago, New York and Los Angeles.

Art Good the concert promoter made the Catalina Island Jazz Trax Festival a reality in 1987 despite many roadblocks. His is a truly inspiring story of a man who refused to give up his dream. "In retrospect, when you realize how many obstacles that are in your way," Good says, "you're amazed that you were ever able to make it. It took someone like me, who was young and stupid with stars in my eyes, who really wanted to do it from the heart, to go in and accomplish [the Festival]." He resented being told it couldn't be done because he wasn't a concert promoter, even though he had learned the ropes by building up Humphrey's Concerts by the Bay. He didn't listen when they told him that Catalina didn't have enough hotel rooms or adequate transportation to the island to support an event of this magnitude. These were just a couple of the pitfalls he faced in making his vision come true. Before he booked his first act or sold his first ticket, Good went on the air boldly announcing the festival and the types of bands he planned to have.

He didn't get discouraged during the week before the festival, when tickets weren't selling. Instead, he was out scrambling to borrow money. He lived on a third of his salary for the nine months following the first festival, using the other two-thirds to pay back lenders. Things got worse. The night of his first festival, Earl Klugh's road manager demanded cash before allowing Klugh to go on stage. If the headliner didn't go on, the whole festival would collapse. Good would be broke and would probably have to leave the state. "I only had one thought in my mind that first night," he remembers. "To get Earl Klugh on stage." And he did! The festival is now in its sixth year and a smashing success, with plans to expand. Problems and frustrations still exist, but Good has learned to surround himself with talented people who free him from sweating the details and allow him to concentrate on what he does best – creating new ideas.

Not one to rest on his laurels, Good's future involves starting a jazz club in San Diego to support up-and-coming jazz acts in a setting that befits jazz lovers. Good feels that he is where he is for one reason: "It's very simple. It's because I never stop going after it. There is a basic talent that is there, and a good ear for what we're doing, but basically I just don't stop despite the many frustrations along the way."

Roger Hedgecock
Radio Talk Show Host

Roger Hedgecock, the well-known former mayor of San Diego, has been the host of the number one radio talk show in town for the past seven years. "Right now, I'm doing the very best job I possibly can, having as much fun as I can. Doing that has led to success in radio," he says. Hedgecock brings his listeners a wide range of fresh perspectives, entertaining insights, lively discussions and timely commentaries week-day mornings on KSDO 1130AM radio. Although he has achieved success in more than one field during a very interesting life, he has had to overcome some sizable obstacles along the way. "Perseverance is about the only virtue outside of having fun at what you do that I think you can pinpoint as common to everyone who has been a success in any field," he points out.

Growing up in the San Diego of the late 1950's and early 1960's was a magical experience for Hedgecock. He spent his youth enjoying every natural resource San Diego had to offer: land, sea and air. "I did everything I could to be part of the natural environment here," he remembers, "to be exposed to it." Two old-timers taught him to surf in Mission Beach, and he's been hooked on surfing ever since. In addition, he spent his days swimming and diving in the ocean, flying, hiking and camping in Mexico. "We'd go down to Baja and it was a wilderness down there," he says. "It was like being on the end of the earth. I mean, there was no one down there!"

The San Diego of thirty years ago was very different from the metropolis we now call America's Finest City. "When I was growing up here, it was wonderful. Imagine San Diego with half the population. It was a time when things seemed a lot simpler, a lot more one-dimensional. Sure, there were hardly any good restaurants back then, but who could afford good restaurants anyway? We lived simply and we enjoyed the simple pleasures of the San Diego lifestyle."

Hedgecock looked to his father as a source of inspiration and as a role model. His father taught him about perseverance and overcoming adversity. After growing up in the Depression, the elder Hedgecock went to World War II as an infantryman. He saw plenty of action, including the Battle of the Bulge. He returned home to marry and start a family, and that's when Roger entered the picture. About that time, the elder Hedgecock contracted polio. "In those days, it was nearly a death sentence, or at the very least confinement to a wheelchair," Hedgecock says. "They told my dad he'd never walk again, and he told them that he had to – he had a family and he had work to do. He got up and was able to walk out of sheer determination." Hedgecock's parents still live in the house on Point Loma where he grew up, and his father is still a fighter. "A couple years ago, he had two or three different kinds of cancer, and he beat them all through sheer determination, diet, exercise, keeping busy..." Hedgecock says proudly, "He's just an amazing role model for me."

Hedgecock attended St. Agnes Elementary School and St. Augustine High School. At St. Augustine in the early 1960's he managed a popular local rock band called The Esquires, booking them at high school dances. When he graduated to San Diego State University, he managed and provided bands for all the fraternity parties. He continued his education at UC Santa Barbara, graduating in 1968. While there, he became involved in student government and began bringing big-time acts to the school. He was on the cutting edge of the music scene at the time, promoting concerts with heavy hitters such as The Doors, Jimi Hendrix, Janis Joplin and Country Joe and the Fish. "I did a lot of promotion of top shows and, in that same period, I promoted the first outdoor rock concert in San Diego," Hedgecock remembers, "Mother's Day 1969 at the Aztec Bowl, featuring the Grateful Dead." The following July he promoted another big concert at Balboa Stadium, featuring Ten Years After. People still remember those shows.

In 1971, Hedgecock took his law degree from Hastings College of Law in San Francisco and became a successful, practicing attorney with Higgs, Fletcher & Mack. From 1974 to 1976, he was City Attorney of Del Mar. From 1977-1983, he served as a San Diego County Supervisor and was elected mayor of San Diego in 1983. What should have been the highlight of his professional career turned into his worst nightmare, and he eventually resigned from San Diego's highest office in 1985. Although he faced a long legal battle, one which cost him his job, damaged his reputation and put him deeply into debt, Hedgecock tackled his problems head-on and ultimately was able to clear his name.

"As much as you hate going through the tough times, and I've been through the toughest times you can imagine," Hedgecock says, "the fact is the wisdom and the poise and perspective I gained from it was priceless. I couldn't have purchased the kind of maturity I got from the combat I went through. I would be a very different person today if it hadn't been for those difficult times." He further explains, "You just have to smile and remain upbeat, keep your hand on the tiller and head through the stormy times with an eye towards the other end and better days ahead. And when you get there – and you will get there – you will appreciate those better days more than you ever did before."

The end of Hedgecock's political career actually opened up new doors for him. He was offered the opportunity to become a talk show host on local radio. The *Roger Hedgecock Show* debuted on KSDO Radio on January 20, 1986. The top-rated show has become an influential public forum for callers and listeners to discuss the issues facing the city. Although he admits that he didn't have a clue what he was doing at the start, Hedgecock was able to use his experience as a politician to give listeners a clearer understanding of how things work behind the scenes of local politics. Not one to pull punches, he tells it like it is. This style has brought his show notable ratings success over the past seven years, causing many to comment that he has more influence and is more effective as a talk show host than if he were mayor.

Hedgecock has met and interviewed some of San Diego's most successful and influential people on his show, and he has observed that they do in fact share common characteristics that play a part in their success. "There are two things that contribute to anybody's success," he says. "Number one, and the absolute foremost thing, is they are having fun at what they do. The fact that they're having fun makes what they're doing attractive to everyone around them, and they attract other successful people. They attract help in business and every other good thing that is attracted by somebody who enjoys what they're doing and does it well. Perseverance is the number two thing, because you're going to get all kinds of flack, all kinds of obstacles. You will undoubtedly get terribly discouraged no matter what you do. There's only one thing to do. Smile, put on a party hat and keep moving, because when you move through those things you're going to find tremendous success."

Hedgecock credits his wife, Cindy, with much of his success. Her support over their seventeen years of marriage has been invaluable. They have two sons, and Hedgecock proudly says that his number one goal in life is to be a good father to Jamie and Christopher. They all share a love of surfing and can be found riding the waves nearly every day.

Hedgecock is truly blessed. He faced adversity head-on and became a better person for it. He has a wonderful family, loves his job and is making a difference in the lives of his listeners and in the city.

Jeff and Jer
On-Air Personalities

Jeff Elliott and Jerry St. James, better known to most San Diegans as Jeff and Jer, are B-100's highly successful morning team. Their loyal listeners have kept them at the top of the ratings for the last four years. They arrived in town in March, 1988 and took a relatively unknown station, Y-95, and turned it into a top contender in the morning drive time (5:30 a.m. to 10:00 a.m.) ratings war. Their popularity was growing when they joined B-100 in the spring of 1990, and soon Jeff and Jer were household names.

In 1981, Jer, who'd had many partners, was sent out by his station to search the country for a suitable new partner. Nothing was happening for him until he met Jeff. They clicked immediately and became best friends almost as fast. They teamed up for the first time in Detroit, but when they went to Chicago things really started cooking. That's where they began the format they still use. They go on the air having lots of fun as themselves, not using any pre-recorded material. They're two easy-going guys who talk to each other and their audience. They're not announcers, and there's a naturalness in their friendship that comes across the airwaves, making them both believable and refreshingly funny. They open up their show in a way that gets everyone involved. It's a fresh approach that took San Diego by storm.

Jeff Elliott was born in Wooster, Ohio in 1955. For as long as he can remember, he wanted to be in radio. His teacher once told him he'd never be able to hold down a "real" job. Fortunately, he doesn't consider working in radio a "real" job. He got his first job in radio at a station in his hometown when he was fourteen. He went from there to graduate from Oral Roberts University with a degree in radio and broadcasting. He has two children, who live with his ex-wife in Ohio. He now lives in Alpine and is engaged to a woman he met while working at Y-95. They share not only similar careers but an equal commitment to God. Jeff enjoys participating in sports and working at his computer in his free time.

Jerry St. James was born in bustling Washington D.C. in 1951. He got his first job in radio while attending the University of Maryland as a speech and dramatic arts major. Since then he's worked in many cities with a variety of partners. Like Jeff, Jer was divorced and remarried since he came to San Diego. Divorce was extremely difficult and sad for both men, but they helped each other through it and became even closer as a result. Jer lives in Point Loma now, and is seriously working on a novel, a screenplay and a movie of the week. His early morning schedule allows him plenty of time to pursue his other career as a writer. He's a diligent goal-setter who not only has long-range goals but also sets daily goals. A good friend of Anthony Robbins, Jer has participated in Robbins' seminars and uses those goal-setting techniques to help shape his future.

Both Jeff and Jer would say that the secret to their success in radio is the result of hard work, enjoying what they do, mutual respect and being able to be themselves on-air. They've tried using pre-recorded skits, canned humor and character voices, but found that just being themselves was and is the magic ingredient to their achievement. Today, their show is filled with zany pranks, celebrity wake-up calls, answering-machine olympics, bonehead jeopardy and car phone dating games. They spend each morning chatting as only best friends can. Sure, they play music, but it's these two guys who make their show so popular.

This story would not be complete without a few words about Tommy Sablan, better known as "Little Tommy," the highly-rated morning show's producer. Although Jeff and Jer jokingly say "He does all the things we don't want to do," in reality, Sablan is an integral part of the team. He often puts in seven-day work-weeks and always manages to pull off the impossible for the show.

"Shotgun Tom" Kelly
Long-Time San Diego Radio and TV Personality

For as long as he can remember, Tom Irwin (aka Shotgun Tom Kelly) wanted to be a broadcaster. As a kid growing up in San Diego in the 1950's, he idolized local disc jockeys. His goal was to be the man on the radio in his hometown. He always wanted to be the one with the microphone in his hand. "When we played kickball, I'd pick up a hose and be the announcer," he says in his signature booming voice. At ten, he got to see his first disc jockey at work. "His name was Frank Thompson," Kelly remembers. "I saw him playing records on remote from Oscar's Drive-In. He had two turntables and a microphone, and I was just in awe." Kelly went home and built his own radio station in his bedroom, broadcasting a midnight show to five friends with a 100-milliwat transmitter. He wired his friend's radio so it received his signal at midnight without even having to be turned on. The problem was, the midnight show couldn't be turned off, either. When his buddy went away on vacation, his parents were perplexed at the late-night noises coming from his bedroom. They tried to turn it off and had no luck until they figured out the culprit was their neighbor, young Tom.

Shotgun Tom Kelly

Yearning to increase his audience, Kelly bought a twenty-five-watt transmitter and went on the air for thirty days, covering the La Mesa and Spring Valley area. He even traded air time for food at a local restaurant before being shut down by the FCC.

His first exposure to television came when he took a tour of the Johnny Downs kid show at what is now KGTV studios. That experience left an indelible impression. Since then, Kelly has delighted two generations of San Diegans and continues to entertain kids and adults alike. Today he's known as much for his bushy beard and ranger hat (he personally presented a smaller version of the hat to then-President Ronald Reagan) as he is for his patented on-air yell (something like "Breeeee-Owwwww!"). He's currently seen hosting KUSI-TV's *Kids Club* and heard locally on oldies station K-BEST-FM, as a voice on commercials and as a television announcer on stations as far away as Florida.

Kelly's start in legitimate radio began on a Junior Achievement show on KOGO while he was still in school. Captain Mike Ambrose of Channel 10 was his Junior Achievement advisor. He worked at KPRI-FM, spinning jazz records while attending Mt. Miguel High School. After that, he wanted to be a "Boss Jock" for KGB-FM, but even back then San Diego was considered a major market, and you didn't just become a big-time DJ without paying your dues. After getting his FCC license in 1960, Kelly worked in towns like Merced, Ventura and Bakersfield. During this time, his name evolved in typical radio fashion to become "Shotgun" Tom Kelly. "I remember walking into the station (KACY) for the first time and the guy says, 'Hello, Bobby.' I go, 'You've got the wrong guy. My name is Tom. Tom Irwin.' He says, 'No, you're Bobby.' I said, 'I'm the new guy you hired.' He said, 'If you're gonna work here, you're gonna be Bobby McCallister, because I have a jingle that fits Bobby McCallister.' I said okay but God, I hated that name." The DJ who went on before him started calling him Bobby "Shotgun" McCallister, and from there it developed into "Shotgun" Tom. Then a station manager in Bakersfield asked him to change his last name. He thought "Shotgun" Tom Carson sounded too much like Johnny Carson and "Shotgun" Tom Collins reminded him of a drink. Since he's Scot-Irish, he chose Kelly and the name stuck.

When he returned to San Diego, he did become a "Boss Jock" for KGB in the early 1970's. From there he moved to KCBQ for six years. KGTV Channel 10 hired him as the host of their new syndicated game show, *Words A-Poppin'*. "They held auditions for all the qualified people from all over town. They would call five people at a time. One of the guys they called in to audition was an old childhood hero of mine, Johnny Downs," Kelly remembers. "As soon as I saw Johnny there, I said, 'Hey, listen, you've got the show. I'm outta here.' He calmed me down and said, 'Relax, sit down. Here's a cup of coffee.' and he told me, 'You have just as much right to audition for this show as I do.' So I auditioned, and I got the job. I've never seen Johnny after that, and I've always wanted to thank him."

The show earned Kelly two local Emmys and endeared him to a whole generation of San Diego youngsters. In 1976, Kelly became B-100's morning guy, winning *Billboard Magazine's* top national DJ award in 1976. He was fired when the station switched to a more mellow format in 1980. "I try to be a positive person as much as possible," he says, while admitting that B-100's action hurt him. "Obviously, there are negatives that come into your life, but I try to aim for the positive things." He has since worked for KFMB and on weekend nights he broadcasts live from the Corvette Diner in Hillcrest. In July, 1992, he switched to K-BEST 95, playing oldies, while working as the popular host of KUSI-TV's *Kids Club.*

Kelly devotes much of his free time to making appearances around his hometown for a number of worthy causes. For the past eighteen years, he's co-hosted the local Muscular Dystrophy Telethon. He received the Jaycee's Top 10 Citizen of the Year award for two years in a row. He's such an icon in San Diego that he can't go anywhere without being recognized and hounded for autographs. Sometimes parents ask for two — one for themselves and one for their kids.

As a child, Kelly dreamed of meeting a president. With the help of local politician Duncan Hunter, his dream came true. Kelly had the chance to swap broadcasting stories with President Reagan in the Oval Office at the White House. "If you see something you want, overcome your fears and move forward and do the necessary things to make it happen," he says.

Kelly met his wife of over fifteen years while they both worked at a local radio station. He says that one of the pluses of Linda's being in radio is that she understands the radio lifestyle. They have two children, Nicholas (eight) and Melanie (fourteen).

Modern technology allows him to spend more time at home doing voice-overs in his own studio. He's the announcer for a television station in Florida. They fax him his lines, he records them and sends them back by express mail. He hopes to expand this part of his work to include voice-overs and commercials all over the country without ever having to leave his beloved hometown. It doesn't matter how far his voice travels, "Shotgun Tom" Kelly isn't going anywhere.

Ken Kramer
Talk Show Host/Producer

To the humble Ken Kramer, success is something he may never achieve. But anyone else looking at his track record as a radio and television personality over the past twenty years in San Diego would find it impossible not to call him successful. Kramer has won ten Golden Mike awards for his news, feature and documentary work. He received several San Diego Press Club awards and a coveted Emmy for television sports reporting. As the producer, writer and host of *About San Diego,* a show with fascinating facts about the history of the city, he's become a favorite local story-teller. He also hosts *The Ken Kramer Show,* a call-in talk show heard weeknights on KSDO. He's doing what he's wanted to do ever since he built a transmitter and hosted his first talk show as a kid. The only difference is that today he earns a comfortable living doing it.

Born in Pasadena in 1948, Kramer was always intrigued by the technical side of broadcasting. He worked as a dishwasher so that he could afford his first tape player in his early teens. His parents, who tolerated his interest in radio, were not pleased when they turned on their car radio only to hear their own son broadcasting from his bedroom on a homemade transmitter. His father quickly put an end to Kramer's pirate radio station. Undaunted, he focused on working in broadcasting. He never gave up, and ultimately earned an Associated Arts degree from Pasadena City College and his Bachelor of Science in Radio and Television from San Diego State University in 1974.

Kramer's real career in radio began while he was at SDSU. He spent thirteen years working full-time at KPBS, where he produced and hosted *About San Diego* while serving in a variety of other capacities. He found his job very satisfying and comfortable, but chose to leave to build the *About San Diego* show. He quit with no other job possibilities. "I let go of one trapeze, not sure the other one was out there," he says ruefully. "And with no net." He became his own sponsor of *About San Diego* for several months. "It got real lean for awhile," Kramer admits. "It got to the point where I had rental furniture in my apartment and I had to let it go. I had to have them pick it all up and take it away. For a time, I was sleeping on an air mattress underneath a trashbag in my apartment. It wasn't that I couldn't have called my mom or dad and gone home. They would have welcomed me with open arms. But I just felt something was about to happen any day. I already had *About San Diego* on the air here at KSDO, but essentially I was eating the cost of doing the show. The money I had saved for the project was going out, and I was getting very close to the zero mark." Just in the nick of time, Jack Merker, the program director at KSDO, offered him some news work, out of which came his talk show.

Kramer delivers his stories about San Diego's colorful past in a unique style that always keeps the audience guessing. His superb talent for storytelling makes this series both educational and entertaining. He knows his subjects intimately and has great admiration for San Diego's early movers and shakers, including Alonzo E. Horton. "They saw opportunities, they saw possibilities, and they didn't dwell on why it couldn't be done," Kramer says. Some of the characteristics of those early entrepreneurs can be found in today's successful people. "They didn't know the meaning of the word 'no.' They just pushed on," he continues. "They also were goal-oriented and determined to get there. Back then, because of the simplicity of life, you could just do it. That same kind of simplicity can exist in your mind today."

When Kramer starts talking about his future plan to produce *About America,* a national radio and television version of his local show, you get the feeling that when he says, "I will do it," he means it. Even if the national show doesn't pan out right away, he feels comfortable continuing with his talk show and adding to the over 1,000 *About San Diego* shows already in the can. For a man who once lived in a rented apartment with no furniture, today this proud homeowner is a success, whether he believes it or not.

Ernie Myers
Veteran Radio Personality

Whose warm and witty voice has helped you get to work every

Ernie Myers

morning for the past ten years? It's Ernie Myers, of course. Along with George Riley and Bruce Binkowski, he can be heard weekdays on KSDO-AM's top-rated morning news. A veteran of over thirty years in San Diego radio, Myers has had the talent and flexibility to be number one on three separate San Diego radio stations with three entirely different formats.

Myers was born in Glendale, California on November 25, 1931. As a kid, he was a horse fanatic, and today he still is. When he was very small, his dream was to become a jockey. However, it only took one look at his feet for trainers to say, "No way. You're going to grow into those." So he gave horseback riding lessons instead. In his high school yearbook, Myers wrote that he wanted to become a foreign correspondent like his childhood idol, Edward R. Murrow. He did eventually broadcast for Armed Forces Radio during the Korean war, serving as a news anchor and broadcasting from the old Tokyo Rose studio. Before that, he acted in a soap opera filmed in New York, NBC's *The Right to Happiness*. Myers' journey to San Diego radio came via Los Angeles. He and a friend were working at a little station in the San Fernando Valley when they heard that a station in San Diego was holding auditions for one opening only. Neither of them really wanted the job, but they decided to fly down in a private plane anyway. Neither Myers nor his friend had a private pilot's license, but the friend had been taking lessons. They took turns at the controls, landed successfully and Myers got the job. After two years at XTRA playing rock and roll, and nineteen years with KOGO playing middle-of-the-road music, he left to join KSDO, and he's been there ever since.

Myers enjoys what he does and takes an active role in his success. "When I was successful at 690 [XTRA], I picked all of my own music," he says, "and I'd slip in Tony Bennett along with the rock and roll. It worked. At KOGO, I programmed all of my own music and had complete control of my show when I was number one." He also worked as co-anchor for the noon news on KGTV Channel 10 and hosted *Dialing for Dollars* on both KGTV and KNSD Channel 39. He's a huge horseracing fan, and at one point in his career he left every Friday night to fly his Cessna 175 (he finally got his pilot's license and has over 1,400 hours in the air) to places like New Mexico to announce races. He now hosts one of horseracing's most popular national satellite TV broadcasts from Del Mar.

His other passion is golf, and he emceed the Andy Williams Open before Charlie Jones did. Weekdays he's on the radio until 9:00 a.m., then heads off to the golf course or home to tend to his prolific vegetable garden. Myers is single and has no children although, he points out, "I have a German shepherd." He hopes to remain on KSDO for years to come, turning down job offers from Los Angeles to stay in San Diego. Why leave when you're on top, work less than half a day and love what you do?

Russ T. Nailz
Comedian/DJ

The zany part of 91X-FM's morning team of Berger and Prescott is definitely Russ T. Nailz, who does over twenty character impersonations. The former Russell Stolnack (his father gave him the nickname) has also established himself as one of San Diego's most popular stand-up comedians. His Emmy Award-winning voice is behind the humorous radio ads for the *Union-Tribune's* classifieds section. Maybe you've seen him hosting KUSI-TV's *Kids Club* or delivering punchlines for charities. With his clever name and talent for making people laugh, he isn't easy to forget once you've caught his act or heard him on the radio. He loves the San Diego lifestyle and hopes he can carve out a long-lasting career here, much as "Shotgun Tom" Kelly, Rod Page and Bob Dale have done before him.

Born June 17, 1957 in Illinois, Nailz's family moved to San Diego when he was three. In fact, he celebrated his third birthday somewhere between Chicago and San Diego on Route 66. "All I remember is the birthday cake and the U-Haul," he laughs. He grew up in La Mesa, where his parents' divorce had a devastating effect on him (he was twelve). "The break-up of my parents stopped me and helped me get in touch with my serious side," Nailz says. "Those were bad times. Up until that point, there seemed to be something funny about everything."

A student at Helix High School, he graduated a year early, in 1974, after using his summers to pile up credits. Not really athletic, he had a tendency to put on weight, until he discovered bodybuilding. "It was a high in itself doing that, and watching my body go from blubbery boy to muscular man," he says. After high school he started a photography company that dealt with half-a-dozen radio stations in town and put on multimedia slide shows at local schools sponsored by B-100 FM and KPRI FM. The experience of getting up in front of teenagers got his feet wet and taught him how to handle a crowd before he took to the stage as a stand-up comedian. In 1985 he entered the Improv's first annual

Laugh-Off and placed third. The following year he was runner-up and he won the event in 1987, beating out more than eighty other comedians.

Nailz began working in radio ten years ago, after going down to the 91X studios in Tijuana to hang out with his high school pal, Chris Kay. The two of them were fooling around on the air and, as a result, were hired as the station's new morning team. Unfortunately for Kay, 91X almost immediately replaced him with sexy newcomer Sue Delany, while keeping Nailz on. He left briefly to go to Los Angeles to do stand-up full-time. "My wife and I tried to go there," he remembers. "I had a manager and an agent, auditions set up, but I just didn't like the L.A. rhythm." He wants to stay in San Diego to be close to his family while he continues building a career in his hometown. He accepts the challenge of constantly having to come up with new material in order to perform locally on a regular basis. "I'd like to think my career will snowball or at least stay the same size and keep rolling," he says.

Nailz has great sources for fresh material: his wife and two children. He met his wife when they were both working at the Improv in Pacific Beach. "She worked at a hospital during the day and part-time at the Improv to offset the depression that came from the hospital gig," he explains. He's glad he waited until he turned thirty to get married and have children. He wanted to be sure he was mature enough to handle the responsibilities and commitment of marriage so his children would never have to endure the hardship of divorce that he suffered.

His wife Marsha stays home and takes care of the kids, a difficult job which he fully understands and appreciates. He admits, "That's more work than I've ever done." Because of his schedule, he's able to take an active part in the children's upbringing, sometimes spending eight hours a day with them. Getting up at 4:30 a.m. leaves him feeling a bit tired, though. He's never become a morning person, even after all those years in morning radio. "Between coffee and napping, I'm able to make it through the day," he grins.

Many people think Russ T. Nailz never gets nervous when he's performing. He offers the following advice for getting up in front of a crowd, advice handed down to him from Larry Himmel: "Even if you're petrified, don't let it show. Don't let them know you're afraid. A lot of new comedians go onstage and the first thing out of their mouths is,

'Look, I'm not really good, I've never done this before, I'm probably gonna suck, but let's see what happens.'"

Seasoned pro though he is, making the crowd laugh is still one of Nailz's greatest thrills. "The payment for doing comedy is not the money," he says, "it's the laughs."

Briefs

Bill Ballance

After on-air success in the Midwest and Los Angeles, "Billo," as his listeners affectionately call him, settled in at KFMB in 1978. Over the past fifteen years, the late-night talk show host has built up quite a following as he discusses love, relationships and broken hearts in a way that only he can.

Don Howard

Once called "Mr. Music" and "The Dean of San Diego Radio," this San Diego native and graduate of San Diego High School became one of the area's most popular DJ's in the late 1940's and early 1950's. He had an instantly recognizable voice and the innate ability to sell practically anything over the airwaves. He spent forty years in local radio.

Hudson & Bauer

The morning team at KFMB-760 AM for over seventeen years, Mac Hudson and Joe Bauer have delighted their listeners with zany character voices, comedy routines, open phone lines and, of course, news, weather, traffic and sports (with help from Ted Leitner). The key to their on-air success and lasting friendship? "We don't take ourselves seriously, and we certainly don't take each other seriously, either," says Bauer. After working together for so many years, the two are able to make their show seem spontaneous, and for good reason — it is! "If you rehearse, then by the time you do it on the air it's lost the charm," Hudson explains. "We try to surprise each other, so we won't even tell each other what we're going to do — if we even know. A comedy bit is kind of like a piece of jazz music. You know how you're going to get in, know what some of the middle is and know what the punchline is, how you're going to get out. When Joe and I started working together, we had no idea what we were going to talk about, let alone how to get in, how to get out or where the middle was." In the very beginning,

Bauer did try to bring structure to their show, even scripting some parts. "We'd start and I would give the first line from the script and I'd look up and he'd be talking about something else," Bauer remembers. Hudson and Bauer don't need a script to keep their listeners in stitches. They instinctively know how to get the most out of each other. Just call them the jazzmen of morning comedy.

Harry "Happy Hare" Martin

He became a teen idol for many in San Diego in the mid-1950's while he was spinning rock 'n roll records for KCBQ AM. He once convinced the late Ritchie Valens to play his hits (La Bamba and Donna) for the students of Clairemont High School in the late 1950's. He's also famous for performing Cupeno Indian rain dances.

J.D. Steyers

With over two decades in local radio, all at one station (KFSD FM), Steyers is the current dean of San Diego radio. Over the years, his name has become synonymous with KFSD and classical music.

Nick Upton

A graduate of Escondido High School in 1973, Upton has been employed full-time by KSON radio for the past fifteen years. During that time, he has worked nearly every on-air shift for the country music station. Since 1980, he's been their music director, and he can also be heard middays and as the host of the highly-rated weekend Top 30 Countdown, which he also produces.

Media

Chapter 10: Print

Tom Blair

Nick Canepa

Jack Dunning

Mary Ellen Hamilton & Jody Sims

Harold Keen

Martin Kruming

Julie & David Mannis

George Varga

Briefs

Thomas K. Arnold · Hugh Baillie

Don Bauder · Simon Casady

James S. Copley

Eileen Jackson · Clint McKinnon

Neil Morgan · Willie Morrow · Jack Murphy

Sean Patrick Reily · E.W. Scripps

Ed & Gloria Self · Lionel Van Deerlin

Tom Blair
Columnist

For over a decade, thousands of San Diegans have been unable to start the day without first turning to Tom Blair's column. Filled with bits of information, news, gossip and humorous anecdotes about the people of San Diego, his column generally reflects the lighter side of the city. "People do tell me they start the day with my column," says Blair, "and it gives me a great sense of fulfillment. It's quite a kick!"

For the past five years, Blair's mornings began with his two daily radio reports. But the recession and budget cuts forced the station to "ax just about everybody who talked," including him. He and other staffers awaited the dreaded pink slip as the *San Diego Union* and *Tribune* newspapers prepared to merge. "I didn't know until the last minute whether I was going to continue writing a column five days a week," he says. Fortunately, he still writes his popular city items column for the new paper. And he was able to realize a musical dream by joining the Big Band Jazz Machine as lead vocalist.

Born July 22, 1946 into an upper-middle-class family in Adrian, Michigan, Blair's father was a family doctor and his mother stayed at home to raise their children. When Blair was eight, his father died and his mother, whose background was in music, went to work entertaining as a singer and pianist. A year later, she decided that just wasn't going to work. "A year after my father died," Blair remembers, "my mother showed some steel. She sold the house, bought a station wagon, loaded the kids into the new car and drove 3,000 miles across country to start a new life." She landed in La Jolla, where she settled with the three kids, got a job as a secretary and started over.

Blair always expected to follow in his father's footsteps and become a doctor, but he'd inherited his mother's musical bent, and also considered a singing career. And there was a third option. "I was always the kid with the big mouth," he says. "And I thought I was smarter and wittier than everybody else. So writing seemed a way to prove that."

His mother instilled in him a work ethic that began early. "I guess I've had a job, in some form or another, since I was twelve," Blair says. "Whether it was delivering telegrams on my bike or selling *Tribunes* on a street corner or washing beakers and test tubes at Scripps Clinic, I was always doing something." While attending San Diego State University as a journalism major, he put money in his jeans as a part-time grocery clerk and singer with a rock band. Hearing the band one night, an agent from Los Angeles offered to represent Blair. With his journalism degree in his back pocket, he went off to L.A. to conquer the world of show business. By night, he sang with a number of different bands and combos. By day he worked in the back of a Burbank McDonald's, mixing shakes and serving up hamburgers. Eight months later, he decided to pack it in and head back home. "I just knew I didn't have the one thing it takes to really hit big in that business – an all-consuming passion to make it," he says.

Writing was his first love, and he decided to make it a career. "Back then," he quips, "it was a fairly honorable profession." His first job was as a typesetter for the *La Jolla Light* in 1972 at the meager wage of $1.50 an hour. Three months later, he was tapped for the Copley Training Program, winning a spot at the *Evening Tribune* and a chance to prove himself. After working as a general assignment reporter and assistant city columnist for the *Tribune,* he started his own column for the *Union* in 1982.

About succeeding, Blair says, "I'm not sure that I know even after all these years what success means to me. I used to think success meant not having to worry about money and being known to people. Fame and fortune. I suppose I have something like fame here. My name is fairly well known in San Diego. I don't have fortune, but then I didn't choose a profession where fortune comes fast. One out of two isn't so bad." He's quick to add that his children, Amy and Tom III, and his marriage of twenty years to Wendy are his greatest accomplishments. His greatest fear is "That one day I'll wake up and people will say to me, 'You've fooled us long enough. You're not a columnist, you never were a columnist and nobody's reading your column!'" So he works harder, keeping the pressure on himself.

"I've always chosen things that required me to prove myself over and over. Meet this deadline. Do live radio and have two deadlines a day. Do a column, have five deadlines a week. Stand in front of a big band and, if you do it right, everybody's applauding. Screw it up, they're all looking straight at you. I suppose I'm always putting myself on the spot," he admits. When the stress level gets too high, Blair says he wants to chuck it all, become a professional bum on an island somewhere, singing when he wants, playing a bit of bridge and writing song lyrics. Right, his wife tells him. He'd go crazy in a week.

Nick Canepa
Sports Columnist

Ever since Nick Canepa was a senior in high school, he knew he wanted to write sports for the paper he used to sell as a kid growing up in San Diego. Now, after two decades writing for the *Union-Tribune,* he has his own sports column, and he couldn't be happier. "I've often wondered what I'd do if I didn't do this," he says. "I really can't come up with any answers. Manual labor would be out. The only job I've ever had is working for this paper." Always a sports fanatic, Canepa has been able to attend the Olympics, Super Bowls, World Series and All Star games — all in the line of duty. He's also had the opportunity to work with one of his childhood idols, the late Jack Murphy, and meet another, the legendary Red Smith. "I'm doing what I always wanted to do — and in my home town. I don't know how you can do better than that," he says.

Nick is a second-generation native San Diegan whose grandfather came here from Italy in 1906. His father, like many who lived in the Little Italy section of San Diego at the time, was a commercial fisherman. Born September 5, 1946, Canepa remembers growing up in a much different San Diego than we live in today. Back then, going to Escondido was an all-day affair, the El Cortez Hotel was the tallest building downtown and dirt roads and farmland lay where the *Union-Tribune* building now sits.

Growing up, Canepa rarely strayed from his part of town, and sports filled his days. They played football on the grass next to the Civic Center on Pacific Highway and watched baseball at Lane Field near the waterfront. "When I was really little," he remembers, "like six or seven,

I started selling papers. I lived on India Street in the Italian district. There used to be a Safeway there, and one of the guys used to bring *Evening Tribune* green sheets by and I started selling them that way." Later, he and his brother would go downtown to get the green sheets, making four cents profit on each paper they sold. They worked their way back home, sometimes stopping in bars to sell papers. "We used to get in fights every day. Every day. A lot of it was territorial. There would be times when guys would be cutting us out, taking our customers. We used to flatten guys' tires on their bikes and wrap up their chains – anything to slow them down," Canepa says.

He remembers how in high school he wasn't sure what he wanted to do until he picked up a copy of a book by Red Smith. It was the best piece of sports writing he'd ever read, and the catalyst that turned his thoughts towards journalism. While attending Mesa College and San Diego State University, he was hired as a copy kid in 1971. At first he did prep sports on Friday nights, then moved on to the action line column designed to help with consumer problems and was finally hired into the Copley Training Program. "I worked my way up from a prep writer to Aztecs writer to Clippers writer to Chargers writer, and then I was given the break of writing the column in 1984," Canepa says proudly. He earned that column.

At the 1980 Super Bowl in Los Angeles, he met Red Smith, the man who all unknowingly got him started. "A bunch of us had gone to the media party on Friday night and I walked into the hospitality room," he remembers. "It must have been eleven o'clock at night, and Jack Murphy was sitting there with Red Smith. Jack waved me over and introduced me. [We] sat and talked for over two hours."

"Journalism isn't always glamorous," Canepa says. He's often had to deal with hostile athletes in sweaty locker rooms for limited pay. "Our business has changed dramatically, and I'm not saying it's for the better," he admits. "I kind of long for the days of the smoke-filled newsrooms and the hard-drinking, cigar-chewing, cigarette-smoking guys who used to scream and holler." He vividly remembers the PSA plane crash that earned the staff a Pulitzer for its intense and sensitive coverage. "I was working the desk that morning, and we found out at about 8:30 a.m. that Don Coryell was being hired as head coach of the Chargers, which is a pretty big story here," he says. "A half hour later, the plane goes down. This place just went nuts. It just emptied, and I went down to the news side to help out. That was a news day!"

Canepa loves sports, but he keeps them in perspective. "Sports are important as entertainment and escape or as a conversation-maker, but in the scheme of things it means absolutely nothing," he admits. He's more concerned with the educational system and how his son will fare while attending a state college. He's also more interested in what's happened to his hometown. "This is a city that is still trying to find an identity, because everything happened to it so quickly," he says. "It's like all of a sudden you woke up tomorrow and you were seven feet tall, and you hadn't grown into your body yet. You're gangly and stumbling. I think that's what has happened to this city."

Jack Dunning
Publisher/Author/Entrepreneur

Jack Dunning always wanted to start a business. He tried several small ventures before he founded *ComputorEdge* magazine in 1983, along with partner Edward Stopper. They built a successful business by combining computer knowledge and publishing to help educate people in a rapidly changing field. Since the magazine's inception, tens of thousands of San Diegans have learned to overcome their fear of computers with Dunning's non-threatening explanations. The publication is free, and addictive. As an author and publisher of computer books, Dunning has reached readers all over the country by focusing on the human side of computers. The topics covered in his nearly twenty reader-friendly titles range from "How to Make Money With Computers" to "How to Understand and Buy Computers." His business continues to thrive because he provides readers with clear and simple information about all aspects of computing. And, as more and more people buy and use computers in their homes and offices, his potential readership gets larger and larger.

Dunning, who turns forty-two this year, first came to San Diego as a fourth grader. The son of a Navy captain, he followed in his father's footsteps and graduated from the Naval Academy in Annapolis, Maryland, with a degree in physics. He served in the military for seven years, including a tour in Vietnam. Deciding not to become career Navy, he went to work as a program manager for a local defense electronics firm, attending night school to earn his MBA. He purchased his first computer and printer through the mail in the early 1980's for $5,000 and taught himself how to use it. He realized that there was no good way to market computer products or services available in San Diego, and decided to start a trader-type computer magazine.

With the help of Ed Stopper, Dunning designed a magazine modeled loosely after *The Reader,* where Stopper worked at the time. They liked the idea of free distribution and free classifieds, and incorporated those ideas into their publication. The magazine was originally called *The Byte Buyer,* but was changed because of possible copyright problems. "We started from the ground up," Dunning remembers. "As far as we know, when we were starting this there was no other computer magazine that was doing this kind of thing. Since it wasn't a proven concept at the time, we had to operate on the faith that we were doing the right thing." In the beginning, they worked late into the night, using Dunning's living room as their office. Dunning risked everything he had to make it work, including his life savings and his house. "I think part of what happens when you're first starting a business is that you don't realize how big the risk is," he says. "I look back on it and say, 'God, I was crazy. I could have lost everything!'"

One of the common themes found among successful entrepreneurs is a supportive spouse. Dunning's wife agreed that the magazine was a good idea, "One of the few I'd had," he laughs, and felt it was worth pursuing. In the beginning, the business didn't make enough for him to draw a salary, so the family made sacrifices and tightened their belts. "You last longer with the same clothes. And you use discount coupons," Dunning says. "You always buy the cheapest cut of meat and you strictly budget everything you do. You just can't think about all the terrible things that could happen. When you start a business, you have one major goal – to survive. You must have absolute stupid faith in what you're doing, a goal and a plan. What you do is work towards that goal following the plan, focus and continually move in that direction."

As the money began to run out, business started to pick up. Readership increased and the magazine began to catch on. Dunning was able to move into a 900-square-foot office and hire a full-time editor. Today, the company has over thirty employees and occupies an entire floor. He formed Computer Publishing Enterprises to publish computer books, and the business is thriving despite some growing pains.

Dunning tends to want to move on once a business is functional, and has dabbled in advertising and graphics. He told his wife about an idea he had for a new business. "She gave me this apprehensive look and said, 'I know you. You'll do it!' Dunning grins, "and that's what she's always been afraid of."

Mary Ellen Hamilton & Jody Sims
Publishers

Mary Ellen Hamilton and Jody Sims are partners in Community Publishers, Inc., created expressly to help other women business owners like themselves excel. They publish a Yellow Pages for women-owned companies and services as well as the *Women's Times,* a free monthly newspaper with a circulation of over 35,000. By showcasing women's success stories, they hope to build their readers' self-esteem.

They built their own business on a shoestring, and became two of San Diego's best success stories as well as women role models. They started out in 1989 as a two-person home-based business, with the idea of publishing an annual directory for women. "We realized this was a business you could start with very little money. You need a computer and a salesperson. You collect the money and then you print the book. It wasn't until a year later that we realized you really need some capital for this to work well," Sims says.

It took them three years of sixty to seventy-hour weeks to get their business going. At times, they lived hand-to-mouth, feeding their company before feeding themselves. It was difficult, but fun and exciting, too. Today, they work in an office in Mission Hills with a complete staff to help them handle what has become an enormous workload.

Both Hamilton and Sims know the horror stories about failed partnerships, but their complimentary talents and personalities proved to be the perfect ingredients for a successful business. Sims is a graphic artist and does all the design work. She's the detail person who handles the day-to-day work flow. Hamilton is the big-picture person, the people person who loves to sell. Hamilton says, "We both share the ability to see something and take it and run with it... to take action. We also share a passion for what we're doing. I wouldn't have had the courage or the vision on my own to do it." Sims adds, "I was smart enough to know that I don't have the rapport with people that Mary Ellen does, and I wouldn't have been able to keep a staff. I knew from the beginning I would have to find the right partner."

Growing up wasn't easy for Jody Sims. Early on she noticed the inequities between the sexes right at home. Her childhood was troubled, and from her senior year in high school through her early twenties she showed a self-destructiveness that eventually had her standing on a bridge contemplating suicide. She got the help she needed to put her life back on track, and today she's totally positive. When things get crazy at the office, she says, "They're not going to put us in jail and we're not going to die from this." Before starting Community Publishing Inc., she worked in banking, sold knives door-to-door and drove a delivery truck. She always earned extra money doing freelance art on the side, but didn't make it a career choice until a back injury made her quit the delivery job. She realized that desktop publishing was the wave of the future and hired a tutor from UCSD, rented a computer and taught herself computer graphics. "I'm doing what I love and have a passion for," she says. "It's the ultimate, because I'm doing what I always wanted to do right now."

Mary Ellen Hamilton comes from a traditional family. She sensed at a young age that she'd entered a man's world. Her father was a fireman and her mother stayed at home, raising seven children — five of them boys. Like her partner, she noticed the inequities between men and women, but she played the traditional role and dropped out of college to marry, stay at home and raise two children. She took several part-time jobs during her marriage, but it wasn't until after the fourteen-year union ended that she went to work full-time. At first she took conventional women's secretarial jobs, but eventually branched out into sales at Cash Lewis Co. Inc., selling computers and fax machines. She'd finally found her niche.

Hamilton excelled at sales, working her way up to branch manager, earning over $50,000 a year. Taking up with Sims was a real leap of faith. She says, "I believe in taking risks only if you've really taken a good look at what you can do and there is an unmet need that you can fill."

Hamilton and Sims are two gutsy women who have met a real need. Their advice is to listen to others who have succeeded in business before. Go to classes on marketing, business planning and decision-making – these are offered by the Small Business Administration at a relatively low cost. Learn how to do what you're doing because, once you do, nothing can stop you. "When you make it, after taking all the necessary little steps along the way and you eventually reach your goals, it's really satisfying," says Sims. "I've never been happier."

Harold Keen
Newsman

In almost half a century of covering San Diego news, Harold Keen was one of the town's most respected media personalities. Often referred to as "the dean of San Diego newsmen," Keen kept a hand in almost every aspect of the news business, working at least two and sometimes as many as five jobs at the same time. Over the years, he wrote a monthly column for *San Diego Magazine* and served as a correspondent for the *Los Angeles Times* as well as *Newsweek, Life* and *Time* magazines. In addition, he appeared weekly on KPBS-TV's *Telepulse,* a news talk show, and *Keen's People,* a thirty-minute interview show. He also appeared regularly as the station's editorial director. Keen received several Golden Mike awards for best television commentary and was such a well-known presence in town that he literally became a San Diego institution.

Keen was born in New York, lived in Chicago as a child and came to California in 1926, where he attended UCLA and wrote for the campus newspaper. He graduated with a degree in English during the Depression and found it next to impossible to find a job in journalism. He took a position as a social worker for almost two years before he was able to work in his chosen profession. He sent out over forty letters to newspapers all over Southern California, and the only reply he received was from *The San Diego Sun,* where he promptly went to work. When the *Sun* folded in 1939, he went over to the *San Diego Tribune,* where he worked as a reporter for eleven years. In the early 1940's, Keen was asked if he could handle a daily local radio news program in addition to his writing assignments. He not only pioneered radio news in San Diego, in 1949 he began a daily television program called *People in the News.*

His roots firmly in the Depression years, Keen was driven to work more out of insecurity than economic need. But his years of working extremely long hours eventually caught up with him. After two heart attacks, he was forced to cut down to eleven hour days, seven days a week. Still, although he had opportunities to take his success to the national level, Keen chose to stay in San Diego. His life here meant more to him than national recognition.

Martin Kruming
Lawyer/Editor

Martin Kruming sees success as having fun at what you're doing and finding calmness within yourself. It's hard to imagine this over-achiever – editor of the *San Diego Daily Transcript,* attorney, teacher, lecturer and devoted family man – finding inner calm, much less having time left over for fun. "I think the number one philosophy for success is having fun at whatever you're doing," he emphasizes. "Success to me is first enjoying what you do and being able to keep your life in perspective."

Born in New York City in 1943, Kruming's early idols were Yankees ballplayers, particularly the Bronx Bombers, Mickey Mantle and Roger Maris. He was crazy about baseball, but he dreamed of becoming a journalist. To that end, he went to the University of North Carolina at Chapel Hill. "I was not a super student," he admits. "School didn't come easy for me." What got him through was a work ethic instilled in him by his parents and an ability to put his nose to the grindstone. After graduation, he worked at a number of jobs in his chosen field, including a stint as a writer for Associated Press, before deciding to become a lawyer. He moved to San Diego in 1973 to attend Western State Law School. Kruming is very proud that he persevered and became a practicing lawyer. "I think anything is possible," he says. "The fear many times is just thinking about something and creating a picture of a mountain too huge to overcome, whatever it might be. Always try taking a little bit at a time. Set a direction and do what you say you're going to do."

Kruming is definitely a doer. After four years of practicing law in San Diego, an opportunity arose for him to get back into the newspaper business in a management position. He jumped at the chance to become editor of the *Transcript* in September of 1984. Under his direction, it has become San Diego's best source for business and legal news. In addition to his duties with the paper, Kruming still gives legal advice to writers and authors. "I enjoy working with writers because I think I understand their problems," he says.

He has taught at the college level for sixteen years and is currently an instructor in writing and public relations at National University. He stays actively involved in the community he serves, keeping tabs on community and business groups. Yet he always finds the time to participate in the lives of his children, coaching Little League and soccer games and going to Cub Scout meetings. "One of my problems is trying to juggle too many balls in the air," Kruming admits. "Something had to give, and at different times it was journalism and law. I don't think you can be all things. You have to carve out some niches and say what are my strengths and what are my weaknesses... and build on those."

Because his children are seven and thirteen, Kruming is tremendously concerned with what the future holds for today's youth. He suggests that many of today's problems with kids stem from a breakdown in the family structure and a lack of direction in a lot of young people. "If we care about kids, we can't simply pay them lip service," he emphasizes. "There are some pretty dark clouds on the horizon unless we can clean up our neighborhoods."

He's both cautious and optimistic about San Diego's future. "I think you have to look around and say what's good and how can we work together as groups of people and go forward with some sort of vision. San Diego, while it's had its share of problems — economic and otherwise — is still a pretty decent place to live."

Kruming says what really turns him on are people who have good ideas and the ability to turn those good thoughts into reality. And Martin Kruming just happens to be that kind of person.

Julie & David Mannis
Publishers

It used to be that if you wanted to know the latest goings-on in your neighborhood, you picked up the party line. Today, you pick up one of two successful San Diego community newspapers – the *Beach and Bay Press* or the *Peninsula Beacon*. Both are published by the high-powered man-and-wife team of Julie and David Mannis. "We publish more news about the communities we cover than any other publication in the world," Julie says. That's been their goal from the beginning, and they've carved out a special niche since they began publishing the *Beach and Bay Press.* "David and I started the paper in 1988, literally doing everything – building it, selling it, doing the accounting and even delivering it," she continues. Between them, they can handle any job that has to be done to get the papers out. Now they have over twenty-five dedicated, full-time employees and a combined press run of over 45,000.

David Mannis, a native San Diegan, met Julie when he was publishing his own successful paper in El Centro. Julie worked in sales for that paper, despite her extensive background in graphic arts. David is more business-oriented, spending much of his time out of the office and in the public eye. Julie's time is spent in the office, working with the employees, handling production, accounting and the classified section. The two have developed a good balance, splitting responsibilities in half. "People still consider me the wife and say, 'Oh, you work with your husband,'" Julie says ruefully. The fact is, each brings separate and necessary talents to the business.

A whole day can go by with neither seeing or talking to the other, each absorbed in their own project. Still, they spend more hours together than most married couples. Julie comments that, "Our personal life is the business. We eat, sleep and live the business." They can't even escape when off in exotic places. Once, vacationing in the Caribbean, David insisted on visiting the local newspaper offices. But it's not all work and no play. They enjoy traveling together, working around the house and both are looking forward to having children. But for right now, the business is their baby – and boy, is it growing fast!

The Mannises' weekly community newspapers cover Pacific Beach, Mission Beach, Ocean Beach and Point Loma. They take great pride in providing information about the issues and concerns of the communities they serve. Their purpose is to be the main source of information for these areas. And they truly care about what they're doing. Julie says, "I sit down and read our papers on the weekends and find myself saying, 'This reads very well.' I can objectively say that I learn a lot about the communities, and that gives me a great deal of satisfaction."

Much of their success is a credit to their knowledge of publishing, their ability to wear many hats and their positive and optimistic approach to business. Julie points out, "There are always going to be stumbling blocks along the way. Just look at it as a challenge and, rather than a negative, turn it into a positive. Say, 'What good can come of it?'"

They listen to their own advice. While other papers are struggling through tough economic times, the Mannises see the recession as a chance to emphasize their strengths. Instead of going after a few giant accounts, they survive on many small accounts, shifting their emphasis to volume. They believe they'll be even stronger heading into better economic times. The future looks bright for this dynamic husband-and-wife publishing team.

George Varga
Music Critic

George Varga is a success because he's doing what he loves most – writing about music. "If success is judged by monetary gain, then I wouldn't qualify. But that's not the motivation to do what I do," he says. Varga firmly believes in the adage, "If you find something you love, you will never have to work a day in your life."

Although his job with the *San Diego Union-Tribune* has allowed Varga to attend hundreds of concerts and interview some of the biggest stars in music, it's not as glamorous as it seems. The way he goes to a concert involves a lot of hard work. Once there, he's constantly taking notes and checking his watch to make sure he can meet his deadline. Even before the show starts, setting up interviews can take months of phone calls and letter-writing. His philosophy about getting an interview applies to getting anything you want in life: "If you really want something, you just pursue it and pursue it and don't give up until you get it."

Varga was born in Louisiana but spent his early years growing up in Frankfurt, Germany, where his father was stationed in the Air Force. When they returned to the States, they were stationed in San Bernardino. This was a difficult time for Varga, who suffered from culture shock and found it hard to fit in. His thick German/Hungarian accent was a source of amusement to his peers, who called him derisive names like *Kraut.* He vowed to graduate early from high school and move back to Germany, and he did.

At an early age, Varga began writing, especially about music. He began playing drums at twelve. In 1972, just before his sixteenth birthday, he got his first paying job writing record reviews for an American magazine in Germany, earning him a whopping five dollars per article. He also served as editor of his high school paper and says, "By the time I graduated from high school, I had over two years experience in writing and getting paid for it." He has no regrets about choosing writing over drumming as a career. He jokes, "I can actually impress somebody [on the drums] for about three minutes." He backs his belief that you learn by doing. He wrote over 226 stories in one year. "An insane amount," he admits. Varga attended City College and San Diego State University, but came to the realization after taking a variety of courses "That I already had a feel for what I wanted to do," and that he didn't belong in college. "It's not that I feel I wouldn't have benefited from earning a degree. It's simply that I was learning more through the doing of it." After freelancing for both the *Reader* and the *Union*, Varga set about proving himself worthy of a staff position at the *Union*. He did that by writing as well and as much as he could. It paid off. At the age of twenty-six, he became a full-time writer covering the music scene for the *San Diego Union.*

After interviewing literally hundreds of successful people in the music field, Varga feels there are certain traits they all have in common.

One is their incredible belief in themselves and what they are doing. Despite the tremendous odds against making it in the music business, they would never think of doing anything else, and they dedicate their entire lives to making their vision a reality. "There are plenty of successful people with minimal talent, and there are plenty of incredibly talented people with limited success. To be successful you have to have your own unique vision and a distinctiveness to what you do," Varga says.

Briefs

Thomas K. Arnold

In his lengthy and successful journalism career in San Diego, Arnold profiled everybody who is anybody. His work can be found in *San Diego Magazine, San Diego Executive Magazine* and the *Reader.*

Hugh Baillie

Regarded as one of the world's top newsmen, his career spanned over a half a century. He interviewed some of the most influential people of his era — Hitler, Mussolini, Eisenhower and FDR, to name a few. A former president and chairman of United Press International (UPI), he came to La Jolla on vacation in the early 1930's and built a home there in 1940. He died in March, 1966.

Don Bauder

Coming to San Diego from the Cleveland bureau of *Business Week Magazine* in 1973, this distinguished financial analyst is financial editor of the *San Diego Union* (now the *Union-Tribune).* He wrote the best-seller *Captain Money and the Golden Girl,* published in 1985. It deals with the J. David Dominelli saga in San Diego. Bauder has received the Harold Keen Award for Journalism and the Press Club award as print journalist of the year.

Simon Casady

Known as "Cyanide Si" during his days as a reporter, editor and publisher, Casady was never afraid to speak his mind — and often did in the pages of his paper, *The El Cajon Valley News* (now the *Daily Californian).* He wrote such steamy anti-establishment editorials that the FBI began keeping a file on him which he obtained through the Freedom of Information Act of 1974 after a two-and-a-half year battle. The feisty Casady put his money where his mouth was when the long-time Democrat ran for mayor in 1979 at the age of seventy-one. He lost to Pete Wilson, but not without a good fight.

James S. Copley (1916-1973)

After his parents died when he was just four years old, James was adopted by the Copley family. His tycoon father, Colonel Ira C. Copley, sent him to the best schools. After graduating from Yale, he began an apprenticeship in the newspaper business. Copley spent several years learning reporting, advertising and circulation. During World War II he served in the Navy, achieving the rank of Captain. When the Colonel died in 1947, Copley inherited one of the world's largest privately-held newspaper groups. As the chief executive officer, he successfully ran four dozen papers in Illinois and California, including the *San Diego Union* and the *San Diego Evening Tribune,* until his death at the age of 57 on October 6, 1973. During his years as head of Copley newspapers, the former Mr. San Diego (1958) gave generously to the arts and hospitals, medical centers, libraries, the zoo and other worthy causes. This philanthropic trend has continued since his wife, Helen H. Copley, took over following his death.

Eileen Jackson

One of San Diego's most respected journalists, Eileen Jackson has been the city's premier society reporter for more than half a century. She knows San Diego and its people better than anybody, and San Diegans have come to depend on her for all the news of social importance. The accomplished columnist has written for several San Diego papers, including the *San Diego Sun,* the *San Diego Daily Journal,* the *San Diego Chronicle* and the *Union* and *Tribune.* She began her career while still in her teens. At San Diego High School, she became the first female editor of the school paper. Over the course of her distinguished career, the charming Jackson has interviewed royalty, many First Ladies and has covered six national conventions. In 1992, Jackson and her husband of sixty years (renowned painter Everett Gee Jackson) were honored as Mr. and Mrs. San Diego. This marked the first time a woman has been honored in the history of the award.

Clint McKinnon

The long-time Pacific Beach resident first came to San Diego in 1918. Even before he reached his teens he was selling newspapers — the *San Diego Union* in the morning and the *Sun* in the afternoon. He continued in the newspaper business, successfully owning papers in Brawley and Los Angeles before starting the *San Diego Journal* in 1944. The *Journal* featured such noted local columnists as Neil Morgan, Eileen Jackson and Lionel Van Deerlin. McKinnon also started KCBQ radio, represented San Diego for two terms as a Congressman and owned several other local papers, including the *La Jolla Light.*

Neil Morgan

Journalist, author and editor, Neil Morgan is one of San Diego's best-known writers. A reporter's reporter, he has been honored with numerous awards during his over-forty years of daily columns and innumerable magazine articles. A columnist with the *Tribune* since 1950, his column now appears three times weekly on page A-2 of the *Union-Tribune.* He is also the author of eleven books, many promoting San Diego and the West Coast, including *Westward Tilt, The California Syndrome, My San Diego* and Time-Life's *The Pacific States.* He was named associate editor of the *Tribune* in 1977 and served as the editor of the afternoon paper from 1981 to 1992. The long-time La Jolla resident has brought both recognition and acclaim to San Diego through his writing and has shown the world that "there is more to brag about in San Diego than the climate." His many honors include both the Ernie Pyle and Bill Corum Memorial Awards, and he is also a two-time winner of the grand prize of the Pacific Area Travel Association. Morgan wrote the California essay in the new *Encyclopedia Britannica.*

Willie Morrow

Morrow is publisher of the *San Diego Monitor News,* a weekly newspaper for the local African-American community. The paper is only one of this self-made millionaire's many successful business ventures. He was born and raised in Alabama, working in the fields until he began cutting hair for family and friends at the age of twelve. Soon he was writing instructional books about the proper way to cut curly hair. At twenty, he opened up a barber shop. In 1969, he traveled the globe for the U.S. Army, training military barbers to cut black men's hair. Internationally renowned in the hairstyling field, he launched a multi-million-dollar business developing and selling a wide range of hair care products.

Jack Murphy

San Diego Jack Murphy Stadium was named after the man who unselfishly worked to bring major sports to San Diego and made sure to have a stadium built to accommodate these new teams. An award-winning sports editor and columnist for the *San Diego Union,* he also authored two books, *Abe of Spoon River* and *Damn You, Al Davis!* Murphy died of cancer at the age of fifty-seven in September 1980.

Sean Patrick Reily

When Reily published his first issue of *San Diego Metropolitan* magazine in October 1985, the odds were stacked against him and his publication. Many downtown publications before his had come and gone. And Reily had never published a magazine before. In the beginning, he was editor, salesman, art director and publisher. Seven-day work weeks were common for him and his staff of two. The magazine is now celebrating its seventh year and has spawned another publication in the Golden Triangle as well as a tourist guide to downtown.

E.W. Scripps (1854-1926)

This newspaper mogul was among the most influential and powerful men of his day. The publishing giant founded or acquired a chain of over forty-five newspapers, an incredible feat just in terms of numbers. To start a paper, he put up the capital and retained fifty-one percent of the stock, leaving a hand-picked staff with forty-nine percent and the incentive to make the paper successful. He got his start in the newspaper business selling subscriptions for a Detroit paper owned by his brother James. Scripps moved on to reporting and eventually became the city editor. At the tender age of twenty-four, he established the Cleveland Penny Press and underpriced the competition. He began buying out or starting new papers and, by the time he was thirty-six, he was a millionaire. When he first visited San Diego in 1890, it was a broken-down boomtown of 16,000 people. Looking for a place to get away from it all, he made his home in an area sixteen miles north of downtown, purchasing 400 acres of land for $5,000. Eight years later, he completed a forty-seven room mansion on the ranch he called Miramar (now known as Scripps Ranch), where he lived for thirty-six years. Never really retiring, he controlled his newspaper empire from the mansion while personally running the *Sun* in San Diego. Called "the damned old crank" and "cantankerous," Scripps was a champion of the little man who believed in making it harder for the rich to grow richer and easier for the poor to keep from growing poorer.

Ed & Gloria Self

For the past forty-four years, Ed and Gloria Self have guided *San Diego Magazine,* the oldest and one of the most successful city magazines in the country. Introduced in October, 1948, the magazine made American journalism history as the first city magazine, becoming a role model and inspiration for dozens of other city magazines across the country. When the Selfs published their first issue, San Diego was one-sixth the size it is today. As the city grew, so did the magazine, always maintaining high standards of excellence.

Lionel Van Deerlin

This veteran newsman began his career as a newspaper man, then co-founded *Point Magazine,* served as a news commentator for local television and was elected to Congress in 1962. He continues to write for the *Union Tribune.*

Chapter 11:
Big Business

Gary Biszantz

José "Joe" G. da Rosa

Anthony DeSio

Gail Stoorza Gill

Jack W. Goodall

David Lloyd

Corky McMillin

Janathin Miller & Lindsey Ware

Judi Sheppard Missett

Fred H. Rohr

T. Claude Ryan

Suzy Spafford

Gary Biszantz
Co-Founder of Cobra Golf

Native Southern Californian Gary Biszantz and Australian-born Tom Crow are the co-founders of Cobra Golf in Carlsbad. This leading manufacturer of golf clubs, with distributorships in Canada, Europe, Japan and Australia, has seen annual sales increase an average of twenty-five to thirty-five percent. They expect 1992 sales to top forty million dollars. Ask Biszantz about the success of Cobra, and he'll tell you it's because of the successful chemistry between the two men.

Tom Crow, former Australian Amateur Champion and highly-regarded golf club designer, came to the United States in 1974 and founded Cobra I in 1975. In 1978, Gary Biszantz, an avid golfer, left his twenty-five year career in the automobile dealership business and he and Crow started Cobra II. Biszantz says, "Tom is a brilliant designer of clubs. I'm the other end of the operation, the one who designs the business strategy. It was always a dream of mine that someday I'd be able to get into a role where I could do it all, be involved in the research and design, the manufacturing, the retailing and the service – all of it."

Biszantz' marketing concept was to work more from the educational and technical side of the picture as well as the marketing and promotional side. He enhanced the thinking of on-course pros across the country to help them understand why the Cobra product was better than other clubs. Quality was the key. They went after a specific market – the serious country-club golfer who doesn't buy off-the-rack clubs. Now, thanks to a new, lighter graphite shaft, more than fifty percent of Cobra's business comes from women and senior citizens.

Since Cobra's prices are at the upper end of the spectrum, they are very small in the retail or discount market. They manufacture very little stock equipment. Instead, they build clubs to order, most of their business coming from golf course pros. Three out of four high-end golf shops around the country feature a Cobra display. Word of mouth is also a large factor. When their record of service and responsiveness to individual needs gets around, more inquiries and sales result.

Biszantz's management style stresses the team concept, personal involvement with one's work and quality consciousness. Most of their employees have been with the company for a long time. They experience very little turnover. He says, "Our people are proud of their work, and they know that what they're doing is important." At Cobra, the goal isn't necessarily to sell the most clubs or make a certain amount of money. It's to make the best product, a quality product, figuring sales and volume will follow.

After years of steady growth without a premier tour player endorsing their clubs, Cobra's greatest coup was getting Greg Norman, golf superstar. Because of his close friendship with fellow Australian Tom Crow, Norman seemed the logical choice, and he respected Cobra's reputation and "go for it" style of business. He's sole owner of their Australian operation, which allows him to actively participate in the business community of his native country.

Named San Diego's Entrepreneur of the Year in 1991 by the *Union Tribune,* Gary Biszantz is proud of his success, both personally and in business. He says, "To be a successful entrepreneur, you have to be a competitive person who likes challenges, likes to work and can face disappointments." He also says, "My advice to anyone starting a business is to start with very strong convictions of what you want to accomplish – a real solid game plan with a procedure for how to reach that end – and make sacrifices so that you are moving closer to the end result you want."

In his personal life, success takes on a slightly different meaning. "A person who is healthy and feels good has it all and should feel blessed every day," he says. "You can own a lot of things and be very wealthy, but lose your health and then absolutely nothing means anything. I'm not one who measures success by wealth or by what you own. Money is meant to be earned and spent. Your family and your children are far more important than how much money you accumulate."

Biszantz's thirty-five-year-old hobby – horse racing – is now becoming his second business. He bought his first thoroughbred in 1956 for $400 and he now has a stable of thirty-two horses, plus five in Kentucky. "Golf and horseracing are a good mix," he says. "You can play in the morning and get back to the track in the afternoon."

Biszantz's philosophy says it all. "No one can ever win anything if they're not fully prepared to lose," he warns, "because if they play too conservatively they caution themselves at all times. They never reach out and they never challenge themselves, because the fear of failing is too great. So they never stretch, they never try, they never make the effort that it takes to really become successful because they can't stand the defeat."

As for the toughest time in his life, Biszantz says, "The hardest thing in my own personal life, by far, was the divorce from my first wife after twenty-three years of marriage. It was a devastating experience for me. I had a very hard time financially with four daughters to raise. I lost enthusiasm, initiative and a lot of the things that had originally made me successful. I had to start over again from scratch. A couple of years went by and I met my current wife [of ten years], and she helped to change my life. She added a lot to my life, and we have two lovely girls. I have recaptured everything I had lost, and now I look at the overall situation and I think I'm the luckiest guy in the world. It was a tough time, and I hated every minute of it. But as I look back on it, it was just an absolutely positive experience for me to learn and grow from and, hopefully, become a better person."

Biszantz believes 1993 will be a terrific year for Cobra Golf. The introduction of the all-new King Cobra oversized metal woods and irons has been fantastic, and he believes Cobra could well achieve a huge growth in 1993. "Vision is essential, because you're only as good as your next innovative idea," he says. Cobra will continue to move forward in technical research and the company is likely to have a bright future in a highly competitive industry. Biszantz smiles, "As golfers say, 'When you're playing good, you don't think of hitting a bad shot and when you're playing poorly you never think you'll hit a good shot." Gary Biszantz always thinks, "Good shot!"

José "Joe" G. da Rosa
President and CEO of Balboa Travel Inc.

Serving as the president and CEO of San Diego-based Balboa Travel Inc., Joe da Rosa, along with his sister, Mary Alice Gonsalves, have built their travel marketing organization into a sixty-million-dollar company with more than a hundred employees. The company they've owned since 1971 has operations in both Southern and Northern California as well as other parts of the United States. The bulk of Balboa Travel's business is in corporate travel, but the organization also handles government travel and leisure travel. Its Motivation Strategies division focuses on incentive travel and meetings and the Balboa Institute provides specialized travel education.

Brother and sister went into business together "despite some trepidation about going into business with family," buying a little travel agency. Gonsalves had been a travel agent for a number of years and da Rosa wanted to get into business for himself. The partnership has worked well. The two have celebrated twenty-one years in business, many of them as the largest travel agency in San Diego.

A San Diego native, da Rosa was born in October 1937 into one of the pioneering tuna-fishing families in San Diego. A first-generation Portuguese-American, his parents immigrated from the island of Pico in the Azores. "My father and his brothers were part of an energetic and determined group of immigrants that arrived in the 1920's," da Rosa explains. "At one time, the Rosa boats caught twenty-five percent of all the fish canned by Chicken of the Sea." Growing up in what was then the small neighborhood of Point Loma, da Rosa always had some type of job — unloading fishing boats and boxcars, mowing lawns or working as a dishwasher. After graduating from Point Loma High School in 1955, he attended Menlo College before graduating from UC Santa Barbara in 1959. He went on to study at the University of Coimbra, Portugal, staying in Europe another year to teach school and dub films in Rome. He recently completed a three-year summer management program at Harvard University's Graduate School of Business.

Da Rosa worked in Santa Barbara as a reporter for a community newspaper which won the California Newspaper Publishers Association's award for outstanding community service. Fluent in several languages, he volunteered for the Peace Corps in 1962, serving two years in the Caribbean. On his return, he focused on freelance writing, turning out a book-length manuscript, among other things. "I was a good craftsman and got a New York agent interested in me," he says, "but I discovered I wasn't the Shakespeare I wanted to be."

Recruited back to the Peace Corps as a staff member, da Rosa served six years as a Foreign Service Reserve Officer in Latin America (his wife Marly is from Brazil) and Washington D.C. His last assignment was as Deputy Director of the Latin America Training and Development Center in Escondido.

In 1971, da Rosa and his sister purchased a small travel agency that had been run part-time by a retired widower and former officer of the Royal Navy. At that time, there were sixty-five travel agencies in San Diego (today there are around 600). With a staff of three, the company doubled its volume within the first six months, then settled into a steady growth pattern. "Our growth has been a lot like a bulldozer moving forward," he says, "not too fast, but nothing can stop us!" Early on he realized that you need to set goals — realistic goals that will also make you reach. Think big but at the same time guard your resources and don't overextend yourself. This strategy helped build Balboa Travel into the powerhouse organization it is today. He points to four other key factors for their success: determination backed by plans and strategies, focusing in on customers' needs, looking ahead and being alert to opportunities and then taking action to take advantage of them. Then there's the importance of a close, caring staff.

Da Rosa has a keen interest in the role his company takes in the affairs of the community it serves, and he has been active on numerous boards and committees in San Diego. "I think when people talk about the problems with our city they are comparing San Diego to what it used to be, wishing San Diego could continue as a place time forgot, as an elegant cul de sac, and they're *really* dreaming," he says. "I can look back on fifty years, and we long ago passed the point of no return. San Diego is not a little town anymore."

Da Rosa sees better times ahead if we seize our opportunities. These include our unique association with Tijuana and Mexico, our strategic position on the Pacific Rim, our climate and the wealth of outstanding institutions of higher education in the county. "Mexico holds great promise for us," da Rosa believes. "Many people know very little about our neighbors in Tijuana and often view Mexico as a problem, something to be protected against. In reality, it may be our greatest opportunity. There are great needs in Mexico — and wherever there's need, there's opportunity."

Anthony DeSio
Mail Boxes Etc.

What began as a post office alternative in Carlsbad in 1980 is now giving the Postal Service a run for its money. Mail Boxes Etc. has grown into one of the largest and most profitable businesses of its kind in the world. But when Anthony (Tony) DeSio first explained his idea to money lenders, they laughed. How could an entrepreneur go head-to-head with the Postal Service? It was too new, too radical, and no one was willing to listen. They're not laughing anymore. Now, the franchiser operates the nation's largest chain of postal, business and communications service centers, with approximately 1,800 offices nationwide in fifty states, plus Canada, Mexico, Jamaica and Spain. Recently, master licenses have been awarded to centers in the United Kingdom, Germany, France, Italy, Brazil, Australia and New Zealand. DeSio's long-term goal is to have 2,500 centers by 1995 and 5,000 by the year 2000.

Anthony DeSio, president and CEO, was born in 1930 in New York City, where he lived until World War II, when his father moved the family to Connecticut. After serving in the Navy during the Korean War, DeSio worked his way through college, graduating from the University of Connecticut in 1957 with a Bachelor of Science degree in electrical engineering. In 1958, he moved to California and joined Lockheed Missiles and Space Company. As he moved up the ladder, he eventually managed one of the nation's most important classified space programs. In 1972, DeSio was sent to Washington D.C., where he spent two years assigned to the Executive Office of the President, helping establish policy for the national space program. After leaving the Space Council, he joined General Electric's Space System Division. He was later recruited by Western Union to implement their new space communications subsidiary. In 1978, DeSio's position was eliminated when the subsidiary was sold.

Unemployed, he decided to move to San Diego to pursue owner-ship of his own business. "I was so successful in my career in industry that I just never got to the point where I had any time to be an

entrepreneur myself," he says. "That is, until the company I was working for was sold out from under me, and I found myself needing
something to do." He joined a San Diego business brokerage firm with
the idea of gaining first access to a business coming on the market. In
1980, his opportunity arrived when an individual approached him with
a floundering private postal box business. DeSio felt that by including
other services, the company's potential could be significant. He acquired an equity in the company and joined them as vice president in
1981.

DeSio and three partners opened their first outlet in Carlsbad but,
although the concept proved popular, they couldn't get capital for
expansion. They turned to franchising. From 1980 to 1982, the chain
expanded rapidly, but his partners became impatient and tired of
waiting for a return on their investment. Disputes arose about DeSio's
management approach which eventually resulted in a proxy battle over
control of the company. When shareholders supported DeSio, the
partners offered to sell their equity. DeSio and an outside investor
bought them out in 1983. In order to do so, DeSio had to use his house,
his savings, even his wife's jewelry for collateral.

"I knew from the beginning that we were going to make this
business successful, in spite of the fact that some of my original partners bailed out along the way," he says. "My nature as a person is that of
someone who is totally dedicated to the achievement of the goals I
have established. In the early days, there were many who doubted that
this type of business could succeed, but I always had faith in the
concept. Even though we had all sorts of problems and distractions
along the way, we remained true to our long-term strategic plan."

He found the strength to hang tough for the next two years,
continuing the same slow, steady growth pattern. "We turned the
corner in 1984," DeSio says. "That's when we made our first substantial
profit." In 1986, Mail Boxes Etc. went public. Now MBE is the leader in
its field. "The nice thing about this business is that not only have we
helped thousands of individual entrepreneurs get started as Mail Boxes
Etc. franchises," he says proudly, "but each of them in turn has helped
many home-based businesses by providing them with all kinds of office
support services."

MBE was named San Diego Entrepreneur of the Year by *Inc.*

Magazine in 1989 and inducted into the Entrepreneur Hall of Fame, being ranked eighteenth among the "Top 100 Franchises" by *Success Magazine,* rated among best bets in "100 Best Franchises for Women" by *Women's Enterprise* in 1990, ranked ninetieth among "200 Best Small Companies" by *Forbes Magazine* in 1991 and 1992 and, in January of 1992, rated sixteenth in *Entrepreneur's* "Franchise 500" listing.

DeSio's role model was his father, "Who, although uneducated, was an independent person who wanted to do his own thing. He was in his own business for most of his life. Although I studied engineering in college, I think I always had this latent desire to be an entrepreneur," admits DeSio. He feels that goals are one of the most important aspects of succeeding in business. In 1983 their goal was to have 1,000 franchises in place by 1990, and they didn't let anything distract them. "We just hung onto that goal and did, in fact, achieve it," he says. "We have never varied from our goal of network growth because we realized that the key to success in this business is to have a large network."

At the rate Mail Boxes Etc. is growing, DeSio's loftiest goal will undoubtedly be attained. "We're going to be the McDonald's in this business," he says.

Gail Stoorza Gill
Businesswoman/Community Leader

For a woman who started out representing dairy farmers whose cows were pastured in fields where Mission Valley Center and Fashion Valley now stand, Gail Stoorza Gill has come a long way. Today she is the head of one of California's leading independent public relations/ marketing communications firms, as well as head of one of San Diego's newest and most prominent advertising agencies. Gill is chairman and CEO of Stoorza, Ziegaus & Metzger, Inc., the public relations firm she founded in 1974, as well as chairman and CEO of Franklin Stoorza, a newly-formed full-service advertising agency. Her public relations firm has offices in San Diego, Sacramento, Los Angeles and Riverside, with an impressive list of clients that includes PacTel Cellular, San Diego Unified Port District, the San Diego Convention Center, Travelodge and other local and national businesses and organizations. In March, 1992, her company acquired Franklin & Associates, one of San Diego's largest advertising agencies, and merged it with ADC Stoorza, her firm's advertising arm, to create Franklin Stoorza, now one of the biggest agencies in town.

Gill got her start in the public relations department of Phillips-Ramsey, Inc., an ad agency. She hadn't even heard the term *public relations* until then, but she quickly learned the business. She went on to become an account representative, but she really got perspective on public relations when one of her clients, Rancho Bernardo, Inc., offered her a job. Becoming their director of advertising and public relations, she began to see how lacking public relations firms were when it came to forming partnerships with their clients. The idea of being a true partner to the people you serve is a unique and important part of Gill's philosophy.

When Rancho Bernardo, Inc. was bought by a development company, Gill suggested a new job to her boss which turned into an opening and opportunity as she became director of corporate communications. At this time she had a chance to see the agency side from the client's viewpoint – and knew she could do better. So she put together a plan where she and a secretary started an agency, and presented her plan to the president of the company. She got where she is today by proving that she could do better.

Gill is currently on the board of directors of the Economic Development Corporation, a trustee of the Scripps Memorial Hospitals Foundation and is committed to other organizations as well. Her honors fill pages and include a 1992 HumanUnity Award from the National Conference of Christians and Jews and the 1988 Equal Opportunity Award from the Urban League of San Diego. She was named one of the eighty-eight "San Diegans to Watch" by *San Diego Magazine* in 1988; named Small Business Person of the Year for San Diego and Imperial Counties in 1984 and PR Professional of the Year by the Public Relations Club of San Diego in 1982.

To Gill, "Success means peace of mind, and that encompasses financial security." But, she adds, "It's not all about money and career advancement, but a healthy balance between work and family." Her suggestion for success is, "Hard, hard work. The thing that frustrates me most about young people is they want to get ahead but they aren't willing to work hard for it. They do just enough to get by, but they lack initiative. That's one of the major reasons I got ahead – I always took the initiative, and I took advantage of opportunity."

Gail Stoorza Gill attended North Texas State University and the University of Texas at Arlington. She lives in San Diego with her husband, Ian Gill, and their daughter, Alexandra.

Jack W. Goodall
Foodmaker President, CEO and Chairman

A chain of drive-through hamburger stands, Jack In The Box restaurants were founded in San Diego back in the early 1950's. The first Jack In The Box opened at 63rd Street and El Cajon Boulevard in 1951. At that time, a hamburger cost roughly eighteen cents. Jack Goodall joined the chain as a lessee in the early 1960's as a twenty-three-year-old. At the time his unit, located at the intersection of 70th Street and University Avenue, was one of about seventy-five Jack In The Box locations, and the cost of a hamburger was still less than a quarter. Advancing rapidly through the company, Goodall became a vice president in his late twenties and by June of 1970, still in his early thirties, he became the company's president. As president, CEO and chairman of San Diego-based Foodmaker, Inc., he has overseen the company's explosive growth from eighty million dollars a year to a staggering $1.5 billion in annual sales. Foodmaker presently consists of some 1,150 Jack In The Box fast service restaurants, making them the fifth largest national hamburger chain. In 1990, Foodmaker also acquired Chi-Chi's, a 206-unit Mexican dinnerhouse chain that now numbers over 230 restaurants. Foodmaker employs over 60,000 people, 450 of whom work locally.

So how did this San Diego native with a degree in industrial management from San Diego State University become head of a billion-dollar-a-year restaurant chain? "The best way to succeed in business is to have people around you who are excellent," Goodall says. "I have always tried to hire people who were smarter than myself, people who would work harder and were at least as dedicated as I was." The same philosophy can also work for the small business owner, because many of the same principles apply to businesses both big and small. "There isn't a whole lot of difference between running a big business and operating a small one," he advises. It's also important to treat people with respect. "It's simple. Treat people how you yourself would like to be treated," Goodall recommends.

As part owner of the San Diego Padres, he applies much of what he's learned in business to dealing with ballplayers – it's just a lot more expensive. "Ballplayers' salaries have just gotten out of hand. The whole thing is nuts. Yet it's the owners' fault," he points out.

Born in San Diego in 1938, Goodall was married at nineteen to his high school sweetheart, Mary Buckley. They had their first child before he graduated from SDSU. He remembers having just a few hundred dollars in the bank and scraping together $625 for a downpayment on their first home (total price: $16,000). After earning his degree, Goodall worked nights at General Dynamics and attended graduate school by day. Around this time, he ran into a friend from high school who was making better money than he was – with no experience, no college education – working in the burger business. Soon thereafter, Goodall joined Jack In The Box and began paying his dues on his way to running the company.

Over the years, Goodall has been recognized for his outstanding accomplishments as a successful businessman. He received SDSU's School of Business Distinguished Alumni Award in 1974 and 1989, was the *Union-Tribune* Headliner of the Year for Business in 1987 and the Academy of Marketing Science Marketer of the Year in 1992. In 1988 he was named Multi-Unit Food Service Operators Executive of the Year. Goodall was inducted into the Junior Achievement Business Hall of Fame in 1992. Yet, as much as he appreciates the accolades, he maintains that the key to success is not awards or money. "A balanced life is the key to success," he says earnestly. He has achieved that as a husband, father and grandfather. He and his wife, Mary, have been married for over thirty-four years and have four children and seven grandchildren. He and his wife are actively involved in helping other families as well, volunteering their time in the Child Abuse Prevention Foundation in San Diego. Goodall is Chairman of the Board and Mary is a director of the Foundation.

How does this 1992 City Club of San Diego Citizen of the Year feel about the future of his hometown? "By nature, I guess I'm an optimist, but the short-term business outlook for San Diego is a very, very frightening scenario," he says. "Long term, San Diego and California *have* to prosper simply because of geography. It's the premier location in the world in terms of weather, in terms of proximity to the Pacific Ocean and because it's sitting right next to Mexico, which is a country of vast, untapped resources. California is also in a unique position to take advantage of trade with the Pacific Rim. There are a whole lot of very strong reasons to relocate and establish a business here."

Still, Goodall is a realist, pointing to some of the obstacles to full recovery for San Diego, particularly the need to replace lost jobs with equally qualified jobs. "A job for a job isn't necessarily a good thing if you replace the deficit of jobs lost in San Diego — primarily high-tech, biotech and aerospace jobs — with lower-paying service jobs," he says. "We've created this elitist society in San Diego where you are either well-to-do or you're struggling to get by." Even with these realistic observations, Goodall is optimistic. He has high hopes for San Diego and its ultimately bright future.

David Lloyd
Shipbuilder

"I tell kids all the time that it's not the car, the clothes or the house that determines the quality of life you're going to have," David Lloyd says. "It's what's inside that counts. Very few people understand that, but the ones who do are wealthy people." Lloyd should know. He rose from poverty to build one of the largest minority-owned shipbuilding companies in the country, and his story is the stuff that dreams are made of.

David Lloyd, a native of Monroeville, Alabama, remembers growing up poor, cold and hungry. He learned early in life the value of hard work and always doing more than what's expected of you. He began working odd jobs at the age of eight, picking cotton, baling hay, washing cars and later working at an auto dealership where he learned how to paint and repair cars. He learned about integrity and determination, too. "The first role model I ever had was a skinny little white man who wasn't all that bright, but he was the wealthiest man in that town. This guy had integrity and determination, and I admired that. He wouldn't let anything slow him down. I would just watch him. He fascinated me," Lloyd remembers.

At nineteen, armed with an eighth-grade education, a willingness to work hard and a determination to make the most of what he had, Lloyd headed west, arriving in San Diego in the mid-1950's. He'd seen a movie about San Diego when he was a kid, and had always wanted to come here.

Once in San Diego, he had to find steady work. "I was a teenager who just wanted a job that paid me enough money to stay out of trouble," he says. He applied for a job as a city garbage collector, but failed the qualifying test. He found work as a janitor and then as a painter. First he painted houses, which he learned how to do in part from studying a book in the library. He soon found that painting boats was much more profitable, so he went to work for several ship repair firms, learning all aspects of ship repair.

He went to trade school to learn more about drafting, painting and welding, determined to do every job a little better than anybody else. He became known for his excellent work, and tuna boat owners asked him to work on their boats. To earn extra money, the resourceful Lloyd scouted the marinas to find boats needing a paint job and left a picture of a freshly-painted boat with a price and a phone number. It was only a matter of time before he had as much work as he could handle.

In 1968, Lloyd and a friend, Tex Johnson, started their own shipbuilding and repair business, concentrating their efforts on small tuna boats. In 1971, they added two more partners to form Bay City Marine, Inc. Things took a turn for the worse when the Mexican government discouraged fishing in its waters by vessels not built in Mexico. The company was overextended and went deeply in debt, but Lloyd refused to declare bankruptcy and vowed to turn the company around. "When you're committed to something and things go wrong, the thought of bailing out never occurs," he declares. He temporarily stopped shipbuilding and diversified by concentrating on an industry that was booming, doing steel work for high-rise construction in downtown San Diego. To save the company, he also began selling off unnec-

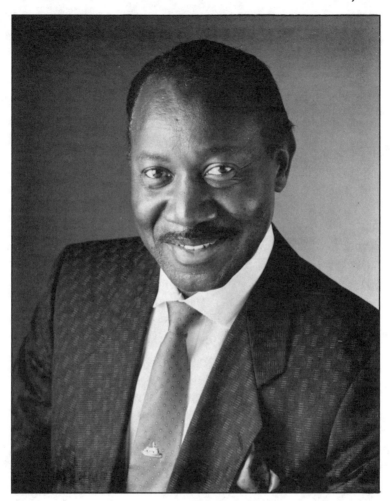

David Lloyd

essary equipment and working out agreements with creditors. "I had to downsize drastically. At one time, I had about ninety employees and I had to go down to about twelve. Once I started to realize the full impact of this thing, I sold the largest facility we had and moved into a smaller place. I knew it would take a while for me to get back up to that size again. It was a very hard thing to do, because it took a lot of hard work to get the company to that size, but it was survival. You have to put those emotional feelings behind you and move forward," Lloyd says. He and his company did move forward, and he was able to buy out the other three principals in the original corporation, becoming sole owner of Bay City Marine, Inc. in 1978.

Lloyd's principal customer became the Kelco Corporation, which manufactures products from kelp. Kelco was based in San Diego until 1978, when they expanded to Oklahoma City, cutting the workload at Bay City Marine significantly. Faced with this setback, Lloyd just worked harder. He was welding when his employees arrived in the morning and welding when they left. On Saturdays and Sundays, he worked on the old equipment. "Many people in hard times wallow in self-pity," he says. "I never could understand that."

In March, 1978, Bay City Marine submitted papers for a Master Ship Repair contract with the Navy. After nearly a year of intense negotiations, Lloyd was awarded the contract, becoming the only minority-owned firm in the country to hold such a contract. Bay City Marine also became part of the United States Small Business Administration's 8(a) program in May of 1979.

Perseverance, quality workmanship and dedication paid off for Lloyd as he reached many of the goals he set for himself and the company in the years that followed. "The goal is the most important part of success. You can't be committed to a goal that you haven't set yet. Once you set that goal, then you commit yourself to it and you can go about accomplishing it," he says. Taking his own advice, Lloyd went about accomplishing some extraordinary goals for himself and his company. Bay City Marine has completed some 600 ship repair contracts for the U.S. Navy, worth in excess of $200 million. The company also designed and built an Orbiter Lifting Frame for NASA and the Air Force in 1980. They built three new Ice Breaking Tugs for the Coast Guard.

Racial considerations have never been an insurmountable obstacle for Lloyd. He was awarded contracts based on his reputation for quality work and for his competitive bids, often finishing the job under budget and ahead of schedule. He won't deny that racism and discrimination still prevail, but he refuses to let it get in his way. "Discrimination exists, but the thing of it is I'm fifty-six years old and I'm used to being black," he says. "I'm a black man in a white world. You can't complain it's not fair, you just have to make the most of what you have."

David Lloyd has made it as an entrepreneur in San Diego, and he confidently states that if he had to, he could do it all over again. "It would be much easier, because I don't have the insecurities anymore, all the self-doubt," he says. "Many times I would go into a place and somebody would tell me, 'We don't think you qualify.' That happens to all of us, and people take that personally. Somebody tells me that today, that I can't do something, and five minutes later I wouldn't even remember. Back in those days, I'd take it home with me and cry." If he were applying for a job today, the first thing he'd do is go to the library and learn the fundamentals of that particular type of work and research the company he was applying to. "If somebody comes to me [as an employer] with that kind of knowledge," he says, "I'll hire them right away. But if somebody comes to me applying for the job and then asks me what do I have to do with that job? – chances are I'm not going to hire them."

If he were going to start a business today, he'd research the business he was trying to start very carefully. "Here in San Diego, the largest investors are the Navy. Next is construction and next is tourism, so that's three areas where there are plenty of opportunities. Most businesses are affected by those three things or the support for those three things. So when you look at that, you can start eliminating risks," he says, admitting that you can never eliminate risks entirely. "Has your life been perfect up till now?" he asks. "You have experience with things going wrong in your life, so pull on those experiences and learn from them!"

Corky McMillin
Home Builder/Off Road Racing Champion

What started out as a $12,000 loan and a commitment to excellence three decades ago led to a real estate empire unsurpassed in San Diego. Macey "Corky" McMillin built his family-owned and operated construction business into nine distinct companies, ranging from interior design to mortgages and including an off-road racing team. His residential resale firm, McMillin Realty, is the county's largest independent real estate company.

McMillin's longevity in the field is attributed to his commitment to customer satisfaction by stressing teamwork, honesty, fairness, value and a partnership with the community. The proof of his outstanding reputation lies in the fact that "The children of buyers of my homes twenty-five years ago are now my customers." In an interview, McMillin said, "I've found that if you do a good job and satisfy the customer, two more people will want you to do that job for them, too."

Born in Missouri sixty-three years ago, McMillin came here as a young boy, where he and his parents lived in a homemade house trailer. His father was a building contractor, and McMillin learned the trade from him. He attended Sweetwater High School in the early 1940's, when the school was so crowded it had a seven-day-a-week schedule.

In 1960, McMillin decided to start his own construction business. He borrowed $12,000 from the equity in his own home in Bonita to build his first house. The earnest young builder dug trenches, laid cast-iron pipe and did most of the carpentry work himself, from framing to cabinetry. With his wife Vonnie's help, he sold the results for $15,000. As his National City-based company grew, he started hiring people to help him, buying lots and building houses. "I would borrow money and build two houses, then they'd give me the money for seven, then thirty, then eighty. In 1975 I was still a little company working out of National City, concentrating on the South Bay," he says.

As demand for McMillin homes grew, the company grew, too. "I put a big emphasis on customer service, customer satisfaction and the quality of the house," he says. Along the way, McMillin developed many friendships. From one neighborhood to the next all across San Diego, he used the same framers, cabinetmakers, plumbers, electricians, dry-wallers and painters. These days, it's not unusual to find two generations of one family working on the job.

In 1972, with twelve years of homebuilding under his belt, Corky formed McMillin Realty to sell previously-owned homes. In 1974, when new home sales declined, his realty business was going strong. In 1991, this real estate brokerage had nearly 400 salespeople working out of eleven offices. From this first step to full diversification, McMillin continued to build an integrated company of independent enterprises. This helped him get through the recession of the early 1980's, when mortgage rates soared. "From 1960 to 1980, my company grew every

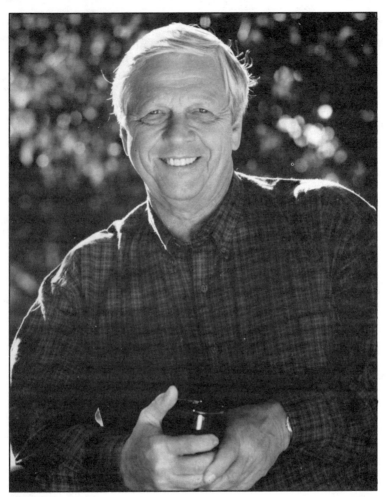

Corky McMillin

year," he says proudly. "I continued to add people, training programs, seminars that we went away to, and we continued to bring in trainees. In 1980, for the first time, I had to cut my company by thirty percent, but I hung on to as many people as I could. I hung on to people that from a business standpoint I shouldn't have. But I wanted to be sure that I had the resources when the market came back to be capable of taking advantage of that comeback."

McMillin has been through three recessions now, and he's no quitter. In the fall of 1990, when housing sales ground to a virtual halt, instead of slashing prices and devaluing property, he tightened his belt, cutting overhead by twenty-five percent. "I know that once money loosens up, the economy is going to take off like a rocket," he says confidently.

In 1975, McMillin convinced his management team that his three children (two sons and a daughter) should be trained to inherit the business. Today, his elder son Mark runs the homebuilding side of the business. Daughter Laurie leads the interior design company and younger son Scott runs the resale division and mortgage banking company.

McMillin was inducted into the California Building Industry Foundation's Hall of Fame in 1988. He won the Lee Hubbard Award from the San Diego Building Industry Association in 1991, while being named Builder of the Year by *California Builder* magazine. In 1992 he was named Man of the Year by the San Diego Apartment Association.

His accomplishments don't stop there, however. McMillin and his sons are known as "the winningest team in off-road racing," The McMillin Race Team has amassed an enviable record of performance over desert, mountains and beaches. The same philosophy holds true for all the McMillin family endeavors: Never give up. And never settle for less than the best. McMillin is "very appreciative of the wonderful San Diego quality of life." He and his wife still reside in Bonita. He says, "I've been able to live a great life. I have a great wife, three great kids, and I have seven grandchildren." It wasn't luck that got him there. His good fortune is the result of hard work, a positive image in the community and a willingness to roll up his sleeves and get involved.

Janathin Miller & Lindsey Ware
Businesswomen

Since coming west in the mid-1970's with only a few dollars between them, Janathin Miller and Lindsey Ware have taken their two-woman consulting business and turned it into Access Research Corporation, a multi-faceted, multi-million dollar firm. Access Research has become the only women-owned company in the United States in high-tech automatic test equipment. They have seven offices across the country.

When they arrived in California in 1975, Miller had a Bachelor's degree in broadcast electronics, a Master's in instructional technology and a Ph.D. in education, with an emphasis on systems management. Ware had a degree in social policy, with an emphasis in special education. They came believing they had jobs at San Diego State University, but that didn't work out. "They told us to be here the first of the month. They never told us they meant the month of August, so when we arrived our jobs had already been filled." SDSU did try to contact them, but "We were in our little sports car with our little puppy dogs, driving across country." They had $64.50 to their names when they rolled into town.

Without money or jobs, the two decided to do consulting work out of a small cottage in Alpine supplied to them on a rent now/pay later basis. Their first job was writing a proposal to design a multimedia facility at SDSU's Calexico campus. "Nobody told us where the hell Calexico was or we wouldn't have taken the job," Miller says. They got the $5,000 project and did all the work themselves out of their home. They started a consulting firm called J. Miller Associates. When they moved to a larger house, they became Training Technology Associates. With very little overhead, the two survived those first few years in business. They typed their proposals on a little portable typewriter, cut, pasted and photocopied their letterhead and disguised their voices when answering the phone, trying to sound like the secretary. As their business grew, Miller and Ware had to subcontract the engineering services that were part of the contracts they were getting. Then they decided to hire their own engineers. They then received a big engineering job – one they didn't expect – and in six weeks they had a large line of credit and a staff of forty-eight, forty-three of them engineers.

In 1983, Access Research Corporation was born, and they moved into a North County office building. In 1987, they moved to their current headquarters, a 43,000-square-foot facility built specifically for them in the Golden Triangle. Today, Access Research is on the leading edge of technology, dealing with engineering, training and documentation support services for government agencies, aerospace firms, academic institutions, telecommunications companies and computer hardware and software industries – all highly male-dominated fields. According to Miller, "I've got to tell you, being a woman in this business is the pits. It's a very tough business for a woman. It was particularly difficult for us when we first started. We were young, over-educated, and women. Now we've built a reputation, and we don't run into those problems nearly as often. But we still don't belong to the good ol' boy network – and I don't play golf." Asked if the Equal Opportunity laws didn't help them, Miller insists, "We never won a contract by being a women-owned business, but by being the best at what we do."

Miller and Ware have known each other since their college days at Cornell University. "We're very different personalities," Miller notes. Ware is the detail person, with patience dealing with banks, contracts and the like. Miller is the technical and marketing person. Miller says, "We were young, and you take chances in your twenties that you wouldn't ever consider taking in your forties. Lindsey and I both come from families where our parents were in their own businesses, so we had great mentors. We grew up with that. I don't think we ever thought we couldn't make it. It just never dawned on us that we wouldn't succeed."

A few years ago, Dr. Miller and Ms. Ware decided to give something back to society, so they expanded into the environmental engineering field with Access Resources, a wholly-owned subsidiary of Access Research. Access Resources offers a series of seminars called "Green Futures," targeting the business community. They both feel that San Diego, and California as a whole, are "extremely avant garde in terms of waste management practices, regulatory compliance to toxic waste, non-smoking, recycling, etc."

Now in their forties, the two entrepreneurs have established a place in San Diego and proved to the world that they're here to stay.

Judi Sheppard Missett
Founder of Jazzercise

According to Judi Sheppard Missett, "Being successful is being happy with what you do every day. It doesn't necessarily mean making a lot of money. It doesn't necessarily mean having power or fame." But this fitness guru has achieved all of that. Dubbed the "Passionate

Pioneer of Fitness" by *Working Woman Magazine* (November 1988), she has blazed a trail for her competitors to follow and her industry "firsts" read like the ABC's of success.

Founder of Jazzercise in the late 1960's, Missett brought her love of fitness through jazz-dance to an international level with over 5,000 franchised instructors and half-a-million participating students throughout the world. Her exercise empire, based in Carlsbad, encompasses youngsters (four through sixteen), seniors (seventy-plus) and everyone in between. It includes Jazzercise albums and videotapes, books, a syndicated newspaper column, a nutrition education program, Jazzertogs (a mail order catalog of fitness wear and accessories), a videotape production company and workout studios.

Missett earned the national title of Small Business Person of the Year in 1985 from the USA Small Business Administration. In 1986 she was named Top Woman Entrepreneur (honored by President Ronald Reagan) and received the Outstanding Business Award from IDEA, Association for Fitness Professionals. *Working Woman Magazine* named her Entrepreneur of the Year in 1988 and in 1991 she won a Lifetime Achievement Award (IDEA) and Regional Entrepreneur of the Year, Women-Owned Business Category (Ernst & Young).

In 1988, Jazzercise ranked seventh among 500 franchised businesses and first among franchised fitness businesses in the "Franchise 500" listing prepared by *Entrepreneur* magazine. In 1992, it was ranked fourteenth out of more than a thousand franchises. Also in 1992, *Working Woman Magazine* listed Jazzercise as one of fifteen "Best Franchises for Women." Missett's most recent coup is a multi-year contract with Nike, under which she will use their footwear and apparel, and Jazzercise will feature Nike products in its videos, promotional materials and events.

Judi Sheppard grew up in Red Oak, Iowa, a small town of 6,000. An only child, her mother was an accountant and her father an appraisal engineer. Her mother, who died a few years ago, "lived to see my success and to share it. My dad's so proud of me it pops his buttons," she says.

She started dancing lessons at the age of two-and-a-half and had her first recital at three. By the time she was twelve, she was teaching her own dance classes, and she hasn't stopped since. She says, "Dance is my love, my passion. It's gotten me through every single day of my life."

After graduating from Red Oak High School, Missett headed for Chicago, where she attended Northwestern University, studying theater and dance. She took a degree in theater and radio/television in 1966. She met her husband, Jack Missett, on a blind date while she was at Northwestern. "It was love at first sight," she says.

She began teaching jazz-dance classes in Chicago, but quickly realized that some of the routines weren't for everyone. She watched a succession of housewives stay a few months and then drop out. They wanted a fun fitness workout without the strict discipline of a serious dance training class. To keep them interested, she developed a jazz-exercise class for fun and fitness.

In 1972, Missett, her husband and her young daughter, Shanna, moved to Southern California. Jack, who had been a television news reporter, wanted to try free-lance writing. Missett was all for it. "I'm a risk-taker," she says. "I love change." She also thought that Southern California, the mecca of health and fitness, would be ripe for her new jazz-dance exercise class.

After settling in North County, Missett continued teaching. She held classes at YMCA's and Park and Recreation facilities. As her classes filled and more were added, she found herself becoming hoarse by the end of each week. In 1974, Missett officially named her class *Jazzercise,* a name suggested by one of her students. By 1977, she was teaching all over San Diego County.

Business was booming, but it was beginning to take a toll on her health. Eventually, she selected five of her students, trained them in her philosophy and taught them the routines. When the five new instructors branched out, more classes were started and a franchise was born. In 1991, Missett launched a new program, Kids Get Fit, a free school fitness program. In 1992, over 400,000 children throughout the world participated.

Missett's long-standing passion for dance is the driving force behind both her personal and professional success. "I'm very lucky, because I love what I do, and I can make a good living from doing it," she says. She's always believed that the American Dream is within reach if you "stretch" for it. "We have helped many women realize that they can be businesswomen, and we have given them that little push it sometimes takes," Missett continues.

If she hadn't been fired in 1973 from teaching part-time at the Golden Door in Escondido, she wouldn't have gotten a head start on opening her own business, which today has annual revenues of more than forty five million dollars.

"Being fired was fabulous," she insists. She left work a half-hour early one day to help with a charity performance, and Golden Door owner Deborah Szekely fired her. "Someday you'll thank me for doing this," Szekely told Missett. "You're destined for better things." Little did she know...

"I've really never had any tough times, because I don't view them as tough times. I view them as new challenges and try to find solutions. I try to look at them in a positive way, and I think that is one of the things that has led to more and more success as the years go on. You don't look at tough times as negatives but as positives, and you try to figure out how to make something positive out of them," Missett says.

Ask her how she built a multi-million-dollar business in just a few years, and she'll tell you it was passion. "I never wondered, 'What am I going to do with my life?' I always knew – from the time I was three years old."

In 1979, Jazzercise incorporated and opened its Carlsbad head-quarters, which now employs more than a hundred people. "I very consciously chose North San Diego County to be the place I would make the headquarters for my company and the place in which I would bring up my children," Missett says. "I like the feeling it had of a smaller community, a sort of togetherness, and yet I liked the fact that we were near larger cities where there were cultural advantages." She intends to keep the company right there. She feels that, although San Diego may have problems, San Diegans should view it as a time to take advantage of the situation and look for the positive.

Now forty-eight, Missett is still teaching. Her twenty-three-year-old daughter is also involved in the multifaceted empire and her husband runs JM Television Productions, which films the videotapes for Jazzercise. Missett acknowledges that without them and her nine-year-old son Brendan, success and fame wouldn't mean anything. "My family is the most important aspect of what I do," she says earnestly.

Fred H. Rohr
Captain of Industry (1896-1965)

Fred H. Rohr was a self-made man who rose from humble beginnings to end up as the head of a company with international impact. He took Rohr Aircraft Corporation from a small company with only five employees working out of a tiny garage in 1940 and built it into an industry leader before his death in 1965 at the age of sixty-nine. An important figure in San Diego's economic growth during and after World War II, he was presented with the Mr. San Diego award in 1956 for his years as a leader of local industry as well as his many civic activities. Rohr substantially influenced the aviation and aerospace industry in his over forty years as chairman of the board and CEO of his Chula Vista-based company, manufacturing many crucial parts for the planes of his day. Respected and admired as a leader of men, he was also known as innovative, industrious and talented. A skilled craftsman, he did much of the sheet metal work as a member of T. Claude Ryan's staff, building the *Spirit of St. Louis* for Charles Lindbergh's historic flight.

The son of a German immigrant, Fredrick Hilmer Rohr was born May 10, 1896 in Hoboken, New Jersey, but moved to San Francisco as a boy. Rohr served two years in the Navy during World War I before learning his trade as an apprentice in his father's sheet metal shop. He continued his education at night, taking college and extension courses. He learned his trade well, inventing the drop hammer for sheet metal shaping. After moving to San Diego in 1924, he opened a sheet metal works of his own, beginning his career as a pioneer in the aircraft industry. After helping construct the *Spirit of St. Louis* in 1927 as sheet metal foreman for Ryan Aeronautical, he left to become a factory manager for Solar Aircraft Company (1928-1932) and spent three years at Boeing in Seattle (1932-1935) before returning to San Diego to become a factory manager at Ryan from 1935 until he resigned to organize his own company in 1940.

Rohr's innovations were well received and proved to be functional. In 1941, the company expanded, opening a plant in Chula Vista where it is headquartered to this day. Rohr Industries, now in its fifty-second year, is a billion-dollar company with over 9,000 employees, 4,000 of them in San Diego, and remains a major participant in the aerospace industry.

T. Claude Ryan
Aviation Pioneer/Businessman (1898-1982)

At twenty-four, T. Claude Ryan was broke financially, but blessed with a wealth of spirit and ingenuity. In 1922, he sold his Model T and poured the proceeds into buying a Jenny airplane, which he put to good use giving sightseeing tours over scenic San Diego. He went on to build a multi-million-dollar aerospace company now known as Teledyne Ryan. He became both rich and famous through hard work and determination. In the process, he created some of aviation's most impressive "firsts": the S-T monoplane, the Navy's Fireball jet fighter, the all-jet vertical takeoff plane and many, many more. One of San Diego's earliest aviation pioneers, his company became a major factor in San Diego's economy, drawing attention to the city where Lindbergh's *Spirit of St. Louis* was built by the company he owned.

Born January 3, 1898 in Parsons, Kansas, Ryan first saw a Wright biplane flight when he was thirteen. From that moment, he dedicated his life to flying. Growing up, he worked in his father's laundry business, delivered papers and mowed lawns. Filled with boundless energy and enthusiasm, he was always a hard worker. He tried to join the service during World War I, but he was too young. Determined to get into the air, he finally took his first flight at a civilian flying school at the age of nineteen, after his family moved to Orange, California. He ended up flying for Uncle Sam after all, earning his wings in the U.S. Air Corps. Stationed at March Field in Riverside County, he advanced rapidly, and in 1919 he received the coveted "Pursuit Pilot" rating. Before leaving the military in 1922, he flew for the Aerial Forest Patrol, searching remote Northern California areas for blazes.

Ryan saw a future in commercial aviation, and searched for an area where the weather was conducive to year-round flying. He found San

Diego, sold his car and emptied his bank account to buy a war-surplus Jenny trainer for $400, and he was in business. The ambitious youngster was given free rent at a small dirt airstrip at the foot of Broadway near the waterfront and he began giving sightseeing flights, charter hops and flight instruction, with some barnstorming on the side. With his earnings, he was able to purchase six surplus World War I planes in need of repair. He rebuilt them — and made major improvements. Soon he and a partner were operating the country's first regularly-scheduled year-round flights between San Diego and Los Angeles. The cost was about seventeen dollars, one way. The air service operated on what was then called Dutch Flats, across from the Marine Corps base — basically just a shack and some vacant land. But the flights were popular and the business thrived.

An engineering student in college, Ryan, dissatisfied with the slow-moving commercial planes of the day, had his own ideas about what a plane could and should do. So he designed and produced the M-1, a trim, high-powered single-wing plane. Air mail flyers loved it for its ruggedness, which Ryan demonstrated in flights all over the Western States. Soon his company was receiving orders for the innovative plane. Newspaper reports of the reliable new plane caught the attention of Charles Lindbergh, a young air mail pilot who wanted to be the first to make the historic nonstop solo flight from New York to Paris. The first to do it would collect a $25,000 prize. Lindbergh, with $2,000 of his own and backing from St. Louis businessmen, contacted Ryan by telegraph, asking if he could design and build a plane to do the job, and have it ready in ninety days or less. Although Ryan had sold his interest in the company to his partner, B. Franklin Mahoney, he still served as general manager. He wired back that it could be done. Operating in a factory that still reeked of fish from previous tenants (it was a cannery), Ryan and his dedicated crew worked night and day, seven days a week, in a race against the clock. The plane was ready ahead of schedule (designed and built in sixty days) at a cost of $10,000. Lindbergh test-flew the *Spirit of St. Louis* over San Diego Bay before embarking on the historic trans-Atlantic flight (May 21, 1927) that made him famous. Lindbergh's success also made Ryan famous, and the company was flooded with orders for the M-1. San Diego became known as the flight capital of the nation, and the city created the airport known today as

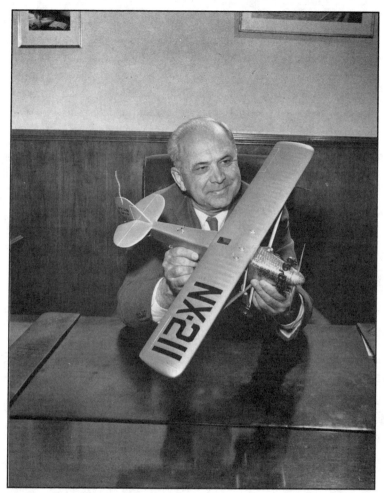

T. Claude Ryan, circa 1957

Photo courtesy San Diego Historical Society,
Union Tribune Collection

Lindbergh Field.

The following year, Ryan established the Ryan School of Aeronautics, one of the first civilian schools to train military pilots. The Ryan Aeronautical Corporation, which he also founded, became an industry leader, producing some of the finest planes of the day. The San Diego-based company was able to survive the lean years of the Depression and thrive during the years that followed under the canny leadership of 1966's Mr. San Diego, T. Claude Ryan. When Teledyne Inc. acquired Ryan's company for a reported $128 million, he was not only famous and well-respected, he was also very wealthy. He stayed on as a consultant to the company for many years.

A member of the San Diego Yacht Club, Ryan spent some time on the water, but aviation was always in his blood. In his late seventies, working out of a Kearny Mesa garage, he formed Ryson Aviation Corporation with his son, Jerome, to design, build and test an affordable powered sailplane called the Cloudster. He was working on the plans until the day before he died in 1982 at the age of eighty-four.

Suzy Spafford
Artist/Entrepreneur

As the founder and president of Suzy's Zoo, Suzy Spafford has many friends, some with odd names like Jack Quacker, Hugo Bear, Suzy Ducken, D.J. Ducken, Corky Turtle and Ollie Marmot. These are animal characters created and drawn by Spafford for her greeting card company. Suzy's Zoo, started in her apartment twenty-five years ago, has a line of over seven hundred all-occasion and seasonal cards. Her designs have expanded to stuffed animals, Mylar balloons, clothing, coffee mugs, calendars, giftware, stationery and other paper products. All but the paper products are licensed to other companies world-wide because of the time, inventory and hassles involved in producing these lines. "We're paper," Spafford says. "Remember, we're paper."

Born in Ohio in 1945, Spafford began drawing as a child and always knew she wanted to be an artist. But in her wildest daydreams she never envisioned herself as an internationally-acclaimed commercial artist. She drew for the love of drawing. When she was in the ninth grade, she started doing surf paintings in oils, and wave-riders began to buy her paintings. Later, at the urging of her high school art teacher, she took watercolor lessons, and she started selling her drawings at art marts.

While she studied art at San Diego State University, Spafford's watercolors sold well at weekend art shows and helped to pay her tuition. She created pastel and watercolor drawings, particularly cartoon characters, while children watched, and she would dress the animals and modify her characters to please them. Their suggestions worked, and the pictures sold well. Despite her part-time success, Spafford planned to give up the art and begin teaching school when she graduated. Her plans changed during her senior year when, at the last art mart she went to, a man suggested they team up and start a greeting card business. The man was Bill Murr, a medical instrument manufacturer vacationing in San Diego from Berkeley. He provided $6,000 for printing and Spafford created eight card designs. 80,000 cards were printed, her partner handling the manufacture and distribution from Northern California. Between March and June 1968, the cards sold so well that second and third print runs were needed. By the end of the year, twenty new designs were created. Murr took ninety percent of the profits, but Spafford felt it was a good opportunity. Suzy's Zoo was on its way.

During 1968, sales totaled $29,000. In 1969 they hit $42,000, then $78,000 and by 1971 sales had risen to $180,000. Murr decided he didn't want to handle the day-to-day operations anymore, and Spafford saw her opportunity. She reversed their financial arrangement, bought the inventory from him, paid it off in two years and became her own boss. She realizes now that what she learned during her first year in business was that her years at the art marts had honed her talents and prepared a product for public acceptance. She had tailor-made her art to the demands of the public and anticipated what people were going to want next. However, she says, "In the early stages, people told me what to do, and I let them tell me because these were the people that were buying the product." Stores would suggest new product ideas. "We wanted to build a greeting card line, and we needed to learn what it meant to be in this industry. We let the industry tell us how to do it."

From that point, the business really took off. Sales moved up steadily every year. By the mid-1970's, the greeting cards were being distributed nationally and her characters were appearing on other novelty items. Sales rose more than twenty times in eight years. With sales moving up so quickly, Spafford moved to a 13,000-square-foot facility. In 1980, more room was needed to handle the ever-expanding business, so she added 22,000 square feet.

"I always knew it would be a business. There was something magical once it got into print," she says. "I knew in the back of my mind that it would go on and on, but you're not supposed to be thinking that at that young age." The key to her early success was in keeping the company small enough to produce on demand. No warehousing costs and low overhead allowed Suzy's Zoo to completely turn its inventory around three or four times in a single year, a routine the company still tries to practice. Spafford recommends, "Once your company is up and running, don't overextend yourself. Make sure you can handle the orders. Otherwise, you wind up sacrificing quality for quantity." When the economy is off and times are tough, Spafford gives the following advice: "It's always a juggle to pay your bills and re-order. The way you deal with that is to get the lowest minimum you can to get the most competitive price. You never cut corners on quality." She recommends taking a conservative approach to running a business. If she had to choose between ordering a large quantity of an item with a high discount or a smaller quantity with a lower discount and not risk dead inventory, she would choose the latter. "Get the largest margin of profit with the least amount of capital outlay," she recommends. "You've got to really watch your cash flow. It's very critical."

Spafford makes all the major decisions regarding the company except for personnel and financial matters. She is, in fact, the company — one run mainly by women for women customers. Though she does most of the drawing, she has a few other artists, supervising them to make sure the characters stay true to her image. It's very difficult for other artists to create original art for the cards, but they can be trained to emulate her special style. "Suzy's Zoo is Suzy herself doing all these little characters, and how interesting can I really make it? What if people get tired of that little smiley duck and those little frogs and turtles?" she asks. "I want these characters to be commonplace in families' homes. I want them to be there for a long time to come, and I want them to be classics. I love what I do. It's that simple. And when you thoroughly enjoy your work, you never get tired of it."

Though Suzy's Zoo isn't trying to compete with the giants of the industry (Hallmark and American Greeting Cards), Spafford has created a niche of her own in the market with a devoted following. She'd like to write children's books in the future — it's something she wanted to do even before she got into greeting cards — and make videos using her characters. But whatever her goals may be, there's no doubt she will reach them.

Business

Chapter 12:
Local Businesses

Jerry G. Bishop

Rachel & Michael Brau

Dan & Ray Hamel

Diana Lindsay

Michael H. McGeath

Martin Mann

George White Marston

Mic Mead

Ira Glenn Opper

Lisa T. Richards

The Rubios

Jerry G. Bishop
Restaurant Owner/Local Media Personality

This veteran broadcaster has had over three decades of success in radio and television. You may remember him from *SunUp San Diego,* the live morning television talk show he hosted from 1978 to 1990. For the past decade, Bishop has also found success as a restauranteur. He and his wife, Liz, own and operate both the Greek Islands Cafe and Asaggio Pizza, Pasta in Seaport Village.

A Chicago native, Bishop played guitar and sang with a folk music group in his late teens and early twenties, but by 1962 came to the realization that they were never going to be the next Kingston Trio. He studied broadcasting in college to have something to fall back on, then "fell back" in a big way and made it his career. His first radio job was with a classical music station in Evanston, Illinois, but he moved into rock 'n roll, working in top stations in Washington, Cleveland and Chicago. He was one of twelve journalists picked to travel with the Beatles on their first American tour in 1964.

Bishop took a break from broadcasting in 1975 to do something he felt was more worthwhile — helping other people. "I'd done nothing but broadcasting all of my career, up until 1975, when I went to work for the National Easter Seal Society. I was Director of Corporate Affairs and co-produced the national telethon. That was the first *real* job I ever had," he says. It entailed involving corporate sponsors in the telethon, and he was directly responsible for over $11.5 million for the disabled served by Easter Seals. He returned to broadcasting when he accepted an offer to host *SunUp San Diego,* a live morning television talk show on KFMB-TV Channel 8. "I came here in 1978 and became the third host of *SunUp* and did it for twelve years," he remembers. Over those twelve years, he conducted some 14,000 interviews, including authors, celebrities and politicians. His most memorable interviews include Charleton Heston ("He did an impression of a camel!"), Alan Alda ("Who broke down in tears talking about the death of his father."), Gerald Ford ("Boring — but, hey, the guy was *President!*"), Tim Conway

("The silliest!"), G. Gordon Liddy ("The scariest!"), Cheech & Chong ("Totally stoned!") and Catherine Deneuve ("The most beautiful. I spilled coffee on her white Chanel dress!").

When the Bishops moved to San Diego in 1978, they decided to open a small business, both as a sideline to broadcasting and as an insurance policy. Six months later, Bishop discovered the yet-to-be-completed Seaport Village. The Bishops took one look at the construction site and saw the exciting possibilities. "We looked out on the bay from the deck and saw the fishing boats and said, 'This looks like a Greek restaurant,'" Bishop remembers. Their choice of spots ensured them of at least three ingredients to success: location, location and location.

"When my wife and I started in this business years ago, we didn't know where the running water was. We'd never been in business before, let alone the restaurant business." Bishop shakes his head. "We just took a shot at it, and so far, so good!" The Greek Islands Cafe was followed by Asaggio, an Italian eatery directly next door. The two provide 2,000 square feet of casual ethnic dining enhanced by spectacular views.

Since 1990, when *SunUp San Diego* went off the air after thirty years, Bishop has devoted his energies to the restaurant business, freelance radio and television performing, commercial and industrial voice-overs and videos and a variety of charitable projects. In addition, he's a highly sought-after emcee and speaker for dinners and community events. His children, Melissa (a Continental Airlines flight attendant) and Chris (who graduated from USD in 1992) both help out the family business in their spare time.

Jerry G. Bishop has touched many lives with his talents as an entertainer and his efforts on behalf of the disabled and others in need of help. If, indeed, the way to one's heart is through the stomach, you might say Bishop has touched many thousands.

Rachel & Michael Brau
Founders of Baltimore Bagel Company

Take one single man, one single woman, mix in a chance meeting at a party, add a large dash of mutual desire for a good bagel and you have the recipe for a beautiful personal relationship and a successful bagel business.

As many East Coast transplants know, the day you realize you can't find a decent bagel in California is the day homesickness really sets in. Transplants themselves, the Braus decided it was time for somebody — them — to start baking great bagels. Today, Baltimore Bagel sells over 21,000 bagels a day to a diverse group of customers, particularly Californians trying to eat healthy, good-tasting, high-quality food. In addition to twenty-five varieties of bagels made from 100 percent natural ingredients, Baltimore Bagel serves sandwiches (on bagels, of course), spreads and homemade desserts.

The first Baltimore Bagel shop opened in a strip mall in La Jolla in 1980 and the second followed in 1981. Today, there are eleven shops, nine in San Diego and two in Orange County. The secret ingredient of their success is a service-oriented approach and understanding the marketplace. According to Michael, "Each new location brings a host of new challenges. But some aspects must remain constant: our commitment to customer service, quality products and staff opportunities."

Brau was born in Easton, Pennsylvania, one of two children. He graduated from high school in Easton and went on to Franklin & Marshall College, where he received a Bachelor's degree in political science. In August, 1973, he came to San Diego to attend graduate school in marriage and family counseling at USIU. He opened a small business called Michael's Plants in September 1973 to help pay the costs of school. What began as plant parties turned into a thriving business selling and maintaining house plants for families and businesses. Three years later, Michael's Plants was a success, with a retail store in La Jolla.

In December, 1978, he attended a party in Los Angeles where he met Rachel, an advertising executive newly arrived from Baltimore. The two had much in common, both agreeing that they desperately missed good bagels and that San Diego was an exciting market for business opportunities. Since neither knew anything about making bagels, it was decided that Michael would take a two-week crash course, learning the bagel business in a bagel shop owned by friends of Rachel's family in Baltimore. Oddly enough, Michael and Rachel expanded their business while the Baltimore company had problems. Michael says, "This is an example of the student learning more than the teacher. I really learned from his errors, and in that way it helped me to be more successful."

Rachel and Michael were engaged in September, 1979 and opened their first store the following April. Six weeks later, they were married in Baltimore. Michael sold Michael's Plants to get the bagel business going and he and Rachel worked grueling hours, seven days a week. He baked and Rachel waited on customers. Michael says, "The beginning stages [of starting a business] are terrific. They're the best. I remember when we had our first store we worked twelve to fourteen hours a day. It takes a tremendous amount of energy. That was like our child. We didn't have any children at the time, and we really worked hard, but we really liked it and we were successful."

They ran into classic problems. Their management skills weren't up to coping with rapid expansion, and they were losing control of their operation. They hired consultants to help them regain control and were told they'd have to give up some of their hands-on participation. Michael became president and Rachel became vice president. Michael now runs Baltimore Bagel from behind a desk, admitting, "One thing I miss is customer service. I love selling bagels. I miss customers telling me how much they love our bagels. I enjoy that."

His advice to those planning to expand a business is, "Have a plan of how you're going to expand and have things written down to communicate your culture and your operations to the people who are going to run your business."

His unfinished education in marriage, family and child counseling has helped him manage, talk and deal with people in general. "You have to be able to listen and hear other points of view and be able to have empathy and understanding," he says, adding, "I know I'm the leader in this industry, and I'll continue to be the leader. When you're bigger, you have the ability to make sure your product is the best, to hire the best people and to make sure your stores continue to be upgraded. You have to be willing to take success and put it back into the company and give it back to your staff and your customers. As long as you're doing that, you'll always be the leader."

In their thirteenth year in both business and marriage, the Braus have eleven stores, three sons and success. In addition to their business interests, they are active in the community, saying that volunteerism is a family tradition. They want to set a good example for their children, and they're committed to giving back to the community because they have so much to be thankful for. Michael is involved with the United Jewish Federation of San Diego County, the Lawrence Family Jewish Community Centers and the United Way of San Diego. Together, they have created a recipe for life that's beneficial for everyone.

Dan & Ray Hamel
Retailers/Trendsetters

As owners of Hamel's Action Sports Center, one of San Diego's most popular beachfront stores, the two brothers have built up a reputation as the kings of the beach. "A lot of people would like to do what we do, and have tried, but they lack the know-how and they don't realize how hard you actually have to work and that you have to physically do a lot of the work yourself," says Ray. "A lot of people think we kid around a lot, and we do. But when it comes to our business we are very serious."

Don't be surprised if one of the legendary Hamels is working on your skates or skateboard or waiting on you when you rent a bike. These two are very hands-on, and they work long hours at their store. They love what they're doing, and they've been doing it well for over twenty-five years. In addition to owning and operating the store, they are also major stockholders in one of the fastest-growing sportswear companies in the country, No Fear. The San Marcos-based company was started by Mark and Brian Simo, who came to the Hamels for investment capital. If there's one thing Ray and Dan Hamel know how to do, it's spot a winner. They helped get No Fear off the ground. They also have their hands in boxing promotion and are presently working with a local fighter. And when there's an issue that involves the beach area or the latest beach trend, you can be sure that the media will turn to Ray or Dan for their insightful and colorful comments.

The Hamel brothers are living proof that the best students aren't always the only ones who go on to become successful. Dan explains, "I think many times there is too much emphasis put on education. My brother and I are prime examples that you don't have to be an excellent student to be successful. There's an unwarranted burden on a lot of kids, who aren't necessarily the best students in the world... They're made to feel like failures." The brothers learned to work with their hands, each mastering a different trade. Dan became a painter and Ray a sheet metal worker. They shared a dislike for their jobs and quit, deciding to open a bicycle shop on the boardwalk in Mission Beach in 1967.

"When we started, we never thought about failing. I mean, really, the worst thing that could happen is we would have to go back to work, and at least that way we'd get two days off a week!" says Dan. They built their little shop into a thriving business with plenty of hard work, a keen sense of timing and an awareness of and ability to take advantage of the latest trends. In the beginning, they rented and repaired bicycles, surfboards and rubber rafts at the foot of Ventura Place in Mission Beach. Gradually, they tried new things, expanding into sportswear, boogie boards and rollerskates.

They cashed in on the outdoor rollerskating craze of the 1970's when new technology turned the sport into a national mania. "We used to stay open till at least 2:00 a.m. every Friday and Saturday night, renting rollerskates," Ray remembers. "Fifteen years ago, I said to Dan, 'I bet ya if we'd stay open an extra hour a night we'd make an extra hundred bucks a week.' We tried it and it worked. Then we came up with the idea to have a midnight skate where customers could skate from 10:00 p.m. until midnight for something like five dollars. We took out a little ad and I came down here at about eight o'clock that first night, and you couldn't even get near the store because people were already lined up to rent skates."

When the rollerskating fad ended, it caught many retailers by surprise and left the Hamels in a sticky position. They went flat broke and thought about selling the business, but they backed out at the last minute. "We decided instead of selling, we'd put our noses to the grindstone and try to get back on our feet. We owed a lot of money to a lot of people, and we just called them and wrote them letters saying, 'Hey, you can send us to collection and you'll get fifty percent or you can bear with us and we'll make payments,'" Ray says. They were down but certainly not out, and most of their creditors accepted their offer. Today, Hamel's Action Sports Center is as strong as ever.

One of the reasons for their current success is Rollerblading, a trend they helped create and have capitalized on. Ray can remember a few short years ago when people laughed at this newfangled skate with wheels all in a row. Kids wanted nothing to do with it. Today, in-line skates are one of the most popular new products to hit the market in years. "Rollerblade was a great product, but it was dead in the water and we couldn't do anything with it," Ray remembers. "We tried for almost two years to push it on the kids. Then one day I got the idea to rent them, so I made a deal with Rollerblade and they gave us fifty pairs to put on rentals, and it went from a dead sport to something that not only the kids are into, but adults love it, too." The "Beach Brothers" alerted the media to this new trend and the exposure really helped get Rollerblades going. What's the secret to the media attention the Hamels receive? "We just asked," they say.

The Hamels bought the building they have occupied for over twenty-five years back in 1977. It's been remodeled and renovated and now stands as a landmark and a tribute to the entrepreneurs who have called Mission Beach home since they were kids. They're very active in, and care about, their community and its people. In the early 1980's, when the area was flooded by storms and high surf, the two worked long and hard to help protect their neighbors' property by shoveling sand into sandbags. They donated bicycles to the police patrols. And over the years they've taken a stand on a number of issues, fighting for what they believe in.

A driving force in their shared success is the fact that they know they're able to help young people by employing them, offering them support and direction in their lives. One trait they try to instill in their young workers is never to be a quitter. Ray explains, "For Danny and me, if something goes wrong it seems that it just turns us on and we work that much harder. You can bet that someday you're going to be in the position where the pressures start mounting on you and you go, 'I just can't get ahead no matter what' and you just want to quit. You might lose your job, your wife might leave you, you wreck your car and it's just one thing after another, but one thing you can't do is quit, because eventually it's all going to turn around."

The Hamels remain positive about San Diego's future as well as noting, "The climate is still great." Dan isn't one to give up on San Diego without a fight. "If you talk about doom and gloom all the time," he says, "before you know it, you're keyed into that kind of thinking. I'd rather focus on the positives."

Diana Lindsay
Entrepreneur/Author/Publisher

Diana Lindsay is a successful businesswoman, author, teacher, lecturer, marathon runner, desert naturalist and mother of two who's been happily married for over twenty-five years. She's done and seen enough in her lifetime to fill several books, and she's just the person to write the book, publish and distribute it. Books are Lindsay's business. She's president of Sunbelt Publications, a company she and her husband built from the ground up into a three-million-dollar business publishing and distributing books throughout the Southwest.

Lindsay was born in Winnipeg, Canada but grew up in Japan and Los Angeles, where she developed a taste for adventure as a freshman at UCLA. Wanting to join a bicycling club, she had to go with the best available alternate – the Bruin Mountaineers Outdoors Club. She met her husband-to-be on a twenty-four-hour crawl in a cave under the Sequoias. Lowell was president of the club, and took every opportunity to get to know her better. He strategically put her right behind him, with a large fellow behind her. The large fellow kept getting stuck, and no one could get by until he got unstuck – and so a thirty-year romance began.

Back on campus, they dated until Lowell graduated and entered the Navy. He was stationed at Pearl Harbor for a year and a half before they married. They were separated again when Lowell earned his wings as a Naval aviator and was sent to Vietnam. Lindsay continued her studies at SDSU, earning her Master's in history and geography of the Southwest. Her thesis became her first book, *Our Historic Desert* (Copley Press 1972), the story of the Anza-Borrego Desert State Park. In 1978, she and her husband co-authored the popular *Anza-Borrego Desert Region* (Wilderness Press), now in its third edition after ten printings. *The Southern Overland Route,* a guide for the cross-country bicycling enthusiast, followed.

Living in Texas in the 1970's, Lindsay became a well-known hotline columnist and editor for the *Amarillo Globe-News,* where she responded to readers' questions as *Ask Adam* (Amarillo's Dynamic Answer Man). Her San Diego area jobs have included home teaching in the Sweetwater School District, serving as Physical Director for the La Mesa YMCA and Marketing Director for Copley Books in La Jolla. The Copley job was the link between her writing career and the founding of Sunbelt Publications as a major regional book distribution company in 1985. It was a small step from selling her own books to representing the complete lines of her several publishers. This was the beginning of Lindsay's trademark "win-win" attitude. She won, the publishers won and local booksellers had more and better regional books than ever before.

Lindsay started small, initially selling a dozen titles out of her car. "The first time I went out to attempt to sell books, I took a box of books and headed for the desert, and I came back by 2:00 p.m. My husband ran out to greet me with this distressed look on his face, worried that I hadn't sold any books and that I was returning empty-handed. But I came back with a big grin on my face because I sold out everything. I was home early because I had no more books to sell!"

She filled her car with books and headed to the desert on a regular basis, usually returning with a purse full of cash and no books. Although business was good, Lindsay didn't draw a salary. She invested the earnings into the business, running a one-person operation until the paperwork got to be too much. Her first employee was a bookkeeper. As the business continued to grow, she stepped up to a VW van as her delivery truck, but had to park it on the street with their other car because the garage was overflowing with books — over 300 titles. Since she was always on the road, she hired an office manager (self-styled "garage manager") to take phone orders. She later hired an accountant who demanded that she draw at least a minimum wage salary.

Lindsay had a lot more to worry about than just salary. The weight of the books on long trips took a toll on her van, making it necessary to replace it with another, larger one. "The real crisis point came when

Diana Lindsay

we started selling books to Adventure 16," she says. "They wanted us to handle an additional 300 titles." This forced Sunbelt to move from a 500-square-foot garage into a 1,500-square-foot warehouse in 1987. The move put the pressure on and Lindsay was actually scared for the first time. She knew she had to hustle to make up for the additional overhead. In short order, she added the Navy Exchanges to her account list, as well as B. Dalton, Waldenbooks and, finally, Crown Books. Her territory grew to include Southern California and eventually the entire Southwest.

Through the years, Lindsay has seen the regional book sections of the chain stores grow from a few titles to special sections within the stores. Because they're all in one easy-to-locate section, the consumers are happy and buy more. This makes the bookstores happy, so they expand the section and order more books through Sunbelt. The result has been an increase in book sales for everyone. "I've always felt strongly that no matter what I do, it has to be a win-win situation," Lindsay says. "Otherwise, I really don't want to be a part of it. By bringing positive things into other peoples' lives, I think your own life becomes enriched. When I can reach out to other people, whether in business or a personal situation, and see them grow, I take my greatest pleasure." Through Sunbelt Publications, Lindsay provides opportunities for a growing number of small publishers and authors by giving their books exposure and getting them into bookstores.

"Sunbelt came about because of dissatisfaction, originally as an author. As a fledgling author, you want to go into bookstores and see your book, but it's not there," Lindsay explains. "I was concerned that my book wasn't there. I decided to do something about it, and that meant distributing it myself."

Starting her company with $1,000 and plenty of sweat, she built the business into a three-million-dollar-per-year corporation that employs eighteen people and provides a real service to bookstores, readers, authors and publishers alike – definitely a win-win proposition.

Michael H. McGeath
Fio's Restaurant

If you were involved in a car accident, trapped inside your vehicle for half an hour with broken ribs and various other injuries and had to be pried loose with the Jaws of Life, would you spend the time thinking about quitting your job and starting a new business? When the insurance company says they'll restore your car to like-new condition or pay you a settlement, do you take the money, planning to spend it on a risky venture like a restaurant? How about when almost everyone tells you it's a bad idea and that the location you picked out will never work – do you stick to your gut instinct and go for it anyway? When the development of the restaurant takes twice as long as you anticipated, do you sell your home to keep the project alive?

If you're Michael McGeath, the answer is "Yes!" and the result is one of downtown's most successful restaurants – Fio's Cucina Italiana.

Born in Evanston, Illinois, McGeath had a serious case of asthma as a child. His parents felt a move to the West Coast would be beneficial and the family came to San Diego when he was just eight. McGeath's father, Harlow, took a job at Ryan Aeronautical and later worked for Home Federal Savings in personnel management. "My dad was a real influential person in my life," McGeath says. "He gave me a good feeling for how to deal with people." His mother, Ruth, was a teacher and director of a preschool.

It was evident early on that McGeath's destiny might be in the restaurant business. "I've always loved working in the kitchen," he says. "My mom always used to tell me that even when I was a little kid I used to want to come help in the kitchen. I couldn't ever just make a plain peanut butter sandwich. I'd always have to trim the crust off and cut the thing at a diagonal and arrange it neatly on the plate. I've always just enjoyed being around food." The only time he strayed from his true calling was while he was a student at San Diego State University, where he earned a degree in history in 1972 and went on to study law at Western State Law School for two years. "I thought I wanted to be either a teacher or an attorney," McGeath remembers. "I was going to law school during the day and worked at restaurants at night. When I first started out in the restaurant business, I was washing dishes. At that point, I didn't want to make a career out of it. The restaurant business is a real good way to work your way through college. It gives you a lot of flexibility and you always have some cash in your pocket."

While he was working at the Old Spaghetti Factory in the Gaslamp Quarter, he decided to take a crack at the management side of the business. He went into a management training program and found that he enjoyed it. He learned his trade by doing it. Over a fourteen-year period, McGeath was a restaurant manager for the Old Spaghetti Factory, the Boathouse on Harbor Island, the London Opera House and the Hungry Hunter in Mission Valley. He served as food and beverage manager for the San Diego Yacht Club, was general manager of Stoneridge Country Club in Rancho Bernardo, then Papagayo Restaurant in Seaport Village and, finally, was the opening general manager of Silas St. John Restaurant in Kensington, one of San Diego's most critically acclaimed restaurants. As an employee, he always gave his employers 100 percent of his effort, but in the back of his mind he was beginning to think about striking out on his own and starting a restaurant. Then fate struck a decisive blow.

"Up until Fio's I'd been working for other people and going along with what they wanted to do," McGeath says. "My father instilled in me the fact that if somebody is going to take a chance on you and offer you a position, you owe it to them to give them your all. Which I always did. The whole thing with Fio's came about around the end of 1987 – I was a few months away from my fortieth birthday and I was in a car accident. I had a nice Porsche. I absolutely loved that car." A speeding car ran a red light and plowed into him, leaving McGeath trapped and injured inside what was left of his car. "It makes you think about where your life is going. I'd been thinking about starting my own business, a restaurant. Then the insurance company came to me with an offer." He decided the time was right to start doing something about opening his dream restaurant, so he took the money and from the beginning of 1988 he devoted all of his attention to developing Fio's.

McGeath had no idea how much money it would take to get started or how long it would be before he could open. He began developing the concept, did market research, made financial cost projections, put together patron profiles and much, much more. As a result, it took twice as long as he thought it would, and he began to run out of money. "I was going with basically no income for almost two years," he says. "I used up all my savings from the insurance settlement. I sold off some vintage wines that I had. It got to the point where it was about six months away from opening and I just couldn't afford to keep my house any longer." So he sold his home. "I really wanted this thing more than anything I'd done before, and I was willing to make sacrifices to make it happen. I wasn't dating or doing anything unless it related directly to the opening of the restaurant. I didn't have the finances to do anything but come home at night and work on the books or do planning."

Fio's Cucina Italiana opened on Fifth Avenue in the Gaslamp Quarter in December, 1989 to rave reviews. Restaurant critics, fellow restauranteurs and the dining public all acclaimed Fio's as the best Italian restaurant in San Diego. It became a true success story of the downtown renaissance. "I just absolutely love this business, and to have a successful restaurant is like a dream come true," McGeath says. He looks like a genius now, but when he was in the planning stages and looking for investors, few believed he knew what he was doing. "There were plenty of doubters. It's really hard when you first go out on your own to convince somebody to believe in you. You just have to keep believing in yourself, even though people keep rejecting you," he says. "I probably talked to at least 400 people before I got the thirty-five investors I needed. That means nine out of ten people I talked to didn't really believe in what I was doing. I knew I had a good business plan, but I think the principal reason I got many of the rejections from people was a result of the location. It was kind of a wasteland down there. I just kept knocking on doors until I found people who believed in the project and the location." McGeath hadn't chosen the location arbitrarily. He took into consideration the redevelopment effort in the downtown area, the Convention Center and the lack of competition – at the time – in the Gaslamp District.

Not content to rest on his laurels, McGeath is planning another venture for the historic Gaslamp Quarter. It's unlikely he'll find any doubters this time around, after the success of Fio's. "The misconception is that restaurants in general make a ton of money," he says. "That is simply not the case. There's a fine line between making and losing money in any particular month."

McGeath always tries to negotiate the best deals without compromising the restaurant's high quality and reputation for excellence. He's also constantly training his staff, and he gives them a lot of credit for Fio's success. "I'm just as important as the dishwasher in the back who makes sure the dishes are spotless," he points out. "If the cook doesn't do a good job, or if the waiter doesn't do a good job, the whole thing falls apart. It's a team effort, and I'm just another cog on the wheel." When hiring, he looks for employees with enthusiasm who truly enjoy the business. He doesn't necessarily hire the most experienced person for the job, because he likes to train them in the style of service or the style of cooking that he wants them to have for his restaurants.

"You can't instill enthusiasm or a caring attitude – that's something that has to come from the heart," he says. "If you can find those people and surround yourself with those types of people and you train them and give them direction in the way you want to go, ideally you should be successful."

Martin Mann
Photographer

A career in photography came together for Martin Mann with the three-shot sequence of Steve Garvey's dramatic home run on October 6, 1984 when the Padres beat the Chicago Cubs in the fourth game of the National League Championship series. Since then, his photographic assignments have included celebrities, supermodel Kim Alexis, local sports hero Tony Gwynn and other national and international clients. Mann's work can be seen in *Sports Illustrated* and *Sporting News Baseball Yearbook* among others, and many of his photographs appear in this book.

A San Diego native, Mann became interested in photography as a student at Patrick Henry High School studying Occupational Photography. After learning the basics of his craft, he began to get surfing, concert and public relations photo assignments. To support a growing and expensive hobby, he took work as a bellman at the Hilton Hotel. While there, the enterprising Mann took on extra jobs, photographing conventions, tours and taking publicity shots for the hotel. A vacation in Hawaii sealed his fate when he returned with postcard-perfect photos. He began to formulate the ideas and set the goals that ultimately led to his current success. In 1981, he decided to put it all on the line and turn his passion into profit by becoming a full-time professional photographer. He resigned from the Hilton and, starting with a will to succeed and a shoestring budget, he started paying his dues. "When I first started out, I was doing a lot of work that I wasn't getting paid for, but in the long run it paid off for me," he says. His charitable beginnings laid the foundation for later work, providing him with personal contacts, invaluable experience and referrals.

In 1983, like many other camera buffs, Mann went to Jack Murphy Stadium for Camera Day, hoping to get photos of some of the players in

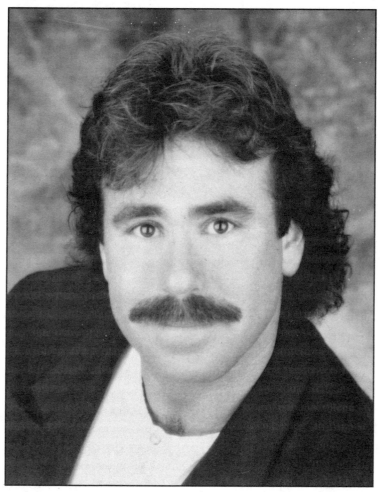

Martin Mann   *Photo by Barbara Baros*

action. His photo of Dave Dravecky caught the attention of *Baseball Gold* editor Fred Rogers, who used it for the magazine's June cover. Several cover shots later, Mann caught the attention of the Padres front office, and Mann was offered the job of Official Team Photographer. "Many people thought I had a cushy job," Mann says, "but in reality it was working long hours, most weekends and holidays, searching for the perfect shot."

His diligence paid off with a great opportunity, capturing on film what turned out to be one of the greatest moments in San Diego sports history. What eventually became known as "the" home run, Steve Garvey's game-winning hit, now hangs in the San Diego Hall of Champions.

Mann also teaches classes in advertising photography at the Advertising Arts College, where he shares technical knowledge and practical experience gained over the years.

George White Marston
Businessman/Civic Leader (1850-1946)

More than a self-made businessman, George White Marston was a civic leader who devoted much of his life helping to establish San Diego as not only a thriving city, but a pleasant place in which to live. After building his tiny dry-goods store into San Diego's finest department store, he used his business expertise for the betterment of the town. He was involved in city planning, developing many of the parks we enjoy today and seeing to it that San Diego's history would be preserved for future generations. He's been called the leading San Diegan of all time and the city's number one citizen. He died May 31, 1946, at the age of ninety-six.

Born October 22, 1850 on a farm in Wisconsin, Marston and his father traveled west by railroad to California when he was twenty. They sailed from San Francisco, arriving in San Diego on October 24, 1870. At the time, San Diego was very much a frontier town, with dusty dirt roads and a population of only a few thousand. Charming and picturesque, it was a town destined to grow, with plenty of opportunities for a hardworking young man like Marston. His first job was as a desk clerk in the palatial new Horton House, the center of public life at the time. Before coming west, Marston had worked in a bank, learning double-entry bookkeeping. After six months at Horton House, he went to work as an assistant bookkeeper for A. Pauly & Sons, the largest store in the city at the time. Located at the foot of Fifth Street, the store was built on pilings at the edge of San Diego Bay and provided supplies to steamships and freight wagons. After a year, he was offered a chance to work with his best friend, Charles S. Hamilton, as a clerk in Joseph Nash's general store.

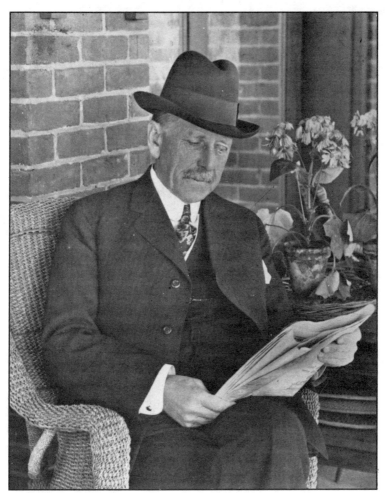

George Marston   *Photo courtesy San Diego Historical Society*

The two friends soon became partners, buying the business from Nash for $10,000. Marston borrowed his half from his father, paying him back in full – with interest – within five years. Theirs was a typical small town store. They sold mostly groceries, hardware and household goods, along with some dry goods and men's clothing. They ran the store successfully from 1873 to 1878 before they decided to split into two stores carrying different lines of merchandise. Marston took dry goods and clothing. They remained the best of friends, marrying sisters and becoming brothers-in-law.

Marston turned his honeymoon into a buying trip, purchasing goods for his new store. The little shop opened August 8, 1878 on the northwest corner of Fifth and D Streets (now Broadway). His first day's sales were a modest $10.50. Deciding he was located too far uptown, Marston moved before the end of the year to a better site on Fifth between Market and G Streets. He worked long and hard, learning more about his products, and it paid off as the store picked up momentum. By 1882, the business outgrew its location and moved once again, this time to the northeast corner of Fifth and F Streets. It remained there for fourteen years, surviving the great flood of 1884, the real estate boom of the mid-1880's and the collapse and hard times of the early 1890's.

Marston built his tiny store into the city's finest department store, paying above-scale wages, offering self-improvement courses for employees and giving many of them a chance to acquire a share in the ownership when the business was incorporated in 1912. Marston's became a place to purchase the latest trends, brought to town from Marston's regular trips to New York and San Francisco. It was not only a place to shop, but a place where friends got together and stayed for lunch. Marston's continued to grow and relocate until it merged with The Broadway in 1961.

Building a successful business wasn't his only goal. George Marston dreamed of a prosperous and beautiful San Diego, giving generously of his money and time. His money and leadership became significant to every major cause that made San Diego a better place to live. He devoted many years of unselfish service as a city councilman, fire commissioner, park commissioner and president of the Chamber of Commerce. He helped organize and was elected the first president of the San Diego YMCA, he was founding president of the San Diego Historical Society... the list goes on and on. Marston put his money where his mouth was, spending $10,000 in 1902 to hire Samuel Parsons, landscape architect for the City of New York, to draw up plans for Balboa Park. He also developed Presidio Park and the Junipero Serra Museum and donated them to the city.

In 1940, on his ninetieth birthday, Marston realized a lifelong ambition as he stepped down as president of the company he built to devote all his time to civic affairs. San Diegans will never be able to repay George White Marston for all he did in seventy-six years of helping to make San Diego into America's finest city. He'll always be remembered as a successful businessman, a great civic leader and a pioneer in the beautification of San Diego.

Mic Mead
Entrepreneur/Owner of Adventure 16

Mic Mead's company has a mission. And very employee there knows it — it's emblazoned on the front of every Employee Handbook. "Adventure 16's objective, within the outdoor industry, is to provide an environment where we can all achieve a balance among enjoyable lifestyles, corporate success and our customers' satisfaction." It's not an empty motto. Achieving and maintaining the balance in that triangle is an ongoing process, regularly reexamined by managers, employees and, most of all, by the CEO himself.

Adventure 16 stores are known to outdoor enthusiasts for their enticing environment, log-cabin ambiance, woodsy incense and nature tapes (thunderstorms included). More than just a place to shop, Adventure 16 stores are destinations in themselves, filled with high-quality products and salespeople who are knowledgeable about their sports and extraordinarily friendly. The San Diego-based company is not only a successful retailer with six stores throughout Southern California (three in San Diego), but also a manufacturer, wholesaler, publisher and general promoter of rock climbing, backpacking and related outdoor activities. The driving force behind it is entrepreneur Mic Mead, although he'll be the first to credit his employees for making the company grow and prosper.

Born in Indianapolis, the Purdue forestry graduate came to San Diego to serve his commission in the Navy in the mid-1950's. Deciding he wanted to make San Diego his home, he purchased a parcel of land on Mt. Helix and proceeded to build his own house from the ground up in eight months. He had no experience building homes, but after he got out of the Navy he went into the construction business full-time. "If anybody said to me, 'You can't do it,'" Mead explains, "I'd tell them they just didn't know Mic Mead."

Along with partners, he completed about thirty homes – then got out of the business. Looking back on this experience helps him remain positive about San Diego's future. "I've been here since 1955," he says, "and while I was in the building game we experienced a turnaround much like what's happening today. We got caught with projects that we couldn't sell for their financing, but San Diego came back, and it's going to come back again. We're going through a cycle. Cycles are always going to happen, and even though people are leaving San Diego now, more still want to come here. I advise people to buy real estate in these down cycles – at the very least to buy their home."

Mead decided his next venture would be something he truly enjoyed, so he started a woodcarving business and ran it for almost ten years. In later years he turned this interest in carving into sculpting in clay, with further success. Several of his bronzes have been sold to collectors, and other pieces of his work adorn offices at his company's headquarters. He had always been a camper and developed a keen interest in backpacking, which is how he first came into contact with a small company called Adventure 16.

Begun by a group of Explorer Scouts in the early 1960's, the name came from the idea of making 16mm adventure films about river running. When the group's interests moved to backpacking, they began to manufacture their own gear in a garage. They set out to improve the comfort of the backpacks available at the time, and their success established comfort characteristics and standards previously unknown. Their innovations were incorporated into Adventure 16's top-of-the-line backpack.

When Adventure 16 took up residence on Gillespie Field next to Mead's woodcarving business in 1968, he began offering suggestions to improve the products, gradually becoming more and more involved. High-quality sleeping bags and lightweight dome tents were added to the production line, and the company started to become internationally known for innovation and quality. The dome tents as well as hip carry-packs were technological and conceptual firsts.

In 1970, Mead financed and incorporated Adventure 16 and the company took its first step toward real growth. By the end of 1971, an old log house in El Cajon became the first Adventure 16 lodge store, complete with its own factory. It soon came to be regarded as a mecca for serious outdoor people as San Diego grew and the backpacking craze took hold. "When San Diego was smaller, I had the market pretty much alone," Mead recalls. "But in my business, as in any business, a growing market encourages competition." Adventure 16 rode the crest of the backpacking boom and continued to do well after the boom faded by focusing on exceptional customer service. "You don't necessarily need a growing market to do well," Mead explains. "You just need to do extremely well within your own market."

How did Mic Mead, once a deputy assessor for San Diego County, build Adventure 16 into the thriving business it is today? "If there is any one key to success, I think it's delegation," he says. "Hire the very best people you can, pay them accordingly and then trust them."

Mead has taken on almost every function in the company himself at one time or another over the years, and he learned that he could always find somebody to specialize in each task and do it better than he could. "The one function I really do serve, as CEO, is to keep everyone focused on a vision," he says.

Mead believes that the entrepreneur needs to be able to realize when he's needed and when he's not. The entrepreneur who moves up to CEO will be the successful owner. "Get out of their way, but keep them focused," he advises. Adventure 16 is thirty-five percent employee-owned, through an employee stock ownership plan implemented in 1987. It's one way of ensuring that the focus of the employees is shared.

Today, the Mission Valley location serves as Adventure 16's headquarters. Mead's office is a log cabin in the center of the store. The building also houses all the other divisions of the company, including a wholesale division which supplies outdoor accessories (many of which are manufactured locally by the company) to over 2,500 dealers throughout the world.

The company that once operated out of a garage has long since become a multi-million-dollar operation. "My goals have always been modest ones," Mead says in retrospect. "With Adventure 16, my goal was for my employees and myself to be able to enjoy our work and to operate on a plateau that was economically successful. It was never to be a giant company. I've always managed to control the growth and keep it within a scale that we could enjoy."

Ira Glenn Opper
Owner of Frontline Video & Film

Executive Producer and President Ira Glenn Opper, along with partner Jim Marino, owns Del Mar-based Frontline Video & Film, a state-of-the-art production company famous for being the leader in producing cutting-edge action sports programs for national cable TV. Over the past ten years, they have carved out a niche in the cable industry and dominated it.

There is never a dull moment for the Emmy-winning production company. Opper has produced and directed over fifty episodes of the award winning *Surfer Magazine,* seen by over sixty million households in the United States. Opper and his hard-core crew, which sometimes includes his wife Gerri, have journeyed to exotic locales all over the world in search of perfect waves. Their travels have taken them to the jungles of Western Java and Costa Rica, to Barbados, Tahiti and Fiji and to Hawaii more times than he can count to capture on film some of the most radical moments in surfing history.

Opper is a true professional who understands all aspects of his business. He's worked every job in his field, starting as mail clerk at KCOP in Los Angeles and moving up to director and producer of his own programs. He has four Emmys, an Ace (for excellence in cable) and, most recently, a Telly for his innovative and imaginative approach to his work. Opper believes in being involved in most of the sports he covers. "I keep my interests and my profession in a nice groove, so that I get a little of both," he says. Many people envy his lifestyle, but he offers the following story to illustrate the less glamorous side of his work: "A friend of mine, Mike, said, 'I'll do anything in the world to go on a trip, see what you do on the show.' I said, 'Okay, in two weeks we're going to Costa Rica. You can carry my bags. That's your job.' At the end of the trip, after three days in the tropical rainforest driving at two miles an hour through rivers to get shots of surf in uninhabited tropical jungle, after taking off in a downpour in a single-engine Cessna from a mud-drenched pasture fishtailing until we got airborne, and after all the rain and all the hassles and all the bugs and other obstacles to getting the show done, by the time we got back Mike said he never wants to go anywhere for free again." Opper thrives on the travel and loves what he does. He feels that getting paid for doing something you're driven to do is the ultimate form of success.

Born January 21, 1949 in Encino, California, his first surfing experience came at the age of fourteen when his grandfather took him and his best friends to Santa Monica. They rented boards and surfed for hours despite the cold. The biggest single influence on his career came shortly thereafter, when he saw the classic Bruce Brown surf flick, *Endless Summer.* "Before Bruce Brown's movie," Opper says, "no one was telling the real surfer's story. It's always been Gidget goes bonkers or idiots dancing on their beach towels – and then along came *Endless Summer* and it validated the surfer's lifestyle. It changed the whole image of the sport." He made *Surfer Magazine* as a modern version of *Endless Summer* after kicking around surf programming on cable television in 1975 with the very first surf show, *Solo Sports.*

At Arizona State University, Opper saw the possibilities that cable presented. "It offered the opportunity to do many different aspects of production, which was more appealing than just being a cameraman or just being an editor," he says. He immediately set his sights and goals on getting into the cable world as a producer. By the time he graduated, he had produced and directed a weekly show and had enough technical expertise to get a job doing anything in a television studio. That early training and diversity has helped Opper achieve success as the undisputed leader in his field today.

Opper feels that parallels can be drawn between success in life and surfing. "The fear you learn in surfing and the challenge of pushing the limits and pulling it off create a feeling of exhilaration. The thrill and rush of adrenaline created by going a little further than your mind thinks you should and the knowledge from that experience give you the edge in the real world and can help get you through situations that would be impossible for someone who hasn't pushed the fear factor," he says.

Frontline Video has five new shows, *Surf Chronicles, Wave Sailing in Paradise, Quiet Storm* (skateboarding), *Hot Water* (jet skiing) and *Hot Air (ballooning).*

Lisa T. Richards
Businesswoman/Founder of Picnic People

What would you do if you were asked to fix up to 2,000 bag lunches every day for three weeks? If you're Lisa Richards, president of Picnic People, it's just another job — hectic, but possible. During the riots in Los Angeles, she trucked that many lunches to Los Alamitos in the wee hours every morning for the National Guard.

Picnic People was born from a casual conversation with a friend in 1979. "We were sitting in a bar in Mission Valley, just talking, and I said, 'Wouldn't it be fun to have a picnic business... and call it Picnic People. We could be the people who would do your picnic.' And the name just stuck." What started as an enjoyable way to spend weekends and a distraction from schoolwork grew into Professional Picnic People, Inc., a San Diego-based corporation which now includes three separate companies: Picnic People, the outdoor division specializing in picnics and beach parties; Festivities Catering and Special Events, a full-service caterer and Destination San Diego, a firm that markets San Diego nationally and internationally as a destination for conventions and special events. Singly and together, they are leaders in the industry. "To remain the leader," Richards says, "we have to continue to be innovative and creative, and that requires being rested and able to observe what other people are doing — to be aware. Everybody is working so hard on the business that we forget to look around."

After leaving the University of San Diego in 1977 with two years to go (which she now regrets), Richards drifted from job to job, disinfecting tuxedo shoes at Sears, waitressing, babysitting and lifeguarding. "I was starving, and I had to make my rent," she says, so she picked up any odd job she could. After that conversation with her friend, a roofing contractor, the two formed a partnership and she began working out of her home with a business phone, cards, the Yellow Pages and a post office box.

In 1979, Richards met her future husband, Rick, when he was in town for a few days from his job in Iran. In 1980 they were married by proxy, Richards here and Rick in Brazil. In 1981 she left the business to her partner and moved to Brazil to be with her husband. Three years later, they returned with a baby and another on the way, and Richards began working for a tour company. Disliking the routine and being away from her children, she decided to reactivate Picnic People. Shortly thereafter, Rick was asked to transfer to Saudi Arabia and Richards refused to go. Decisions had to be made and a rough time followed. Rick eventually declined the transfer and worked out of San Diego until he, too, joined Picnic People.

In 1986, Richards moved her operation out of her home and into 1,700 square feet of space, while her staff expanded as well. They averaged three events per weekend during the picnic season that year. Six months later, the company grew again, taking on a full-time staff of four and a part-time staff of seventy-five. By this time, they were handling six events per weekend. In early 1987, additional staff was added and they were able to handle twenty events per weekend simultaneously at separate locations. Today, the staff has ballooned to forty full-time and over 400 part-time people operating out of 14,000 square feet of space in the Miramar area, space filled with equipment, props, games and prizes. Richards handles sales, administration, personnel and catering, while her husband heads finance, operations and warehousing. She's the "people person" while Rick is the "big picture guy." Although Richards doesn't see herself as a saleswoman, "I could always talk about what I believe in," she says. Someone once said of her, "People buy Lisa."

Richards and her company have garnered their share of awards and recognition since 1988, being named Chamber of Commerce Small Business of the Month in 1988. Richards was Woman Entrepreneur of the Year for San Diego County in 1989 and Small Business Person of the Year in 1991. Richards is actively involved with several local committees and councils and wants to be a good advocate for women in business. Her advice to anybody starting a business is to "get in touch with the Small Business Development Center of the Chamber of Commerce. I go in twice a year and they analyze my business." She also recommends using the services of the Small Business Administration, including SCORE (Service Corps of Retired Executives). She notes the importance of establishing a banking relationship from the beginning.

"It really means just going in and meeting the bank manager where you bank, sharing your concepts for your business and checking in regularly. Then, when you need a line of credit, they know who you are."

Richards is a very good delegator who has surrounded herself with "people who are much smarter than myself. And they are so capable, hardworking and creative that it is very easy to delegate a lot of the day-to-day responsibility," she says. This frees her to do sales, visionary and strategic planning.

The Richardses, who now have three sons, agree that it's not all fun and games working together. It's sometimes hard to leave the work at the office. Richards says, "I have hurdles to overcome every day, that's just part of doing business, and I can get over those. The challenge is to stay as balanced as possible between being married, having children, running a business, staying healthy and keeping friends. That's a constant challenge."

She's very optimistic about San Diego. "I think San Diego is going to continue to grow. I think San Diego has the most to offer of any California city," she says. "Yes, we have problems, but I think we still have a very bright future and I look for pockets of gold." She continues, "I didn't set out to be the largest special events company in town. I set out to be happy and prosperous. But there just isn't an end to the opportunities out there."

The Rubios
"First Family" of Fish Tacos

Rubio's Restaurants, Inc., a family-owned and operated business, is truly a family endeavor. Ralph Rubio and his father, Ray, co-founded this upscale Mexican takeout restaurant chain in 1983. Now, Ray is chairman, Ralph is president, his brother Robert is vice president of operations, brother Richard is vice president of expansion and sister Gloria is vice president of training. The youngest son, Roman, is still in college, but helps out at the corporate level whenever needed.

While at San Diego State University, Ralph and his buddies would head for San Felipe in Baja California on the weekend, and they loved the fish tacos there. In 1978, after declining an offer to start a business

The Rubio family, (from left to right) Ralph, Gloria, Robert, Ray and Richard.   Photo by Martin Mann

in San Diego, Carlos, the street vendor they bought their tacos from, gave Ralph his recipe. Five years later, Ralph's dad provided the nearly $50,000 of his hard-earned savings needed to take over a failed hamburger stand in Pacific Beach. By that time, Ralph had gained experience in a number of different capacities, working at the Old Spaghetti Factory, Hungry Hunter and Harbor House, but nothing had prepared him for running his own business. "There were times when Dad and Robert were helping me cook, Mom was bagging orders and Richard was ringing them up," Ralph recalls. "The first day it was so busy it was a nightmare." He had one woman, a holdover from the burger stand, to help. "I never could have done it without her," he says. They started with $100 a day in sales, but within three years their first location was doing $3,000 per day.

As the curious came to see what a fish taco was, and as the business grew, Ralph remembers, "I was naive when this whole thing started, and I think it was better that I was, because I really didn't know what I was getting into. A lot of people have ideas and a lot of people have money, but you just have to have that go for it attitude, and you almost have to be naive." He also says, "I don't think people realize all that went on during the first few years. It was a completely new business. We made a lot of mistakes, and there were a lot of long hours. Now you see a very smooth operating restaurant machine, but in the very beginning there were a lot of problems." Ray agrees, saying, "Sales were not up to our expenses. It took awhile to educate the public that the product was there and that it was a good product."

They knew from the beginning that the one location at Mission Bay was going to work and they were going to become a chain of success-ful restaurants, or it wasn't going to work and Ralph would end up managing a restaurant for someone else. "My dad's always been a risk-taker," Ralph says, "and he used to tell me, 'If you get a chance to work for yourself, don't work for somebody else.'"

In 1986, a second Rubio's opened on College Avenue near SDSU. That year they sold their one millionth fish taco. From 1986 to the present, Rubio's has opened one to three restaurants per year. There are now twelve in San Diego and two in Orange County – and locations in Los Angeles are on the drawing board. In addition to fish tacos, which account for sixty percent of their sales, they offer Baja-style Mexican favorites. Rubio's is also part of the concessions lineup at all Padres and Charger games at San Diego Jack Murphy Stadium. In 1990, when it was first offered at the stadium, the fish taco was voted the best new food by both Charger and Padres fans. Today, hundreds of South-ern California restaurants have added fish tacos to their menu.

From 1987 through 1992, Rubio's has accumulated a number of awards, including California Retailer of the Year (1987, La Mancha Development Company of Los Angeles), San Diego Retail Business of the Year (1988, Greater San Diego Chamber of Commerce) and *Inc.*

Magazine's San Diego Business of the Year founded by a minority in 1989. They were a finalist in that magazine's 1989 Entrepreneur of the Year contest. They were awarded the 1989 Community Service Award for Economic Development by the Mexican American Business and Professional Association of San Diego County and appeared at number 316 on *Hispanic Business Magazine's* 1991 "Hispanic 500" list of the nation's largest Hispanic-owned businesses, moving up to 259 in 1992. Averaging 10,000 fish tacos a day, Rubio's has sold over six million in San Diego alone. In 1986 the slogan "Home of the Fish Taco" was copyrighted and is displayed at each restaurant.

Ralph Rubio had no marketing or advertising background when the first Rubio's opened. His first marketing experience "was the constant line of media sales reps coming into my restaurant to pitch me," he remembers. "I met reps from all types of media, and they were great customers and a forced education." He learned his lessons well. He made his first media buy, space in the *San Diego Reader,* because he read the weekly newsmagazine himself. Later he went into radio advertising with 91X, because that's what he listened to.

Marketing planning now takes place weekly. "Image is important," Ralph says. "From the type of food to the employees' dress to the decor, all must be part of the marketing concept." Rubio's sells t-shirts with their logo, sweatshirts, caps, bumper stickers and other merchandising tools. They've produced manuals and videos including job descriptions for each of their employees (now numbering approximately 300 full and part-time workers), close monitoring of product costs, and documentation of the recipes by weight of ingredients. "We have been and will remain focused on food quality, customer service and cleanliness," says Robert.

The Rubios are proud to be called Southern California's first family of fish tacos. And they're proud to be part of the San Diego business community. Ralph says, "I've noticed that when I travel, and I go to some nice places, San Diego is the best place. I just can't see myself living anywhere else. San Diego is going through an adjustment that was probably long overdue. It's must a matter of riding it out."

Ray says, "Some people don't realize just how good we have it here."

Business

Chapter 13:
Individuals

Dave Drexler

Mary-Ellen Drummond

Bill Holland

Gabriel Wisdom

Dave Drexler
Man of Many Voices

Bet you don't know his name. You won't be able to describe his face. But that voice – you definitely know that voice. Or some of them. Or at least one of them.

Dave Drexler has been doing character voices for years in local radio commercials. His take-off on Andy Rooney, "Sixty Seconds with Randy Looney," was a huge success for a local car dealership. Drexler's impression sounded so much like Rooney that the advertiser had to add a disclaimer at the end of the spot, stating that the celebrity voice was an impersonation. Drexler credibly parrots close to a hundred character impersonations, from famous politicians to sports personalities to entertainers and cartoons. Not to mention some of his own original voices. He also serves as KPBS-TV's staff announcer when not running his successful radio-commercial company, Outgoing Messages! His impressive client list reads like a *Who's Who* in San Diego Business and he's hawked everything from furniture to autos to hamburgers.

A San Diego native, Drexler realized early in life that he had a rare talent for doing impersonations. At Crawford High School, he used his voice to entertain friends, and it eventually earned him an internship at San Diego State University's radio station KCR, where he became program director after only a year. Drexler got his start as a disc jockey with KPRI-FM at nineteen. They liked his work so much they offered him a full-time job, but he turned it down so he could concentrate on his studies. His parents encouraged him to complete his college education. They both have worked in radio – his father as an announcer in the 1930's and 1940's, his mother as an announcer and actress in radio drama – and they knew very well that radio is not a secure field.

Drexler graduated from SDSU with a degree in telecommunications and film, along with years of valuable on-air experience. He worked for KPBS-FM and XHRM-FM, in his father's clothing store and as an audio-visual technician, which he describes as "basically heavy lifting in a coat and tie." He saved his money so he could travel the world and set out on a "self-questioning" journey to Sydney, Australia and Japan. In Australia, he landed a job as a part-time disc jockey on a Sydney radio station for six weeks. He taught English and did voice-over work in Japan. When he returned to the States, he wanted to become a television movie reviewer or newscaster in a small market like Bakersfield, but nothing like that panned out. After much rejection, he got a break out of the blue while driving home from a fruitless job-hunting trip. He heard Z90, a San Diego station, change its format right before his ears. The following Monday, he sent them a demo tape of his character voices. One of the salesmen heard it and insisted that the station hire him. He worked weekends as a DJ, but the salesman liked using his character voices in his ads. They built a long-standing working relationship that has continued at other stations as well.

When Drexler got serious about using his character voices to make a living, he hit it big. He had the opportunity to learn about production at Z90's fully-equipped studio and by the time he did the Randy Looney ad he was moving closer to his goal of being on radio in a creative and commercial way. While that campaign ran, he was on the air every week with a new commercial, coming up with ideas for over 150 different spots. He now adds *entrepreneur* to his list of credits with his own radio production company. "I enjoy being able to have control over what I do — controlling the product, controlling creativity and being in control of my own affairs rather than being beholden to others for employment. Even though I still work for KPBS-TV, they give me quite a bit of latitude there. Success is being able to do what I want to do and being able to live the lifestyle I idealize for myself," he says.

Drexler takes his business seriously. He works extremely hard and puts in long hours. "I'm a perfectionist, and it doesn't matter how much I'm getting paid for a job. I take it with the same degree of seriousness and put the same amount of effort into it." Can this be the voice behind the man who sells new and used cars? Absolutely.

Mary-Ellen Drummond
Consultant/Speaker/Author/Entrepreneur

Mary-Ellen Drummond was so timid growing up she found it excruciating to make eye contact with anyone, much less squeak out a simple hello. It's truly remarkable that today she's a nationally-known speaker, trainer, motivator and recipient of more than seventy-five awards. "I think because I was so shy I have a lot of empathy for people who are really afraid of public speaking," she says.

Through her company, Polished Presentations, she has made a career out of educating and inspiring people to overcome their fear of public speaking. She helped thousands develop better communication skills, from CEO's to terrified individuals stepping out in front of an audience for the first time.

Drummond took her first step twelve years ago, when she joined Toastmasters. Since then, she's been Toastmaster of the Year twelve times and ranked in the top twenty-seven speakers out of some 150,000 members in worldwide competition. She served as president of the San Diego Chapter of the National Speakers Association and is considered an expert in the areas of communication and presentation skills – and has, in fact, authored a book on that subject, *How to Communicate with Power, Polish and Pizazz* (Pfeiffer & Co.). Never again shy, public speaking and the desire to help others overcome their fears have become her passions.

In the ninth grade, Mary-Ellen resolved to become more outgoing. "I was determined to become friendly no matter how painful it was, and I started forcing myself to say hello to people. I had a goal and I saw what it would take to achieve that goal – that I couldn't be shy any longer, that I had to force myself to overcome the fear." To this day, her proudest accomplishment is being awarded "friendliest senior" of her graduating class of 550 students.

Born September 12, 1947 in southern Illinois, Drummond's family moved to California when she was four. Both her parents were teachers, and it was assumed that she'd go to college. She attended night school at California State University at Fullerton while working full time to support herself. She graduated with a liberal arts degree and no idea what to do next. "In high school and college, I was told that a woman with a college degree can be a librarian, a schoolteacher or a nurse instead of an administrator or a doctor," she says.

In 1975, Drummond signed up for a six-week course at a career planning center in Los Angeles. There she found out that over 500 job possibilities existed for men and only 100 for women with exactly the same qualifications. "It was mind-boggling," she says. "I still remember how shocked I was that that was true. And why was it?" She still can't figure out why some of the inequalities that existed back then prevail today, but offers a possible solution: "I think that the more we can strengthen our own self-esteem and the more we can empower our-selves, the more we'll set a good example for other people to see that we can change some perceptions as well as get women to realize they have tremendous potential."

After her aptitude course, she was told that her best bet was to go into sales in the medical field. She embarked on an incredibly success-ful thirteen-year career with Bristol Myers U.S. Pharmaceutical Divi-sion, where she distinguished herself as a consistently high achiever, earning the title "Sales Representative of the Year" in a field previously dominated by men. In 1979, Bristol Myers sent her to a leadership program to assess her managerial potential. There she saw herself on videotape for the first time. "I was sitting in a chair and I'd cross my legs at the knee. I'd also cross my ankles and wrap my leg around the leg of the chair. I looked like a contortionist," she remembers. "I was fidgeting and looking at the ceiling. I saw exactly what I didn't want to be. I was embarrassed for myself." The man evaluating her offered criticism while leaving her ego intact. He commented that she was great one-on-one but lacked leadership skills in a group. He suggested she try Toastmasters. "I really didn't know what Toastmasters was. I thought it was either people who drank a lot or fixed toasters. I went to a meeting and I thought, 'I really want to do that! I want to be able to have the confidence to stand up and speak in front of a group of people,'" Drummond remembers. "I thought of it as very empowering. It changed my life."

In 1980, Drummond started her own club in Del Mar, unheard of for a beginner. She became the area governor in 1982 and attended over 200 meetings. The following year she competed in the humorous speech contest and went all the way to the regional finals, finishing seventh in a region of 20,000 members. Her accomplishments in local Toastmasters are legendary, serving as an inspiration and example for anyone who feels they could never overcome their fear of public speaking.

In January, 1988 her family doctor and close friend was tragically killed by a drunk driver. Drummond was asked to speak at the driver's sentencing, to represent the medical community and demand the harshest sentence possible. As a result, she became involved in the San Diego chapter of Mothers Against Drunk Driving (M.A.D.D.). She volunteered to train their speakers bureau, with the goal of getting the word out faster. She put together a training video and spoke at their national conference.

But speaking was still just a hobby for Drummond. She was paid fifty dollars for her first speaking engagement in 1981. Now she was speaking more and more, but still working for Bristol Myers. She became utterly exhausted. "I used to get up at 4:30 a.m. to do my paperwork to keep up," she remembers. "I wanted to prove to people that I could do it all, that I could be the mom with a daughter who's healthy and well-adjusted and have a husband who thinks I'm great while continuing to make my goals and be a good rep. That's a lot. I tend to do too much sometimes."

Drummond decided to quit her sales job to become a full-time speaker after her husband assured her that he was behind her 100 percent. Now she runs her own company and has never worked harder. "I find that I could work twenty-four hours a day if I let myself," she admits. "There's always something to do. It's exciting, it's challenging and I love it – and when you love something, it's hard to stop." It wasn't easy for Mary-Ellen Drummond to walk away from the security of her job, with its good salary, expense account, company car and incentive trips. But she knew she had to cut the umbilical cord to realize her full potential and fulfill her goals. She was scared and cried at the beginning of her venture, but she never really doubted that she'd make it. After all, overcoming fear is her specialty.

Stanford University gave their incoming MBA's a report that said your success in life could be predicted by how you answered one question: Would you be willing right now to get up and give a speech? The people who say yes are the risk-takers. If you're not willing to take risks, you're not going to make it. "Because public speaking is the number one greatest fear, the greater the fear, the greater the risk, the greater the reward. If we could only get people to take more risks on themselves," Drummond says. Another factor in determining one's potential for success is the ability to take action. "I see a lot of people who want to be successful, but they never take action on the things they learn. They'll say, 'I could do that!' but they don't do it. It's the ten percent I see who take action, take risks and empower other people who are successful."

Empowering other people is something Drummond does very well. "I feel I'm successful when I have touched someone else and inspired them to take action. It's not enough that I make people laugh or feel good or they have a good time when they hear me speak. I want to inspire action," she says. "They say when you can have an impact on just one person, that person will have an impact on 250 other lives."

Bill Holland
Broker, Broadcaster

Bill Holland's *Money Talks* is KSDO's top-rated afternoon radio show. His financial news report is carried mornings on Channel 10. He works as a broker and financial consultant with Prudential Services. When Bill Holland talks about money, people listen.

Born in Whittier, California, Holland moved to San Diego in 1960. His start in radio came over twenty-five years ago when he was a broker with Merrill Lynch and began giving financial advice on KOGO radio. Holland switched from KOGO to KSDO in 1979, along with San Diego veteran Ernie Myers. *Money Talks* was an experiment that KSDO was willing to try for two weeks. The show was an immediate hit and has remained highly popular for over ten years. Holland answers questions from callers and offers advice on all types of money-related matters from his office while someone from KSDO co-hosts from the studio.

Holland has achieved a healthy balance between work and play, but he had to suffer three ulcers before he did it. Weekdays he's up at 4:00 a.m. and into the office by 5:00 a.m. During the day, he does thirteen financial newscasts for KSDO, serving as their business editor. He also does a morning television spot on Channel 10, *Money Talks* from 3:00 p.m. to 4:00 p.m. and runs a lucrative business as a broker and financial consultant in between times.

He's always tried to keep his broadcasting career separate from his brokerage business, and he makes it a rule never to work on Friday nights or weekends.

Weekends are for relaxation – if you call racing your car around a track at unimaginable speeds relaxing. Holland likes to scuba dive and such, but put him behind the wheel of his favorite Mazda and watch out! This is his passion. He's driven his cars to many victories and championships in the fifteen years since he started racing, and today his team includes his entire family.

One thing that links successful people, he feels, is that they love their work so much they can't help but excel. With Holland, that goes for play, as well.

Gabriel Wisdom
Stockbroker/On-Air Personality

According to Gabriel Wisdom, "Success in and of itself was never my primary goal. The goal was to have a fulfilling life." He began a successful career in radio over twenty years ago at the age of eighteen, and he's now a thriving stockbroker with Sutro & Co. in La Jolla. His path to success is both unique and inspiring.

Wisdom has owned a surfboard repair business, had his own syndicated radio show, interviewed Bill Cosby, Robin Williams and The Who, sold radio time, lived in a treehouse on Kauai while surfing the Na Pali Coast, studied to be a lawyer, completed a doctorate in psychology, served as a marriage counselor and sold real estate. He currently is a stockbroker who does market analysis on television, gives financial seminars, is financially independent and is married to a radio producer. A graduate of Point Loma High School in 1968, Wisdom wasted no time getting his start in radio on KPRI. He wanted to be a disc jockey, but the only job opening they had was for an advertising salesman. He convinced the general manager to give him the sales job based on his vast experience as a paper boy. It was commission only, but at least he had his foot in the door. Soon afterwards he was given his own radio show, taking over for a DJ who fell asleep for nearly three hours while on-air. Wisdom's Sunday show was called *The Joyful Wisdom Hour,* during which he read poetry and played hit records about peace, love and utopia to satisfy the FCC's religious programming requirement.

When KPRI's album-oriented rock format caught on, Wisdom became one of its most prominent and highly visible disc jockeys, emceeing every live rock concert that came to town. He then "crossed the street" to rival rock station KGB, reprising the *Joyful Wisdom Hour* and adding interviews and commentaries. The show became so popular it ended up in national syndication. But even during the peak of his radio career, Wisdom knew he wanted to be a businessman. Today he enjoys the best of both worlds.

A typical day for Wisdom starts out with a 4:00 a.m. wake-up call. By 5:45 a.m., he's at the Channel 8 studios, where he reads six newspapers in preparation for his 6:35 a.m. weekday morning financial report. He then heads to his office to manage millions of dollars for both his clients and himself. "The old adage is to buy low, sell high and use other people's money. But I'm using my own, too, and that makes it even more interesting," he says. In addition to his role as stockbroker and financial analyst, he and his partner also hold financial seminars. Although he doesn't have to work, he really enjoys it, and appreciates that Sutro allows him the freedom to be an entrepreneur while working within the framework of a large firm.

Gabriel Wisdom has seen some financial setbacks on the way to financial independence, however. When he was twenty-one, he lost nearly everything he had sponsoring Dan Hicks and His Hot Licks band. Nearly broke, he was lucky to have his radio career to fall back on. When asked if he'd do it again, he replied, "When a risk-taker really believes in something, he puts everything he has into it, including his money." The hardest times came in 1980 and 1981 when, as a result of real estate speculation, he lost his shirt again. "I didn't really know what I was doing," he says ruefully. "I was buying property left and right on borrowed money, and then interest rates went to over twenty percent and I couldn't sell these properties. I wound up giving them away." Bitter? "It was probably the best education I ever got," he says now. "If it hadn't happened to me, I wouldn't be where I am today."

Chapter 14:
What It Takes
To Be Successful
In San Diego

What It Takes To Be Successful In San Diego (Or Anywhere Else, For That Matter)

1. Goals

Almost every successful San Diegan was able to clearly describe where they were going, how they planned to get there and when they expected to arrive. They knew what they wanted out of life and understood that the best way to realize their dreams was to set and achieve worthwhile goals. To them, setting clear, believable, written goals was the difference between success and failure. With meaningful goals, they were able to accomplish more and were more satisfied with their lives. Many were able to reach their full potential because they knew exactly what they wanted. Their goals gave them purpose and a focus for their talent and energy so they could structure their time towards reaching their objectives. Because they were the masters of their own destiny, they chose goals that inspired and excited them and were able to enjoy the process of working towards them.

For most, the first step on the way to success was to clearly define their primary goal in life. They took the time to carefully choose goals that were challenging and enabled them to combine their talents with work that they truly enjoyed. Some of these goals were fame, fortune, family, health, happiness, career advancement, business success, status, personal or team accomplishments, stability, balance and helping others. Some always knew what they wanted to be; others didn't discover what they really wanted out of life until they were much older – but at some point they were all able to define their talents and their goals. Most had to remain flexible and make adjustments during the process of achieving their goals, but the primary objective stayed the same. Once that was achieved, they continued to set new and more challenging goals.

Once they were aware of the outcome they desired, these men and women were able to formulate a plan for getting there. Having a plan with a timetable for its accomplishment enabled them to direct their energy, focusing on doing the most important thing *toward their goal* at any given time. Their plans included setting a series of short and medium-range goals. Step-by-step, they moved closer to achieving the long-range goal. The plan added aim and energy to their lives, but it also required action and plenty of hard work and discipline to make their dreams a reality. They were willing to pay the price and make the short-term sacrifices necessary for long-term prosperity. Few people are willing to pay the short-term price for long-term success, but those who do are richly rewarded.

The benefits of goal-setting are obvious. Goals are a high priority in almost every success story included in this book. Effective goal-setting is an extremely powerful tool that makes almost anything possible – within reason. Realistic, clearly-written goals are usually what separate the successful from the also-ran. If you're serious about success, determine what you want – your major, long-term goal. Write it down, define and refine it. Then write out a step-by-step plan for reaching it. The effectiveness of goal-setting has been proven over and over again by the successful people in this book. It's a skill anyone can develop, and the ones who make it to the top are those who use goals to focus their efforts and keep them from getting side-tracked. When you make the commitment to a goal, you'll find that instead of wishing you could be successful, you're moving closer and closer to achieving what you desire.

2. Action

The people in this book are not afraid to take action. They are doers. One thing that separates the successful from the not-so-successful is that they knew what they wanted, defined their goals and were able to go after them. By taking action, they produced results. There are always people who are better educated, have more experience, more money, more talent, but it's the individual who takes action and makes things happen who becomes successful. Success usually eludes those who procrastinate, who are afraid to make a decision or take a risk. Indecision is a major cause for failure. Yes, some made wrong decisions along the way, but they learned from those experiences. The people in this book had their eyes on a goal and didn't let anything stop them. The ability to overcome failure or procrastination is within everyone's reach. Successful people find the strength to make effective decisions and take action.

3. Hard Work

There's no shortcut to success. It takes a great deal of hard work. Successful San Diegans worked longer hours, practiced more, were better prepared, made the extra effort, pushed harder and did a better job than the person next to them. Most say their hard work is the major reason for their success. Their goals were important to them; they were willing to pay the price required and work hard for what they wanted. When they were faced with obstacles, failures and adversity, they just rolled up their sleeves and worked harder until they persevered. It should be noted that every one of the successful people in this book enjoyed their work and found it so rewarding that it seemed natural to work hard.

4. Fulfilling and Enjoyable Work

Successful people realize that a good portion of their adult lives is spent working, so they choose a career or business that brings them happiness, fulfillment and purpose. Because they take pleasure in what they do, they work hard and excel. For many, money is secondary to enjoying their work. Some started out earning next to nothing and have gone on to earn higher wages, while others realize they may never become wealthy at what they do, but enjoy their work too much to really care. There are plenty of people in this world who are financially secure but are unhappy and unfulfilled by their work. That is not success. The secret to success is being able to enjoy the way you earn your living. Some of the people in this book quit their jobs, changed their careers or became entrepreneurs in order to find real success and gratification in their work.

5. Desire

Desire, coupled with meaningful goals, action and hard work usually results in success. Successful people who have an overwhelming desire for something have more energy, passion, commitment and purpose. They are able to accomplish the seemingly impossible. Their desire strengthens their focus on success and they are able to overcome incredible odds and adversity to excel in sports, business and career. They are energized, and that energy spreads to those around them. Desire is the energy that fuels them toward greatness and allows these inspired people to wake up earlier, work longer hours, practice harder and surpass others who lack the same passion. For someone with a strong enough desire, there is always hope.

6. Perseverance

Many of the people in this book overcame limitations, setbacks and tremendous odds to become successful. They were usually not expected to be the best in their field. A few were told they didn't stand a chance of making it. Some had success and lost it, but were able to get it back. The thing they all have in common is perseverance and persistence. If the road was blocked, they looked for alternate routes, always working toward their goal. And they never stopped trying. They are strong, resilient people who took challenges head-on and won. They didn't listen if someone told them something couldn't be done or that they lacked the means to do it. Their motto was always "Never say die."

7. Discipline

To a certain degree, all successful people have some self-discipline. Usually the more self-discipline a person has, the more successful and contented they are. It takes self-discipline to maintain your focus on a goal. There are always negative and tempting forces trying to pull people away from realizing their long-term goals in favor of short-term gratification. It's the people who can stay focused and on course who are able to avoid this trap and strive for long-term satisfaction and success in career, relationships and business. Self-disciplined people are able to channel their time, energy, resources and money to the accomplishment of their goals. Self-discipline is not something you're born with, but those who learn it and practice it have a great advantage over those who don't.

8. Adversity

Adversity, frustration, discouragement, rejection and hardship are things almost everyone will have to face at one time or another. How you handle it determines whether or not you will be successful. Winners are able to persevere and rebound from life's toughest challenges. They respond with courage, determination and faith to overcome enormous obstacles on their way to success. Almost every successful person has failed at one time or another. If they try something and it doesn't work out, they try something else. They are able to learn from failure and use adversity as an incentive to rise above and become stronger. Some of the people in this book started with disadvantaged or traumatic childhoods, but these only gave them the inspiration – the need – to strive for a better life and success.

Successful people are resourceful and resilient and don't quit in the face of tough challenges. No matter how bad it gets, they never give up. They look at tough times as temporary situations and, instead of wallowing in self-pity, they look for what can be learned, look at the positives of the situation and often see opportunity where others only see despair. Those who have come through extremely trying times are truly grateful for the experience and find that it gave them a positive new perspective on life.

9. Fearlessness

Even successful people feel anxiety, stress and fear, but what makes them successful is their ability to use that fear to propel them on to greatness instead of letting it hold them back. They realize that by conquering their fears they are able to take the action necessary to succeed. People who let fear paralyze them cripple their chances for success. Everyone possesses the power to overcome their fears. The successful people in this book did it by pitting themselves against their fears over and over again. Many also used preparation as a way to overcome anxiety. Once they were able to control their fears, they took the necessary and calculated risks that helped lead to success. Many people are apprehensive about public speaking, yet most of the people in this book realized what a powerful tool good communications were and overcame their fear in order use it.

10. Efficiency

Everyone begins with the same number of hours in a day. How you use that time is what's important. If you take one day and compare how a successful person uses the time as compared to an ordinary person, the difference is substantial. When you multiply that by weeks, months and years, the difference between success and mediocrity becomes obvious. Successful people realize how valuable time is, so they do their best to eliminate waste. Because they set their priorities based on goals, the most productive thing for them to do at any given time is clear. They know how to plan, organize, take action and, when needed, they know how to say NO!

One of the keys to becoming and remaining efficient is learning to delegate. They realize that delegating helps them grow and allows them to devote their time and efforts to their most productive talents. By developing better time management skills, successful people are able to have more time for their friends, family, fitness – and for themselves. They are able to lead more balanced lives. Sometimes the most productive use of your time is to take a vacation, sleep late, read a good book, spend quality time with your family or simply watch the sun go down.

11. Communication

In many cases, getting ahead didn't necessarily mean being the best for the people in this book. Often it was the person with good people skills who succeeded. They knew what their strengths and weaknesses were and weren't afraid to enlist the help of others to fill in the gaps. Many were team players who understood that one person alone, no matter how talented or brilliant, would never be able to match the collective efforts of a team focused on a common purpose. They cultivated mutually beneficial relationships with others who could help further their goals more quickly. Some needed to be able to communicate their ideas clearly and effectively, others needed to be able to motivate. And nearly every successful person knows the importance of good communication.

12. Self-Esteem

The old sayings, "Success breeds success" and "Fake it till you make it" hold true when it comes to self-esteem. Self-esteem isn't something these successful San Diegans were born with. In fact, some began life with certain strikes against them. But somehow they were able to develop this important element for success. Sometimes it was built up by achieving a series of small successes. Others did all they could to make people believe they had it before they really did. Walking tall, dressing the part, using a firm handshake created the illusion, and eventually the illusion became the reality. It takes hard work, but it can be done.

You can acquire self-esteem by refusing to compare yourself to others, basing your success on the effort you put forth. You don't have to come in first every time, as long as you do your best. Even the great ones don't win all the time. Temporary setbacks are viewed by successful people as just that: temporary. They try to finish everything they start and see things through. They don't dwell on things they can't control – height, sex, race or physical limitations. They take what they're given and make the best of it. They don't take rejection personally. People are going to criticize no matter what you do or how successful you are.

A healthy sense of self-worth allows others to have confidence in you because you exude confidence. Influential people are more willing to put their trust in someone with a sense of self-esteem. These are the people they want to do business with, to hire, to be around.

13. Optimism

There are really only three ways to look at life. You can be pessimistic, indifferent or you can maintain an optimistic outlook. Successful people almost always choose to be positive, hopeful and enthusiastic. They realize that life is a series of highs and lows, but they choose to focus on the highs. Optimism is a way of life – positive thinking brings positive results, and positive results make you more optimistic. Success rarely comes to negative thinkers, because they're too busy suffering from fear, anxiety and conflict. Indifferent people are unwilling to make the commitment and do the work necessary for success. Because positive thinkers are generally happy people who emphasize the good in almost any situation, others are drawn to them and opportunities open to them that often elude others.

14. Balance

Many of the successful people in this book said a balanced life is the key to their success. They try to take time out from their work for their families, friends, hobbies and vacations. They work hard and they play hard. Although they are extremely busy, most take the time to exercise and keep in shape, realizing that without their health, nothing else really matters. Many also credit their spouses for much of their success. These successful people realize that their families and friends are the sources of the most worthwhile and lasting satisfaction in their lives. They are driven when it comes to their work, but they also realize how empty success can be without someone to share it. Many are very appreciative of what they worked so hard to accomplish and feel blessed because they loved what they were doing and were successful at it as well.

15. Health

The hardworking and busy individuals in this book find the time to exercise regularly. They realize that they can't afford *not* to make the time to keep in shape. They've discovered that exercise and healthy eating habits give them more energy, less stress, a better attitude, appearance, self-esteem and quality of life. In the long run, exercise in every case increased productivity.

Successful people have everything to live for and want to have the time to enjoy it. For some, health was a low priority until it was threatened, but then it became priority number one. It's far better to take preventive measures to ensure good health before a problem surfaces.

16. Wealth

To some people, wealth represents security, a good education for their children or grandchildren and a way to provide for their family. To others, wealth is not so important in the scheme of things, and is a poor way to judge success. Money alone doesn't ensure success. In and of itself, it rarely brings happiness.

Many of the people in this book went through times when they were earning little or no money at all but, because they enjoyed what they were doing and did it well, because they were always working toward a goal, the money usually followed. Some had wealth, lost it and earned it back again – which proves that just because someone knows how to attain wealth they don't necessarily understand it or have the skills to manage it properly.

Most would agree that you should set financial goals that include a plan for saving for the future. You must spend less than you earn and have enough left over to save. Surprisingly, even millionaires can be frugal and often shop for the best prices in an effort to stretch their money further.

17. Role Models

Virtually all successful people have role models, people they respect who they can turn to for advice, inspiration, support and direction. By asking for advice or studying the examples of those who have already succeeded, many of the successful people in this book were able to save time and energy and avoid traveling down the wrong paths. Because success *does* leave clues.

18. Education

Not everyone in this book is a college graduate, but most of them believe in some form of education — schooling, mentors, hands-on learning, reading, attending seminars, specialized training or any combination thereof. They know that knowledge is power and they made whatever sacrifices were needed to acquire the skills necessary to get ahead. For most, education is an ongoing process that provides them with a much-needed edge.

19. Integrity

People who are successful and want to stay that way know the value of integrity and a sound reputation. To maintain long-term success, you must build lasting relationships over a long period of time. To do that, you must be trustworthy, ethical and honest. Successful people generally don't want to achieve through deceit or at someone else's expense. They prefer to be part of win-win situations and relationships that benefit all involved, both personally and professionally.

20. Involvement

Many successful San Diegans are generous volunteers who give their time and money. They understand the tremendous fulfillment that comes from giving and helping others. Many have devoted years of their lives to helping causes they really believe in and have been able to make a difference and help bring about positive change. These philanthropists are often joiners who belong to clubs and organizations that help further their careers while building beneficial and lasting relationships for themselves and their businesses.

What It Takes To Make It In Business

Success in business takes many of the same qualities already discussed in this section, but an entrepreneur needs to possess or acquire some additional skills.

It is true that entrepreneurs are risk-takers, yet many of those risks are carefully calculated. Entrepreneurs are usually willing to risk everything they have – including the security of a regular paycheck and weekends off – for uncertainty and seven-day work weeks. They're willing to take those risks on a business or an idea because they truly believe it will succeed. The ability to take risks and a go-for-it attitude are helpful in almost any business, but you must also realize the importance of extensive research to help minimize those risks. Careful planning and the discipline to follow that plan are essential ingredients to success. Thoughtful planning and thorough research, coupled with a willingness to put it all on the line, give an entrepreneur a very good chance of succeeding. Successful entrepreneurs generally are not afraid of failure, although some have failed in the past. They pick themselves up and start all over again, armed with new insights and valuable experience.

Many successful businesses started very humbly. Some entrepreneurs began by working out of their homes or garages. Some were undercapitalized, but their lack of finances forced them to find creative solutions as problems arose. They replaced money with sweat equity and a burning desire to succeed, although having sufficient capital and establishing a good relationship with a bank never hurts. A few used image to create the illusion to their clients that they were bigger than they actually were. Many believe it was a plus to start small and build their business at a controlled pace. Sometimes when companies are small and lean they're able to compete and thrive in situations where larger businesses can't survive. As these companies succeeded and grew, they faced a whole new set of challenges.

In order for their businesses to grow, successful entrepreneurs understand the importance of delegation. They surround themselves with successful people, which allows them to focus their time and energy on the things they do best. Sometimes that is simply providing leadership and giving their company direction. They know what their strengths and weaknesses are, and hire people to fill in the gaps. If they have a problem, they aren't too proud to seek the advice and services of professionals.

San Diego

San Diegans can look forward to a bright future for America's Finest City. San Diego has so much going for it most would agree it simply has to prosper in years to come. We are fortunate to have the finest climate in the country – possibly the world – with sunshine and moderate temperatures all year long. Residing in San Diego encourages outdoor living and year-round recreation. It's simply an awe-inspiring place to behold, with its incomparable natural environment, the blue Pacific and natural harbors contrasted by a spectacular skyline and a revitalized downtown. Probably the city's biggest asset, though, is its people. Over and over again, those who live here and those who wish they still did comment on the wonderful people of the city.

Most of the successful people in this book agreed that, although San Diego has faced adversity, in the long run the city is always better for it. We have some problems and have faced some economically difficult times, but many feel San Diego will rebound and come back stronger than ever. Historically, San Diego has been a boom-and-bust town, but it always found ways to recover and should continue to do so. According to *Fortune Magazine,* "Manufacturing has been growing faster than the U.S. average, with biotech, electronics and telecommunications among competitive local industries. The city is well situated to trade with Mexico and Asia. A healthy twenty-one percent of what's made here is exported." [November 2, 1992]

San Diego is no longer a sleepy little beach town. It's the nation's sixth largest city, the second largest city in California. And it's on its way to becoming a great metropolis, with all the benefits of a big city and all the charms of an unbeatable natural setting. It doesn't take much to realize how good we have it here, watching the sailboats on San Diego Bay, driving the mountain roads or spending a warm September day at the beach. We all share the same good feeling upon returning home from our travels. When the plane circles over San Diego's majestic coastline and glides past the enchanting lushness of Balboa Park, you realize just how lucky you are to be able to call San Diego home.

Just for Fun

Chapter 15:
Trivia Questions

The author wishes to thank Evelyn Kooperman,
author of *San Diego Trivia* and *San Diego Trivia II,*
for her help in compiling these questions.

Celebrities:

1. What Oscar-nominated actress made her Old Globe debut as a belly dancer and once worked as a cook aboard a charter boat in San Diego to support her love of scuba diving?

2. What San Diego native plays Danny Romalotti on the soap opera *The Young and the Restless?*

3. What native San Diegan and Emmy Award-winning actor got his start appearing in commercials, including one in which he was a box of lemon chiffon pie mix?

4. What Emmy Award-winning actress and San Diego State University graduate made her mark on shows such as *Rhoda, The Tracy Ullman Show* and as the voice of Marge on *The Simpsons?*

5. What Crawford High School graduate played an eternally upbeat nun opposite Whoopi Goldberg in the 1992 smash hit movie, *Sister Act?*

6. What famous actor/director was named Most Likely to Succeed by his 1954 Helix High School classmates?

7. What native La Jollan and Academy Award-winning actor rode his bicycle thirteen miles to wash airplanes in exchange for an occasional flying lesson?

8. What actress/comedienne once worked as a dishwasher at The Big Kitchen restaurant in Golden Hill?

9. What San Diego native, who now stars as Mona Loveland on the new *WKRP In Cincinnati,* once worked in a Burger King in Pacific Beach?

10. What Grossmont High School graduate portrayed a sleazy car salesman named Joe Isuzu?

11. What Kearny High School and SDSU graduate won a Tony Award in 1970 for his outstanding performance in *Purlie?*

12. What Academy Award-winning actor and La Jolla native was one of

the founders of the La Jolla Playhouse?

13. What San Diego-based saxophonist was honored as UCSD's Alumnus of the Year in 1991?

14. What popular singer from the 1940's and 1950's has twenty-one gold records to his credit, with hit songs like *Rawhide, Mule Train* and *That's My Desire?*

15. What country music superstar was once Miss Oceanside?

16. What outrageous singer-humorist was joined onstage in 1992 by ex-Eagle Don Henley while performing *Don Henley Must Die?*

17. What rock supergroup – whose debut album *Out of the Cellar* sold more than three million copies in 1984 – included three San Diegans?

18. What longtime North County resident penned hit songs for the Eagles, Glenn Frey and Johnny Rivers?

19. What former Bacchanal nightclub roadie and longtime San Diego surfer is now the frontman for Pearl Jam, one of the hottest rock bands on the music scene today?

20. What San Diego native and former *San Diego Union* paperboy garnered gold records with hit singles *On and On* and *Save It for a Rainy Day?*

21. What UCSD graduate is one of today's most in-demand bass players, performing with Eric Clapton, Michael Jackson, Barbra Streisand and Phil Collins?

22. What jazz-pop singer/songwriter returned to San Diego to write songs for his tenth album, Blue Pacific?

23. What is the name of the Beat Farmers guitarist whose uncle, Nick Reynolds, was a member of the original Kingston Trio?

24. What two Coronado residents, both members of the Kingston Trio, recorded an album together called *Revenge of the Budgie?*

25. What long-time Fallbrook resident was known for making classic

feel-good movies such as *Mr. Deeds Goes to Town, Mr. Smith Goes to Washington* and *It's A Wonderful Life?*

26. What San Diego Zoo Goodwill Ambassador has appeared on *The Tonight Show* roughly seventy times with over 300 unique animals?

27. What is the real name of the five-foot-four-inch Hoover High School graduate better known as The Chicken?

28. Who is the former Channel 10 anchorman now seen by millions on his weekday morning syndicated television talk show?

29. What University High School graduate wrote, directed and co-produced the 1992 film, *Singles?* (Hint: He's also famous for his book and later the film, *Fast Times at Ridgemont High*.)

30. What author of twenty young adult books once worked for the FBI?

31. What is the real name of the author who wrote and illustrated over forty-five books for children, yet never had any children of his own?

32. What best-selling author uses firewalking as a tool to help people overcome their fears and phobias?

32. Anthony Robbins.
Crowe. 30. Joan Oppenheimer. 31. Theodor Geisel (aka Dr. Seuss).
Joan Embery. 27. Ted Giannoulas. 28. Regis Philbin. 29. Cameron
Joey Harris. 24. Nick Reynolds & John Stewart. 25. Frank Capra. 26.
Vedder. 20. Stephen Bishop. 21. Nathan East. 22. Michael Franks. 23.
Mandrell. 16. Mojo Nixon. 17. Ratt. 18. Jack Tempchin. 19. Eddie
Gregory Peck. 13. Hollis Gentry. 14. Frankie Laine. 15. Barbara
Goldberg. 9. Tawny Kitaen. 10. David Leisure. 11. Cleavon Little. 12.
5. Kathy Najimy. 6. Dennis Hopper. 7. Cliff Robertson. 8. Whoopi
1. Annette Bening. 2. Michael Damian. 3. Ted Danson. 4. Julie Kavner.

Sports:

1. What pitcher with over 100 wins in eleven major league seasons was once Tony Gwynn's teammate at SDSU?

2. What San Diego native lefty was named the Sporting News American League Rookie Pitcher of the Year, winning seventeen games and leading the league in strikeouts while pitching for the Seattle Mariners? Hint: He won thirteen games in 1992 pitching for the California Angels.

3. What gold glove third baseman who finished his major league career with 390 home runs and 1,314 RBI's attended SDSU on a basketball scholarship?

4. What former Padres catcher became the first black to play triple-A minor league baseball and was known as the Jackie Robinson of the Pacific Coast League?

5. What San Diego family was the first to have three generations play major league baseball?

6. What famous broadcaster and former New York Yankees infielder earned several medals as a pilot and war hero during WWII and the Korean conflict, flying 120 missions and surviving two plane crashes?

7. What former San Diego Padres utility infielder and his band opened for Jimmy Buffett at his San Diego Convention Center concert in 1992?

8. What San Diego native and Kearny High School graduate was the 1984 World Series MVP when his team, the Detroit Tigers, defeated the San Diego Padres in five games?

9. What Baseball Hall of Famer and San Diego native was known as "The Kid" and "The Splendid Splinter"?

10. What All-Pro defensive back for the Philadelphia Eagles rushed for over 900 yards while a senior at Point Loma High School?

11. What Pro Bowl kicker from San Dieguito High School kicked the

longest field goal in NFL history on November 8, 1970? (His sixty-three yarder set a record that has yet to be broken.)

12. In November 1992, two offensive weapons from the Air Coryell teams of the late 1970's and early 1980's were the thirteenth and fourteenth players inducted into the San Diego Chargers Hall of Fame. Who were they?

13. What former Lincoln High School football legend became the first college player to rush for over 2,000 yards? (He did it in 1981 while playing for USC.)

14. What former San Diego Charger nicknamed "The Howitzer" was the NFL's Special Teams Player of the Year in 1982, setting an NFL record with fifty-two special teams tackles?

15. What former San Diego Chargers kicker took a spin as host of the popular game show, *Wheel of Fortune?*

16. What former San Diego Chargers offensive lineman and San Diego native was once the NFL's arm wrestling champion?

17. What San Diegan was the first Asian-American figure skater ever to qualify for the USFSA World Team when she did it at age fifteen?

18. What San Diego track star made a dramatic recovery from Graves disease, coming back to win the gold in the 100-meter dash at the 1992 Olympics?

19. What All-American sailor from SDSU won an Olympic gold medal in the Star class in 1992?

20. What San Diego native is considered the greatest female golfer of all time?

21. What famous channel swimmer is now a stockbroker in La Jolla? Hint: She appeared in the movie *Bathing Beauty* opposite another swimming great, Esther Williams.

22. What legendary tennis star was nicknamed after the battleship *Missouri?* Hint: She once shagged balls in exchange for tennis lessons at the University Heights playground.

23. What native San Diegan beat Tom Watson by one shot to win the U.S. Open Championship in 1987?

24. What off-road racing legend (nicknamed "Ironman") has his own arcade game?

25. What award-winning Channel 10 cameraman won the welterweight bronze medal in boxing at the 1972 Olympics?

26. What former Helix High School standout and UCLA legend was voted the NBA's MVP following the 1976-77 basketball season?

1. Bud Black. 2. Mark Langston. 3. Graig Nettles. 4. John Ritchey. 5. The Boones: Ray, Bob and Bret. 6. Jerry Coleman. 7. Tim Flannery and "Buffed Out." 8. Alan Trammell. 9. Ted Williams. 10. Eric Allen. 11. Tom Dempsey. 12. Dan Fouts and Charlie Joiner. 13. Marcus Allen. 14. Hank Bauer. 15. Rolf Benirschke. 16. Ed White. 17. Tiffany Chin. 18. Gail Devers. 19. Mark Reynolds. 20. Mary "Mickey" Wright. 21. Florence Chadwick. 22. Maureen "Little Mo" Connolly. 23. Scott Simpson. 24. Ivan "Ironman" Stewart. 25. Jesse Valdez. 26. Bill Walton.

Media:

1. What San Diego media celebrity tended bar at the Sunshine Company in Ocean Beach and named his first child after one of his idols, jazz great Miles Davis?

2. Who was voted the country's best sportscaster in a 1987 national survey?

3. What long-time San Diego radio and television personality is known for his bushy beard, ranger hat and patented on-air yell?

4. What late-night radio talk show host is affectionately called "Billo" by his listeners?

5. What radio talk-show host was the first person to promote an outdoor rock concert in San Diego when he brought the Grateful Dead to the Aztec Bowl on Mother's Day, 1969?

6. Who is the voice behind the humorous radio ads for the *Union-Tribune* classifieds section?

1. Larry Himmel. 2. Ted Leitner. 3. Shotgun Tom Kelly. 4. Bill Ballance. 5. Roger Hedgecock. 6. Russ T. Nailz.

Business:

1. What former *SunUp San Diego* host is the owner of two restaurants in Seaport Village?

2. What is the name of David Lloyd's San Diego-based company, one of the largest minority-owned shipyards in the United States?

3. What civic leader and department store owner who devoted his life to making San Diego a pleasant place in which to live was called the leading San Diegan of all time and the city's number one citizen?

4. What company was founded by a group of adventurous young Explorer Scouts who set out to improve the comfort of backpacks in the 1960's?

5. Who sold his Model T in 1922 and poured the proceeds into a Jenny airplane, which he used to give sightseeing tours of San Diego?

6. The first Rubio's "Home of the Fish Taco" restaurant was located in an old hamburger stand on Mission Bay Drive in 1983. Where was the second Rubio's opened (in 1986)?

7. What multi-million-dollar greeting card company began in the San Diego apartment of its founder in 1967?

8. Who is the host of the top-rated radio show *Money Talks?* (Hint: It's on weekday afternoons on KSDO.)

9. What stockbroker and financial analyst was once one of San Diego's most prominent and highly-visible radio personalities? (Hint: He had a nationally-syndicated radio show in the 1970's called *The Joyful Wisdom Hour.*)

1. Jerry G. Bishop. 2. **Bay City Marine.** 3. George Marston. 4. Adventure 16. 5. T. Claude Ryan. 6. On College Avenue near SDSU. 7. Suzy's Zoo. 8. Bill Holland. 9. Gabriel Wisdom.

Index

Bibliography

Blackwell, Earl. *Earl Blackwell's Entertainment Celebrity Register*, Visible Ink Press, 1991.

Brandes, Ray. *San Diego, An Illustrated History*, Rosebud Books, 1981.

Dunlap, Carol. *California People*, Peregrine Smith Books, 1982.

Fuller, Theodore W. *San Diego Originals*, California Profiles Publications, 1987.

Hopkins, Tom. *The Official Guide to Success*, Warner Books, 1982.

Leftwich, James Adolf. *La Jolla Life*, La Jolla Press, 1984.

Gammond, Peter. *The Oxford Companion to Popular Music*, Oxford University Press, 1991.

Hill, Napoleon. *Think and Grow Rich*, Fawcett, 1979.

James, Bill. *The Baseball Book 1991*, Villard Books, 1991.

Kooperman, Evelyn. *San Diego Trivia*, Silver Gate Publications, 1989. *San Diego Trivia II*, Silver Gate Publications, 1993.

LaBlanc, Michael L. *Contemporary Musicians*, Gales Research Inc., 1991.

McCoy, Doris Lee. *Megatraits*, Wordware Publishing, Inc., 1988.

McNeil, Alex, *Total Television*, Penguin, 1991.

Miller, Max. *I Cover the Waterfront*, E.P. Dutton, 1932.

Mills, James Robert. *San Diego — Where California Began*, San Diego Historical Society, 1985.

Morgan, Neil Bowen. *My San Diego*, Frye and Smith, 1951. *San Diego: The Unconventional City*, Morgan House, 1972.

Morgan, Neil Bowen and Blair, Tom. *Yesterday's San Diego*, E.A. Seeman Publishing, Inc., 1976.

Official 1992 National Football League Record and Fact Book, Workman Publishing Company, 1992.

Quinlan, David. *Quinlan's Illustrated Registry of Film Stars*, Henry Holt and Company, 1991.

Robbins, Anthony. *Unlimited Power.* Ballantine Books, 1986.

San Diego Magazine. *San Diego, Portrait of a Spectacular City*, by Syd Love and the editors of San Diego Magazine, San Diego Magazine Publishing Company, 1969.

Shatzkin, Mike and Charlton, Jim. *The Ballplayers 1990,* William Morrow, 1990.

Silber, Lee T. *The Guide to Dating in San Diego,* Tales From The Tropics Publishing Company, 1992.

The Sporting News NBA Register 1992-93 Edition, The Sporting News Publishing Company, 1992.

Tucker, Joan C. *San Diego and the Southland — Just the Facts: A Guide to Sightseeing.* Rand Editions, 1984.

Waitley, Dr. Denis. *The Winner's Edge,* Berkley Books, 1980.

Who's Who in Entertainment, 1989-1990, Marquis, 1990.

Newspapers and Magazines:

Blade Citizen, Cosmopolitan, Ebony, Entrepreneur, First Thursday, Fortune, Guitar Player, Interview, La Jolla Light, Los Angeles Times, Parade, People, Premiere, Rolling Stone, San Diego Business Journal, San Diego Executive, San Diego Magazine, San Diego Monitor News, San Diego Woman, San Diego Writers Monthly, Seventeen, Sports Illustrated, Success, Teen, The Californian, The Reader, The San Diego Tribune, The San Diego Union, The San Diego Union-Tribune, Time, Tuned In, TV Guide, USA Today, Vanity Fair

Notes from the Author

I have always loved reading biographies, all the way back to when I was a kid. I'm an especially big fan of collected biographies. Over the years, I've spent plenty of time hanging around bookstores, wondering what it would be like to write a book of collected biographies myself. The subject matter would have to be entertaining, yet inspiring. The best stories always seemed to be the ones about people who overcame adversity and achieved success.

A few years ago, I decided to combine my love for San Diego and its people with the principles of success. My first step was to write down the names of the most successful San Diegans I could think of. The first name I put down was Theodor Geisel – Dr. Seuss. Before I knew it, I had several hundred names and files upon files of research. I'm not going to bore you with the details of how I went about researching this book, but I will tell you that I spent months and months doing it. Even though this is not my first book, it still felt like new and uncharted territory – but then, I've always enjoyed a good challenge.

I made writing *Successful San Diegans* my full-time job. I basically disappeared from sight for over a year and a half as I spent every waking hour working on "the book," as my friends and family called it. Although it took many long hours and a lot of hard work, it was essentially a labor of love. My enthusiasm for the subject was catching, and I was able to turn even my biggest doubters into believers that this book was worth doing, and doing well. I put my heart and soul into it to make the book something San Diegans can be proud of. I feel privileged to be the one who gets to share these great biographies with you and I intend to continue to do so in the future.

I've always tried to live my life by the motto, "keep it fun," and I've always tried to live life to the fullest. So far, I've been able to apply that philosophy to every aspect of my life. Don't get me wrong – I work hard, and I'm as ambitious as the next guy, usually even more so. But it's the way I go about accomplishing my goals that sets me apart. When I realized that my life is what I make of it and I can choose to do whatever I want, I chose to become a writer and publisher. Many people wish they could be doing what they really enjoy for a living. I guess I'm very fortunate.

I've always loved being outdoors and taking advantage of the San Diego lifestyle. I hoped becoming a writer wouldn't spoil that way of life. Well, it actually enhanced it. Even though being a writer can be a lonely job, it also offers the freedom of being able to take your work with you, wherever you wish to go. When I wasn't conducting interviews or doing research, I picked small, out-of-the-way places to do my writing. Countless days were spent in my boat, anchored off the coast, writing diligently (with the occasional break for a swim in the ocean). During the heat wave of the summer of 1992, I spent most of my time escaping the sizzling temperatures down at the waterfront, where the cool ocean breezes provided some relief. The sea air also provided inspiration. Sometimes I felt like a modern-day Max Miller as I chatted with passersby who wanted to know what I was writing about. Actually, I learned a great deal about San Diego from some of the legendary characters who dwell along the waterfront. The only real distraction was when I looked up to watch the occasional boat head out to sea. I spent many days holed up at the library or stuck in the office, but that's what it's all about — achieving a balance between work and play, and whenever possible combining the two.

Since I was thoroughly enjoying writing this book, I thought nothing of the seventy-hour weeks and the sacrifices I had to make to do it. Two of my good friends, Cammie Cather and Lee Dulgeroff, thought I needed a vacation from my work. My girlfriend agreed. As hard as I tried to explain to them that when you love what you do it isn't work, they didn't believe me. Eventually I gave in and committed to a ten-day sailing trip in the British Virgin Islands but, much to their chagrin, I brought along ten days worth of work. We sailed our thirty-eight-foot sailboat from one exotic island to another and every morning I was up at dawn, sitting on the deck with a cup of coffee in one hand and a pen in the other. Most evenings after everyone was asleep, I was in the cabin or up on deck writing by flashlight. The only problem with this was when I accidentally lost my tape player and the tape that included interviews with Jerry Coleman and Natasha Josefowitz over the side in the Sir Francis Drake Channel. I had to write their stories from my notes and by memory. I sent them each a rough copy of their stories with a letter explaining what had happened. Neither of these hard-working individuals questioned why I was doing my writing in a tropical paradise!

My love for San Diego probably comes from my father, who came here as a young man in the early 1960's to attend San Diego State University. The day he arrived, he headed down to Mission Beach for a swim in the Pacific Ocean and almost drowned. Since that day, though, my dad has become quite a waterman. He has always embodied the spirit of the San Diego lifestyle. One of the first things he did when he moved here was to trade in his Oldsmobile for a Honda motorcycle. He was able to support himself and pay his five dollars a week rent in Hillcrest while attending college by working odd jobs around town as a part-time busboy, lifeguard and short order cook. My father is a hardworking man who built a successful business out of nothing and was able to retire just before his fiftieth birthday. His retirement only lasted a few months, but that's another story. He has an ongoing love affair with San Diego and its lifestyle which he passed on to his eldest son.

If you happen to see a contented guy sitting under a palm tree overlooking the ocean on a sunny summer weekday afternoon, dressed in shorts, t-shirt, flojos and a baseball cap, working away at a laptop computer – chances are that's me, the luckiest guy in the world. Well, at least in San Diego.

About the Author

Having grown up in San Diego, Lee Silber, like so many others, has tremendous respect and appreciation for America's Finest City and its people. *Successful San Diegans* is Silber's second book on San Diego. He also authored *The Guide to Dating in San Diego,* published in 1991.

Silber has owned and operated five businesses in San Diego and Hawaii. He founded The SuccessShop™, which sells and distributes success-related products. He publishes *Success in San Diego,* a quarterly newsletter for success-minded San Diegans.

Silber is a member of the San Diego Historical Society, the San Diego Hall of Champions, the San Diego Writers/Editors Guild and is a longtime member of Toastmasters. He has made frequent appearances on local television and radio and has been featured in many newspapers and magazines.

When not writing, lecturing or running his various business interests, Silber, a resident of Del Mar, spends his free time traveling, boating, flying, scuba diving, surfing and enjoying the San Diego lifestyle.

SUCCESS

In San Diego • A Quarterly Newsletter

What You Get

The *SUCCESS In San Diego* quarterly newsletter is based on Lee T. Silber's book *Successful San Diegans*. It features new, in-depth profiles of San Diego's most successful people in Entertainment, Sports, Media and Business. These new profiles are not from the book. You will also find:

- **Updates on Successful San Diegans and their latest accomplishments.**

- **Reviews of Music, Movies & Books that include or are by San Diegans.**

- **Year-end picks and profiles of the 25 Most Successful San Diegans.**

- **Practical "what to do" and "how to do it" suggestions from the experts that will help guide you towards success in San Diego.**

How You Get It

The SUCCESS In San Diego Quarterly Newsletter can be sent directly to your home or office. For a complimentary copy of the *SUCCESS In San Diego* quarterly newsletter, please print your name and address below.

Name_____

_____

Address_____

_____

City _____

State _____

Zip _____

Fill out, clip and send to:

SUCCESS In San Diego Newsletter

P. O. Box 4100-186

Del Mar, CA 92014

Order Form

Please send me:

_____ **(copies) of** *SUCCESSFUL SAN DIEGANS: The Stories Behind San Diego's Most Successful People Both Past and Present* @ $15.95 each plus $3.00 for shipping & handling.

Quantity discounts available:
> **5 - 11 books $12.95 each**
> **12 - 24 books $11.95 each**
> **25 or more books $9.95 each.**

(No shipping charge on orders of 5 books or more.)
Please add 7.75% sales tax to total dollar amount of order.

Ship To:

Name _____

Address _____

City _____ State _____ Zip _____

Make check payable to:

TALES FROM THE TROPICS PUBLISHING CO.
P. O. Box 4100-186
Del Mar, CA 92014
(619) 792-5312